Lexical ambiguity in poetry

Studies in language and linguistics

General editors: GEOFFREY LEECH & MICK SHORT
Lancaster University

Already published:

A Dictionary of Stylistics
KATIE WALES

The Communicative Competence of Young Children
SUSAN H. FOSTER

Linguistic Purism
GEORGE THOMAS

Women, Men and Language
Second edition
JENNIFER COATES

Contents

Publisher's acknowledgements

We are indebted to the following for permission to reproduce copyright material;

the author's agent for an extract from the poem 'Babies' by D. J. Enright; Faber and Faber Ltd and Harcourt Brace Jovanovich, Inc for an extract from the poem 'Morning at the Window' by T. S. Elliot.

We have been unable to trace the copyright holders in *Phrase and Paraphrase* by Gleitman and Gleitman (pub W. W. Norton and Co., Inc, 1970); and L. G. Heller for extracts and figures from paper 'Toward a general typology of the pun' from *Language and Style* 1974 and would appreciate any information that would enable us to do so.

Author's acknowledgements

This book is based on my PhD thesis which was submitted to the Department of Linguistics and Modern English Language at the University of Lancaster. It is with pleasure that I acknowledge my debt and gratitude to my supervisor, Professor G. N. Leech, whose incisive comments helped to shape the development of this study. His genuine interest in my work, and his constant support and guidance sustained me through various periods of doubt, despondency and despair. To him, I owe the fruition of both the thesis and book: I cannot thank him enough. I am also very grateful to Dr M. H. Short for commentaries and criticisms, for directing my attention to relevant materials and examples, and for expressing a personal concern in the progress of my work.

I should like to thank Professor R. Hale for introducing me to some simple logic, Dr J. A. Thomas for allowing me to attend her classes on pragmatics, and Professor M. Wheeler for generously loaning me some material on Hopkins. My grateful thanks also to the many friends who have offered support or provided distractions, to G. Tan for his thoughtful gift of a hard-disk card and, more so, for his sound advice and unfailing encouragements, and to my family for their love and belief in me.

Finally, I wish to acknowledge with appreciation the scholarship from the Association of Commonwealth Universities, its smooth administration by the British Council, and the leave from University of Malaya, all of which have enabled me to pursue this project to its completion.

To my mother, Ho Foong Ying,
and my father, Su Hoi Pa

CHAPTER ONE

Introduction

1.1 Aim and scope

> Names are finite and so is the sum total of formulae, while things are
> infinite in number. Inevitably, then, the same formula, and a single name,
> have a number of meanings.
>
> Aristotle, *De Sophisticis Elenchis*, 165

Ambiguity is a pervasive feature of language,[1] and thus deserves to
be studied in its own right. Where ambiguity occurs as a topic of
interest in various disciplines such as literature, linguistics, psychology and philosophy, it is used mainly as a sounding board in the
analysis of other phenomena. For instance, in linguistics, the notion
of ambiguity is fundamental in the treatment of certain arguments
about deep structure and about the relation between syntax and
semantics; in psychology, it can serve as a key to the study of the
human psyche; and in literature, it 'fits itself to contain within the
form of discourse aspects of human experience' (Nowottny 1962: 146).
A fairly recent article (Hagenbuchle 1984), makes use of the concept
of ambiguity to point to the fundamental difference between the
linguist and literary critic in their attitudes to language.

In the various disciplines which discuss ambiguity, the term is
often assumed to be self-evident, but its nature is, in fact, far from
clear. For many, the term is synonymous with 'double meaning', 'lack
of clarity' or 'equivocation'. Some base their concept of ambiguity on
dictionary definitions, usually given as 'a word which has more than
one interpretation, or explanation; of double meaning, or of several
possible meanings: equivocal' and 'doubtful, questionable; indistinct,
obscure, not clearly defined' (as found in Norrman 1977: 6). The term
has also been subjected to an idiosyncratic use to cover 'change' and

'diversity' in addition to 'polyvalence', such as is found in Page (1985: 13). Even within the same discipline, the term is not always used consistently to refer to the same thing. This is notoriously the case in literary criticism where ambiguity, taken particularly at the global level, is sometimes equated with multiple subjective interpretations (which Barthes characterizes as 'infinite plurality' and Eco as 'openness of the work'; see Rimmon 1977: 12–13), or sometimes with indeterminacy, vagueness or suggestiveness. Empson's *Seven Types of Ambiguity* (1961), a seminal book on the subject from a literary angle, has a wide-ranging definition of the term (see section 1.2.2).

In his comment on another term, 'irony', Booth (1974: ix) remarks that: 'Once a term has been used to cover just about everything there is, it perhaps ought simply to be retired; if it can apply to everything, it can hardly be rescued for everyday purposes.' This remark can be extended to 'ambiguity' so that, for the term to be useful once more, it must be rescued from confusion and indiscriminately loose usage. More particularly, for the concept of ambiguity to be useful, the scope of the term should be delimited to fit the purpose at hand, which in the present study is to see how ambiguity is used as a stylistic device for aesthetic effects.

The primary aim of this book is to provide some theoretical clarity about the concept of ambiguity. This task is carried out with the following restrictions in mind.

(a) Although the explication of the concept has general applica-tion, the focus will be on dealing with ambiguity as it occurs in poetry.

(b) The theoretical explication will be illustrated mainly from the poetry of Gerard Manley Hopkins which is marked by ambiguity (see, for instance, Frye 1957: 193), although data gathered from other poetic as well as non-poetic sources will also be included where it serves to illuminate a point being made.

(c) Linguistically, ambiguity has often been dealt with at the levels of phonology, lexis and surface and deep structures (see Kooij 1971 and MacKay 1966); for an in-depth study, this book will concentrate only on lexical ambiguity.

(d) The analysis will be carried out within the framework of stylistics, and hence, the approach is interdisciplinary, making use of linguistics (in particular, semantics), pragmatics and literary criticism and theory.[2]

It seems apt to choose poetry as the register for the study of ambiguity, as poetry is compact and dense; in addition, it allows a unique freedom (commonly known as 'poetic licence') for poets to make creative and innovative use of linguistic resources. Thus, it offers a rich as well as interesting source of data for the examination of ambiguity. However, poetry is not used here only as a source of data to illustrate a theoretical concept, but it is itself to be illuminated through the explication of ambiguity. This forms the secondary aim when we focus on the poetry of Hopkins, a poet whose rich exploitation of ambiguity repays particularly careful study. In fact, a run-through of the critical bibliography on Hopkins reveals that, except for a few articles which specifically discuss ambiguity in his poetry, little has been written substantially on this aspect of Hopkins's poetic works.[3] The hope is, therefore, that the present work will also contribute to highlighting this ambiguous aspect of Hopkins which has, hitherto, been given relatively little attention.

Further, the scope is limited to lexical ambiguity for several reasons:

(a) There is, as Ricoeur (1977: 125) puts it, 'an uncertainty at the very heart of the semantics of word', meaning that the lexical system is non-systematic in some aspects, as compared to the phonological or grammatical systems. For instance, there is a finite number of phonemes or grammatical rules, but the lexical code is relatively open so that it is possible for new entities to be added to it, hence word-coinages, and changes in, or additions to, the meanings of established words. This feature of openness renders the vocabulary 'an unstable structure in which individual words can acquire and lose meanings with the utmost ease' (Ullmann 1962: 195, quoted in Ricoeur 1977: 127). Such instability makes the lexical level an especially fertile area for the investigation of ambiguity.

(b) Word-consciousness is the hallmark of all poets, but in Hopkins, this is a particularly distinctive feature which is seen in the poet's keen interest in the etymology and coinage of words as well as in the use of words in non-standard senses. Much of the poet's deep concern with words can be gathered from his journals and letters. The openness of the lexical system mentioned in (a) is, thus, especially evident in Hopkins's poetry, which provides a rich enough source of data for a study of lexical ambiguity.

(c) From a psycholinguistic point of view, Kess and Hoppe (1981: 77) mark out lexical ambiguity as a special class:

> There is nothing to guarantee that the recognition, processing, storage, and recall procedures that go into dealing with lexical

ambiguity has anything to do with the other types of structural ambiguity . . . . In fact, from the way that lexical ambiguity seems to have been treated, it would appear that treating lexical ambiguity separately is a more realistic approach to the problem.

On the other hand, lexical ambiguity is used a great deal in psycholinguistic research as a kind of test-bed for ambiguity in general. Both these points, in their different ways, indicate lexical ambiguity as a rich area for the investigation of the concept of ambiguity.

Carter (1987: 103) sounds the warning that analysis focused on the lexical level may be accompanied by 'a corresponding analytical narrowing and a failure to perceive the semantic densities which result from an interpenetration of levels'. In anticipation of this potential problem, it could be noted that, although the focus is on lexical ambiguity, the fact that words occur in relation to other words and in particular contexts means that a consideration of other factors such as syntax, text and context will be included. In addition, although the focus is on the *micro-level* of small-scale verbal analysis, for the study to have any significance, this level is to be related to the *macro-level* of ambiguity involving the theme or design of a poem as a whole (see, in particular, Chapter 8, section 8.1).

1.2 Ambiguity in poetry: a critical survey

Since the concern of this book is with the concept of ambiguity as it occurs in poetry, and particularly, the poetry of Hopkins, one of the first steps to take is to survey the literary field of already available material on the subject. Two main sub-sections are given, the first dealing with aspects of ambiguity and ambiguity-related issues which are of most concern to critics, and the second with what is more directly relevant to our purpose, i.e. the definitions of ambiguity in poetry and literature. For the latter subsection, only certain works are selected either because they are seminal to the subject or because they are representative of the general literary approach to ambiguity.

1.2.1 The status of ambiguity in poetry

Literary studies of ambiguity seem to agree that this phenomenon receives much more attention now in the twentieth century than in most earlier ages. Schaar (1965: 157) quotes Mahood's observation in *Shakespeare's Wordplay* (1957: 94): 'Where the Augustans disapproved of Shakespeare's wordplay and the Victorians ignored it, we now acclaim it. A generation that relishes *Finnegan's Wake* is more in danger of reading non-existent quibbles into Shakespeare's work than of missing his subtlest play of meaning.' Ambiguity is seen to be so prevalent in literature possibly because, as Frye (1957: 72) observes, 'The conclusion that a work of literary art contains a variety or sequence of meanings seems inescapable.' Frye calls this 'the principle of polysemous meaning', and this pluralistic nature of literary texts leads to the realization of extensive ambiguities.

Explanations of why literature is pluralistic are not necessary here, but an indication can suggest reasons for the interest in the study of ambiguity, and point to the aesthetic value of the phenomenon. According to Braendlin (1988: 3), the literature of earlier times contains many expressions which suggest irresolvable ambiguities in order to realize the potential for idiosyncratic expression. Recent and modern literature admits ambiguities as a reflection of modern man's 'inchoate and complex experience' (Nowottny 1962: 149) with its insistent ambiguities. It will be seen in subsequent chapters (especially Chapters 7 and 8) that these two reasons pertaining to artistic use of language and perception of real life by means of ambiguity (though not as the sole means) are also found in Hopkins.

The pluralism of literary texts leads some critics to claim that ambiguity is central to poetry. Empson, for instance, declares that 'the machinations of ambiguity are among the very roots of poetry' (1961: 21), and he is not alone in regarding ambiguity as a crucial and valuable poetic device. New Critics such as Cleanth Brooks in *The Well Wrought Urn* (1947) consider literary texts to be fundamentally ambiguous; similarly, to Wellek and Warren (1963: 23) literature abounds with ambiguities, and Jakobson (1960: 371) considers ambiguity to be a 'corollary of poetry'. These observations of ambiguity as poetically valuable and intrinsic are closely connected to the commonly held view that the more different, interesting interpretations a poem evokes, the better it is (Kasher 1976: 81), and may be summed up in the representative view of Widdowson (1975: 114): 'It is the nature of poetry to be ambiguous and no one interpretation can capture the meaning of a poem in its entirety.'

If ambiguity is considered to be a poetic device, as mentioned in the preceding paragraph, then it must perform a function. This function is usually regarded as one associated with the poetic use of language to enrich the aesthetic experience. In studies such as Schaar (1965), ambiguity is seen as a method of reading or interpreting literary texts, with an important role of deepening our understanding of the texts. Positive value is given to ambiguity in literature because the process of producing a literary piece, involving numerous rewritings and revisions, reduces the likelihood of accidental ambiguities. This leads to the assumption on the part of literary critics that ambiguity in literature, and poetry especially, is deliberate and contributes to the larger design of the work. Richards's observation in *The Philosophy of Rhetoric* (1936: 40), made decades ago, is still upheld by critics today: 'The old Rhetoric [e.g. Aristotle] treated ambiguity as a fault in language, and hoped to confine or eliminate it. The new Rhetoric sees it as an inevitable consequence of language and as an indispensable means of our most important utterances – especially in Poetry and Religion.'

Critics' discussion on ambiguity inevitably revolves around the value of the phenomenon in literature (e.g. Wheelwright 1967; Empson 1961; Nowottny 1962) and this is appropriate. But evaluation is preceded by interpretation and understanding of the term 'ambiguity', so it is really essential to see if critics are talking about the same phenomenon by examining their definitions of the term and concept.

1.2.2   Some definitions of literary ambiguity

In the following sub-sections, some definitions of ambiguity are examined for their strengths and weaknesses.

Empson

Empson's seminal book, *Seven Types of Ambiguity*, is almost a household name with most students and scholars of literature. In fact, it is reasonable to claim that interest in the phenomenon of ambiguity as central to literature has largely been generated by this book, which can boast the triumph of showing how close attention to ambiguity (resulting in, or from, close attention to the text) enriches the experience of reading poetry. However, Empson's use of the term is rather wide-ranging, as will be discussed below.

Empson considers ambiguous 'any verbal nuance, however slight, which gives room for alternative reactions to the same piece of language' (1961: 19). An objection to this definition is that it is indiscriminately accommodating, with no constraint whatsoever on declaring any expression ambiguous. This gives the term 'ambiguity' little use as a designation of a property. We might hang hope on the word 'alternative' but this is insufficient to constitute a criterion for defining the phenomenon, especially when coupled with the rather vague notion of 'reactions' which places the onus of identifying ambiguity squarely on the reader. Empson has, thus, offered no clear definition of 'ambiguity'. Perhaps it is difficult to define the phenomenon in a sentence, but even the 'types' of ambiguity Empson describes only add to the confusion of what he means by the term.

Empson's seven types are summarized in his page of Contents as follows:

(1) 'First-type ambiguities arise when a detail is effective in several ways at once, e.g. by comparisons with several points of likeness, antitheses with several points of difference . . . "comparative" adjectives, subdued metaphors, and extra meanings suggested by rhythm.' This type is so broad that it seems to cover almost everything of literary importance, thus rendering 'ambiguity' too vague and general as an umbrella term for many different phenomena.

(2) 'In second-type ambiguities two or more alternative meanings are fully resolved into one.' Ordinarily, ambiguity is resolved by choosing one of the meanings, but implicit in Empson's second type is resolution by integration. This results in ambiguity becoming indistinct from what Wheelwright (1967: 266) calls 'plurisignation', i.e. multiple meaning or complexity.[4] This confusion is common in the literary perspective of ambiguity as a welding together of acceptable meanings into a unified poetic statement, rather than an opening up of alternatives which are allowed to coexist.

(3) 'The condition for third-type ambiguity is that two apparently unconnected meanings are given simultaneously.' This type seems to correspond to the more commonly accepted definition of 'ambiguity' as the presence of double meaning, each meaning being discrete and alternative in the context. This is a necessary, but not sufficient, condition to distinguish it from some of the phenomena included in this type, such as allegory (see Chapter 7, section 7.2.3).

(4) 'In the fourth type the alternative meanings combine to make clear a complicated state of mind in the author.' This type seems to contravene the 'intentional fallacy' thesis of New Criticism; on the evidence of the text alone, it is not always certain if we can say whether or not an instance of ambiguity is intended, although foregrounding and other poetic devices may indicate the possibility that an ambiguity is deliberate.

Nevertheless, there is no reason to reject any evidence of an author's intended ambiguity, when such evidence (which can lie outside of the text being studied) is available. This fourth type, unlike the first three, is a functional characterization of ambiguity, and rather vague at that, given the difficulty of deciding what the author's state of mind is.

(5) 'The fifth type is a fortunate confusion, as when the author is discovering his idea in the act of writing . . . or not holding it all in mind at once . . . .' Like type four, this one relies on knowing what goes on in the author's mind; in fact, it is even more incredible than the fourth type as it tries to locate ambiguity in the author's mind *while* he is in the process of creating a poem. The very fluid and dynamic nature of the process of creation makes it difficult, if not impracticable, to discover this type of ambiguity.

(6) 'In the sixth type what is said is contradictory or irrelevant and the reader is forced to invent interpretations.' This form of interpretation seems to be, in reality, what psychologists call 'projection', which occurs when the reader imposes his own reading onto a word or piece of text which does not clearly signal that reading. The utter subjectivity inherent in this method of reading makes it suspect as a defining feature of this type of ambiguity.

(7) 'The seventh type is that of full contradiction, marking a division in the author's mind.' Empson considers this type most ambiguous. The second part of this description can be subjected to the objections made for type four; the first part, however, is more acceptable and may, perhaps, be further refined as the kind of disjunctive ambiguity discussed by Kaplan and Kris (1948) and Rimmon (1977), as shown in the next two sub-sections which follow.

The main thrust of Empson's discourse is a psychological perspective on ambiguity, in that he talks in terms of a reader's and author's viewpoint. Ransom (1941: 120) observes that 'Empson is beforehand with his readers.' There is no doubt that Empson is right to direct attention to the reader in his conceptualization of ambiguity, but his weakness is to allow the reader an unbridled liberty to project ambiguity on to any word or part of a text, as represented by type six. This gives rise to the danger of overreading,[5] with no criterion given for how far or in what direction the meanings of words can be stretched. This occurs because, in the words of Norris (1978: 81):

'Empson had been concerned with the "vertical" reaches of association, or what Saussure calls the "paradigmatic" dimension; the
meanings called out by a word's associative properties, without any
clear or decisive controls of context.'

The indication that the reader plays an important role in the
concept of ambiguity should not be dismissed, and will be developed
in Chapter 5 of this book. However, constraints by means of context
and an explication of 'meaning' (dealt with in Chapters 4 and 2
respectively) will help to sort out much of the muddle that Empson
has created over what constitutes ambiguity.

Although he leaves much to be desired as far as clarity in the
concept of ambiguity is concerned, Empson's *Seven Types of
Ambiguity* is, nevertheless, important in initiating a heightened
awareness and interest in the phenomenon in the twentieth century.
The next piece of work to be discussed, Kaplan and Kris's 'Esthetic
Ambiguity' (1948), is one of those written as a response to Empson's
book.

Kaplan and Kris

The most obvious difference which distinguishes the treatment of
ambiguity by Kaplan and Kris (1948) from that of Empson (1961) is a
principle or theory that is found in the former but lacking in the
latter. Empson uncovers ambiguities by the method of close analysis
of poems, but what the underlying principles are for such identification are not clear. This is one of the reasons for the confusion
occasioned by his types. By contrast, Kaplan and Kris anchor their
concept of ambiguity in a response theory of meaning.

The authors characterize the meanings of a word in terms of a
reader's responses, a set of which constitutes a 'cluster'. There is a
scale in the degree of response-constancy: high constancy is accorded
to a 'code-word' which 'has a single fixed meaning regardless of the
words accompanying it or the situations in which it occurs' (1948:
416). But there is a greater degree of variation for a 'symbol-word'
which is dependent on the context in which it occurs, and which can
only be specified in terms of a range of responses and their clusters.
The code/symbol distinction here is similar to the linguistic type/
token distinction (developed in Chapter 2, section 2.1.1). However, a
discussion in terms of 'responses' has the danger of degenerating into
emotive associations which are hard to pin down and hard to verify.
The linguistic notion of 'type' and 'token' would be less fraught with
such subjective implications.

Using the above theory of meaning, Kaplan and Kris draw up a continuum on which they classify five different types of ambiguity. The types given are: disjunctive and conjunctive, which have clusters that are sharply distinct; projective, in which responses are diffused and not grouped in distinct clusters; additive and integrative, where multiple clusters are evoked simultaneously. These types are described in greater detail below (1948: 417–21):

(1) Disjunctive ambiguity: 'We call an ambiguity *disjunctive* when the separate meanings function in the process of interpretation as alternatives, excluding and inhibiting each other.' Typical examples are homonyms or constructions with a strictly 'either/or' reading. The illustration given is 'The Duke yet lives that Henry shall depose', which can be read as 'The Duke shall depose Henry' or 'Henry shall depose the Duke.' The authors recognize that this constitutes ambiguity proper (see Beardsley, 1958: 152; and Rimmon, 1977: 26 as well).

(2) Additive ambiguity: 'the separate meanings, though still alternative, are no longer fully exclusive but are to some extent included one in the other. Rather than several distinct clusters, we have a set of clusters of varying range and with a common center. Thus a symbol is additively ambiguous when it has several meanings differing only in degree of specificity, or in what they add to the common core of meaning.' The example given is the word *rich* which may be interpreted in terms of 'abundance', 'value' or 'excellence'. A closer analysis will reveal that this is not such a straightforward category. Overlapping of meanings or clusters occurs in *a rich man* as compared to *rich soil*, both sharing the core sense of abundance but differing in specificity: 'abundance in wealth' for the former use of *rich* and 'abundance in the minerals which promote fertility' for the latter instance. However, the senses of 'abundance' and 'excellence' or 'value' have dissociative underlying markers[6] of QUANTITY (cf. 'a rich man') and QUALITY (cf. 'a rich collection of antiques') respectively. Depending on which senses are called into play, the related or the different, this category could yield ambiguity with the characteristic of the first type. The sense relation for additive ambiguity may be considered not to belong to ambiguity proper, but words seen to be additively ambiguous may also exhibit senses with a disjunctive relation. This is found in many polysemous words which are, without doubt, potentially ambiguous. Chapter 2 looks into homonymy and polysemy as indispensable sources for lexical ambiguity, and examines the difficulty of distinguishing between them.

INTRODUCTION

(3) Conjunctive ambiguity: 'the separate meanings are jointly effective in the interpretation. Rather than overlapping of clusters, there is but a single cluster consisting of paired (or multiple-linked) responses, each member of the pair (or n-tuple) corresponding to a different partial meaning.' This underlies paradox, irony, allegory and so on, which involve the recognition of two distinct meanings that are responded to conjointly. However, this does not make the preceding phenomena equivalent to ambiguity; rather, they become rich sources of potential ambiguity, as we shall see in Chapter 7. For Kaplan and Kris, this could possibly be included as ambiguity proper along with the first type.

(4) Integrative ambiguity: 'its manifold meanings evoke and support one another. There is a stimulus–response relation between the clusters as well as within them. They interact to produce a complex and shifting pattern; though multiple, the meaning is unified.' The example given is *shrunken* in 'the shrunken seas' from T. S. Eliot's 'Sweeney Among the Nightingales'. Kaplan and Kris interpret this as referring to the state of the tides at its lowest ebb (with *shrunken* carrying the meaning of 'withered', 'old', 'dried up'), and to an attitude of fearful expectancy (with 'to shrink' meaning 'to contract, huddle, cower'), and culminating in the interpretation of 'decline or decay, the falling off from past glory embodied in the figure of Sweeney.' In their interpretation, there is a reliance on the suggested associations rather than on the code-senses, which can turn out to be problematic if we aim for clarity in the concept of ambiguity (see Chapter 2, section 2.1.1). Another problem lies in the close interweaving of the meanings which end up giving the reader a single vision: one wonders, then, where is the ambiguity?

(5) Projective ambiguity: 'clustering is minimal, so that responses vary altogether with the interpreter. The term is in such cases said to be "hopelessly" vague, the meanings found being in fact imposed – projected – by the interpreter.' The authors' doubt, parenthesized in 'This type of ambiguity (if, indeed, it is to be called such) . . .', speaks for itself.

Kaplan and Kris consider that the register of poetry makes it legitimate to include all the above types as ambiguity because, in terms of multiplicity, they 'can be treated as generically identical' (1948: 417). Multiplicity, then, becomes the overriding feature for literary ambiguity, and such a characterization perpetuates the

11

confusion that ambiguity is equivalent to multiple meaning. This confusion can be resolved by considering ambiguity as *a form* of multiple meaning, different from, but capable of being evoked by, other forms of multiple meaning such as irony, paradox, allegory, and so on. Multiple meaning becomes a broad phenomenon which is manifested in many ways, one of which is through ambiguity. This view, I believe, helps us to overcome the needless controversy over the (non-)identification between multiple meaning and ambiguity (Chapter 6, section 6.1 delves into this in greater detail). It would, therefore, help to delimit what constitutes 'ambiguity' by restricting it to Kaplan and Kris's disjunctive and conjunctive types; more precisely, ambiguous words having the sense-relations of disjunction and conjunction. (It will be seen in Chapter 3 that these relations occur at different levels: disjunction is required at the semantic level, but conjunction is called forth at the pragmatic level.)

Rimmon

Of recent studies on ambiguity, Rimmon (1974; 1977) is perhaps the one who offers the neatest and most clear-cut view, made possible by the exclusive stance she takes. She defines ambiguity as 'a conjunction of exclusive disjuncts' (1977: 12), which is a definition that depends on operations in logic. The formula she gives is: $a \wedge b$, where a and b are propositions, and the symbol '$\wedge$' is 'a relational sign which combines an exclusive disjunction and a conjunction' (1977: 8). The exclusive disjunction is used in the logical sense of limiting truth to one and only one proposition, and conjunction is used in the general sense of co-presence. Logically, two disjuncts which are exclusive cannot be conjoined giving the same truth value: i.e. if a is true, and b is false, then $a \wedge b$ is true, but $a.b$ is false; similarly, if a is false, and b is true, then $a \wedge b$ is true, but $a.b$ is false. This incongruence comes about in ambiguous texts because the two propositions are equitable, which arrests any choice of one or the other. Such an approach to *literary* ambiguity has the disadvantage of being tied down to the rigidity of true–false propositions.[7] Furthermore, for Rimmon there is only one relation which underlies ambiguity, that of mutual exclusiveness.[8] This means that, in view of Kaplan and Kris's five types of ambiguity, she only considers the first, disjunctive ambiguity, to be strictly ambiguous (1977: 26). As we will argue below, ambiguity is marked not only by an 'either–or' relation, but also by a 'both–and' relation. However, what Rimmon fails to recognize is that, to avoid contradiction, these relations must be defined at different levels (see Chapter 3).

Rimmon's use of the mutually exclusive hypothesis clears away a lot of clutter and muddy thinking surrounding the concept of ambiguity as dealt with by many critics. However, her delineation of what constitutes mutual exclusion is too limiting. She equates 'mutual exclusiveness' with 'incompatibility', which she examines only in terms of the two logical relations of contradiction ('X is black' and 'X is not black') and contrariness ('X is black' and 'X is white') (1977: 7–9). There is no doubt that such contradictory and contrary cases are clear-cut instances of ambiguity since these exhibit a relation of opposition. However, it is arguable that, although incompatibility in the form of these two logical relations gives rise to mutual exclusiveness, it is not equivalent to the latter. Any form of contrast or distinctness between the meanings of utterances will contribute to the feature of mutual exclusiveness in ambiguity. An illustration is provided by Rimmon herself who unwittingly slips in adhering to the strict definition she has laid out for her concept of ambiguity. The example she gives is the following line from Shakespeare's Sonnet 38: 'Shall I compare thee to a summer's day?' (1977: 64). Her focus when discussing this is on phonological ambiguity; the stress may be on 'shall' or 'I', giving the respective readings of 'whether it is desirable or possible to compare the addressee to a summer's day' and whether 'Shall I, or will somebody else, compare thee . . .?' (1977: 64). It can be noted here that the readings offered by Rimmon do not hold a relation of opposition and they are not necessarily incompatible. However, they are obviously different enough to act as a basis for ambiguity. (Mutual exclusiveness as a feature of ambiguity is discussed further in Chapter 3, section 3.2.1.)

Rimmon's use of the logical approach inclines her to regard the exclusive disjuncts as perfectly balanced so that an effect of 'perpetual oscillation' (1977: 83) is produced as characteristic of ambiguity:

> . . . ambiguity posits opposites, two mutually exclusive intepretations according to which the various pieces of evidence balance each other in the scales of contradiction. . . . a reading which recognizes the ambiguity necessarily manifests the symmetry arising from a constant oscillation between the two opposed structures, the symmetry of a seesaw movement.
>
> (Rimmon 1974: 311)

We have argued in the previous paragraph that opposition, including contradiction, is not the only relation that leads to ambiguity. Here, one may also question how realistic it is for Rimmon to insist on perfectly balanced disjuncts. In logic, the rigorous stance adopted by Rimmon in her demand for perfectly balanced disjuncts must be expected, but imposing it on literature may be impractical. As Miller (1980: 112) observes:

> Rimmon's definition of ambiguity, however, is too rational, too 'canny', too much an attempt to reduce the *mise en abyme* of any literary work, for example the novels and stories of James, to a logical scheme. . . . Rimmon's concept of ambiguity, in spite of its linguistic sophistication, is a misleadingly logical schematization of the alogical in literature . . . .

Literature is not logic. Rimmon insists that 'both (or all) the meanings of an ambiguous expression are *equally* basic' (1977: 24; emphasis mine), but this perfect balance of disjuncts is more likely to occur in a theoretical, 'ideal' form of ambiguity than in actual practice. More often than not, the alternatives (local or global) in an instance of literary ambiguity do not have a perfect 50/50 balance, and yet can still be mutually exclusive.[9] The tenable meanings of an ambiguity may be 'unbalanced' in the sense that one can be discerned as being preferable, which is particularly likely where the ambiguous senses are not contradictory or opposite.

It follows that the effect of an unceasing oscillation which results, in Rimmon's account, from an inability to choose between the disjuncts, should also be re-examined. She draws upon an analogy with the visual arts, in particular, the well-known rabbit–duck figure as it is commented upon by Gombrich (1977: 4–5). The rabbit–duck figure allows us to see a rabbit at one instance, and, at another, a duck. This involves a shift in perspective: 'True, we can switch from one reading to another with increasing rapidity; we will also 'remember' the rabbit while we see the duck, but the more closely we watch ourselves, the more certainly will we discover that we cannot experience alternative readings at the same time' (Gombrich 1977: 5; also quoted in Rimmon 1977: ix).

Rimmon draws a parallel from the above visual trick with verbal and narrative ambiguity. She is right to infer from Gombrich's observation the features of mutual exclusiveness, the impossibility of making a choice, the distinctness of the two images or readings and the effect of incessant alternation (1977: x–xi). However, it is arguable that this effect of constantly shifting between two images or ideas operates at a purely linguistic level; at a 'higher' level, where context is fully taken into account, the alternates conjoin as a form of double vision. In Booth's (1974: 127–8) words, 'our minds no longer think of it as either a duck or a rabbit but *as an optical illusion*. Our *chief* pleasure now becomes our awareness of the duplicity.' It would seem, then, that the effect of 'incessant oscillation' gives us only a partial picture of what happens in the perception of ambiguity. The constant shift between meanings or readings is a possible psychological characterization of ambiguity at a linguistic level, but having comprehended both alternates as tenable in a given context, they are allowed to coexist in the mind. There is no longer any need to exercise choice, and consequently, to keep switching between the ambiguous meanings; at this 'higher' level, what has been created may be, to use Keats's term, a 'negative capability' which tolerates 'uncertainties, mysteries, doubts without any irritable reaching after' one solution (cited in Veeder 1980: 67).

The preceding discussion suggests that it would be more appropriate to examine ambiguity on two levels, and it is proposed in this book that these could be carried out at the semantic or textual level, and the pragmatic or interpretative level. We turn to this in the next chapter, but before we do so, an outline of how the book is organized is given below.

1.3 Organization of chapters

In this first chapter, we have seen that the term 'ambiguity' has not been used to mean the same thing in various writings on the subject. This problem stems from an inadequate clarification of the concept of ambiguity itself. We have also indicated that the literary value of ambiguity can be better appreciated when the phenomenon itself is more clearly and carefully explicated. The next two chapters, then, are concerned with a theoretical examination of the concept. For this purpose, the main thrust of Chapter 2 is (a) to elucidate certain essential terms, such as 'meaning', which are often involved in the discussion of ambiguity; and (b) to introduce some useful notions which are explored for their application to ambiguity, such as the 'type/token' distinction, 'actual' and 'potential' ambiguities, 'context', 'reader' and 'relevance'. This chapter serves as a foundation on which the following chapter builds its two-level approach (semantic/ pragmatic) to ambiguity. The thesis of this approach is that ambiguity is primarily a pragmatic phenomenon, but it exists in a potential state at a semantic level. The two factors which are crucial to actualizing ambiguity are the context and the reader: these are developed in Chapters 4 and 5 respectively.

After the theoretical base for considering the concept of ambiguity has been established in these earlier chapters, the sixth chapter further explicates the concept by comparing ambiguity with the cognate phenomena of multiple meaning, indeterminacy, vagueness, obscurity and the pun. Chapter 7 deals with the sources of lexical ambiguity, which include the metaphor and other tropes, lexical innovation and referential uncertainty. Chapter 8 delves into what has been of most concern to literary critics interested in literary ambiguity, i.e. the aesthetic value of ambiguity in poetry. This chapter also takes a look at how instances of lexical ambiguity identified at the micro-level are related to ambiguity at the macro-level; i.e. local, small-scale verbal ambiguities are examined for their relevance to ambiguity as a property of the poem as a whole. Finally, the chapter recapitulates the main thread of concern developed throughout the book, and makes some suggestions for future research in the area of ambiguity.

Notes

1. According to Edlow (1975: 425), this was reported as early as the second century AD on an observation made by a Stoic, Chrysippus.
2. Here, I am not making a clear distinction between literary critics who are more concerned with describing, interpreting and evaluating literary texts, and literary theorists who aim to provide a coherent set of principles which can be used by the critic in his literary tasks (van Rees 1984: 502). In fact, it is not certain to me that the tasks of the literary critic and those of the literary theorist can be so sharply distinguished or separated.
3. The bibliographies consulted are: Tom Dunne, *Gerard Manley Hopkins: A Comprehensive Bibliography* (1976), Edward H. Cohen, *Works and Criticism of Gerard Manley Hopkins: A Comprehensive Bibliography* (1969), and *MLA International Bibliography* (1981–88).
4. Section 6.1 of Chapter 6 examines multiple meaning as a cognate phenomenon of ambiguity.
5. This is the most often criticized aspect of Empson's book: he has been accused of over-ingenuity (Miller 1971: 55), fantastic readings and self-indulgence (Fowler 1987: 8) and solipsism (Jensen 1966: 248). Underlying these objections is the violation of the principle of tenability or relevance, thus giving rise to 'uncontrolled' readings. The significance of the principle of relevance is examined in Chapter 3.
6. See Chapter 2.
7. It could be noted here that, as Mukařovský (1976: 11) tells us, 'the question of truthfulness does not make sense at all in poetry where the aesthetic function prevails'.
8. This parallels the definition given by Beardsley (1958: 126): 'I reserve the term "ambiguity" for linguistic expressions that are doubtful in meaning

because they could have either, but not both, of two possible meanings and provide no ground for a decision between them.'

9. Criticism of the rigidity of this aspect of Rimmon's concept of ambiguity is also given by Veeder (1980: 68–9), who points out that 'Readers of *The Turn of the Screw* could thus recognize that polar interpretations conflict insolubly and yet still *feel* that the evidence for the governess's hallucinations or for the spirits' visitations is stronger'.

CHAPTER TWO

Towards a redefinition of ambiguity

The previous chapter gave a brief survey of the treatment of ambiguity in literature. In the process, some strengths and weaknesses of the various definitions and conceptions of ambiguity were also highlighted. The aim of this chapter is to work towards greater theoretical clarity of the concept of ambiguity, and thus we will examine some essential terms and notions which are related to it (sections 2.1 and 2.2 respectively). As the focus of this study is on the lexical aspect of ambiguity, a section dealing specifically with the term 'lexical ambiguity' will also be given.

2.1 Clarifying some essential terms

Underlying a definition is the assumption that the words used to define are explanatory and capable of clarifying. The problem with defining 'ambiguity' is that in practice the definiens does not uphold the assumption stated. The descriptive phrase most commonly applied to ambiguity is 'double or multiple meanings in a linguistic expression'. The troublesome culprit is the word 'meaning' which is as ambiguous as the term it defines, thus resulting in a problem the extent of which is evident in the following quotation:

> If recognition of ambiguity rests on direct understanding of the meaning of the term in question, and if an appeal to such understanding is unsatisfactory in adjudicating disputes as to the presence or absence of ambiguity, then it would seem that there is no satisfactory method of settling such disputes; unfortunately, both components of the antecedent of this conditional appear to be true.
>
> (Richman 1959: 92)

To define 'meaning' is an impossibly huge task; nevertheless, there are certain relevant aspects to this term which, when analysed, will lead to a clearer view of what constitutes ambiguity. In other words, our task here is not so much to attempt a definition as to select, for our purpose, the relevant senses in which the word 'meaning' is used. In addition, a related term 'significance' will be examined for its bearing on the concept of ambiguity.

2.1.1 'Meaning' and 'significance'

Dictionaries, whether general or more specifically for poetic terms, usually consider ambiguity to occur when a word, phrase, or sentence has more than one meaning. The survey given in the first chapter establishes the inadequacy of such a characterization. However, this general description does point out one inescapable feature of the phenomenon, and that is that the potential for ambiguity is fundamentally a semantic issue,[1] and the term central to ambiguity is 'meaning'. It is difficult to imagine a workable criterion of ambiguity which is totally independent of an appeal to direct understanding of meanings. None of the critics surveyed in Chapter 1 has emphasized the need to discuss 'meaning' as a way to attain greater clarity about the concept of ambiguity.

As Chomsky (1962: 103) points out, 'Part of the difficulty with the theory of meaning is that "meaning" tends to be used as a catch-all term to include every aspect of language that we know very little about.'[2] Perhaps the term is so basic that it should explain itself in the process of examining its usage. This can be carried out by looking at the various ways in which the word 'meaning' and its root 'mean' are used in the examples given below (the phrase in parenthesis is the approximate equivalent).

(1) These pictures mean a lot to him ('have importance').
(2) He may not have pleased everyone, but he means well ('intends').
(3) He feels that life no longer holds any meaning for him ('sense of purpose').
(4) 'I've just seen the President', he said with a meaning look ('suggestive').
(5) A continuous beeping sound means that the machine is faulty ('is a sign').
(6) *Patriotism* means 'love of or zealous devotion to one's country' ('denotes').
(7) He has managed to grasp the meaning of the play ('significance').

The above represent only a few definitions of the term; Ogden and Richards (1923: 186–7) list more than twenty. Those which are of most concern and relevance for our discussion about ambiguity in the context of poetry are found in (6) and (7) above, i.e. the dictionary kind of meaning which gives the cognitive content of the word, and all that is communicated by the word or poem, respectively (Leech 1969: 40). Following Leech, the former will be assigned the term 'meaning', and the latter, 'significance'. These will be discussed in turn.

Denotation, connotation and other kinds of meaning

Regarding 'meaning', there are, essentially, two main types which are of concern here: denotative and connotative. A discussion of these will also lead us to the consideration of the contrast between literal and figurative meanings.

Denotation is used in the sense defined by Lyons (1977: 207): 'the relationship that holds between that lexeme and [its denotatum which may be in the form of] persons, things, properties, processes and activities external to the language-system'. It is characterized by invariance in the criterial properties attributed to the lexeme: *man*, for instance, has the constant features of +HUMAN, +MALE and +ADULT. However, as Zgusta (1971: 30) points out, the problem is that 'there is no universal repertory or inventory of the criterial features valid for each single language'. This means that there is an inherent complication when we denote the properties of a lexical item. Nevertheless, despite the difficulty of quantifying such features, it is safe to say that the denotation of a lexeme captures the core meaning.

The denotative meaning of words is that typically described by means of componential analysis, of which the feature analysis used in the previous paragraph is an instance. In componential analysis, a lexical item is decomposed into sense components or features which may be thought of as universal atomic concepts. Some or all of these components are shared by different lexemes in the lexicon.[3] As Lyons (1977: 319–21) argues, the meaning of some lexemes cannot be adequately handled by merely listing the components; rather, a specification of the way these components are related and combined may be necessary. For example, *brother-in-law* might be characterized by the components MALE, SPOUSE, and SIBLING, and further represented relationally to result in the readings of: 'if x is y's brother-in-law, then x is either both male and the spouse of the sibling of y or both male and the sibling of the spouse of y' (Lyons 1977: 319). In this way, the denotative content of the word is seen to be dual-branching, and, therefore, the word is ambiguous.

One version of componential analysis which is well known is that of Katz and Fodor (1964). Here, lexical information is broken down into atomic concepts by means of semantic markers and distinguishers. According to Katz and Fodor, this approach has the advantage of 'enabling us to exhibit the semantic structure *in* a dictionary entry and the semantic relations *between* dictionary entries' (1964: 496). Markers represent that part of the meaning of a lexical item which is systematic, whilst distinguishers represent that part which is not (1964: 498). Katz and Fodor give us the example *bachelor* which carries the markers (Human), (Animal) and (Male), but since (Human) and (Animal) are 'antonymous' (Lyons 1977: 325), different branching occurs. Amongst the various designations, two are represented below (expressions enclosed in square brackets are distinguishers):

(a) *bachelor* → (Human) → (Male) → [who has never married]
(b) *bachelor* → (Animal) → (Male) → [young fur seal when without a mate during the breeding time]

In this way, different paths for an ambiguous word can be traced. In fact, Katz and Fodor (1964: 499) consider that 'the degree of semantic ambiguity a semantic interpretation assigns to a sentence is a function of the degree of branching within the entries for the lexical items appearing in the sentence, branching into markers, distinguishers, or a combination of both counting equally in determining degree of ambiguity'.

One limitation of Katz and Fodor's method is that it fails to account for non-linguistic facts. It is recognized here that many semanticists, including Katz and Fodor, consider that semantics should not attempt to deal with non-linguistic knowledge, but this does not change the observation made about the limitation of Katz and Fodor's method. For instance, compare the two sentences below (from Saporta 1967: 14):

(a) All bachelors are unmarried.
(b) Paris is the capital of France.

As Saporta notes, the truth of (a) is based on the meaning of its elements, but no amount of analysis by means of semantic markers and distinguishers can establish the truth of (b) which requires extra-linguistic knowledge. Another criticism comes from Bolinger. In his comment on Katz and Fodor's (1964: 489) example *horse shoes/alligator shoes*, Bolinger (1965: 556) observes: 'Where do markers like (Animal),

21

(Physical Object), (Young), and (Female) come from if not from our knowledge of the world? What is strange about (Shoe-Wearing) as a semantic marker – not as general, surely, as (Female), but general enough?'

From the quotation, we gather that (a) the choice of markers is essentially arbitrary; and (b) there is an appeal to non-linguistic context which is not handled by Katz and Fodor's semantic theory. Theirs is a theory of the ideal competence of an ideal speaker, 'unable to explain social competence in all its living contradictions' (Eco 1976: 98). By ignoring the contextual factor, Katz and Fodor's model cannot establish the circumstances in which ambiguity is or is not resolved. Katz and Fodor's objection to a theory of setting is that 'it would be required that the theory represent *all* the knowledge speakers have about the world' (1964: 488–9). This is, in principle, not possible. Nevertheless, to dismiss any consideration of setting whatsoever is unrealistic, particularly so in the world of poetry where so much of the significance can arise from an interplay between different settings, which can, in fact, generate ambiguity. Consider the following example from Hopkins's 'The Wreck of the Deutschland', stanza 23,

> Joy fall to thee, father Francis,
> Drawn to the Life that died;
> With the gnarls of the nails in thee, niche of the lance, his
> Lovescape crucified
> And seal of his seraph-arrival! and these thy daughters
> And five-lived and leaved favour and pride,
> Are sisterly *sealed* in wild waters,
> To bathe in his fall-gold mercies, to breathe in his all-fire glances.

In the context of the lines quoted and of the story of the shipwreck in the poem, *sealed* takes on the sense of 'drowned'. However, Hopkins has earlier on described the five marks, similar to Christ's five wounds, appearing on Saint Francis's body as the 'seal of his seraph-arrival'. Here, *seal* carries the sense of 'stamp' or 'sign' which is a proof of his vision of the seraph and an assurance of heavenly reward (according to *The Little Flowers of St Francis*, all who belong to the Franciscan order would be led from death to eternal life; Phillips 1986: 340). In the context where the five nuns are of the Franciscan order (and their drowning is further on described as 'to bathe'), this sense of *seal* is relevant as well in the second occurrence of the word, so that, at the linguistic (lexical) level there is ambiguity, and beyond this level a play on the ideas of life and death is suggested. Thus, it seems more sensible to recognize the importance of context, and, at the same time, to recognize that it is not necessary to list all the contextual information underlying a given lexical item; rather, a selection of the relevant contextual factors which will help to (or fail to) disambiguate will suffice. The need to consider context (linguistic and non-linguistic) in unravelling the meaning of words will be dealt with in a later section and in greater detail in Chapter 4. But on the whole, despite the shortcomings, the componential approach can still serve as a useful tool to identify the denotative meaning of words and lexical ambiguity.

Connotation is generally taken to be opposed to denotation, and is of undoubted importance in poetry. It is defined as 'the communicative value an expression has by virtue of what it *refers to*, over and above its purely conceptual content' (Leech 1981: 12). More specifically, what goes beyond the conceptual content may include the attributes that are additional to the criterial attributes found in the denotation of a word, or may include the emotive or affective component frequently associated with the word. For example, the word *rose* is typically, though not invariably, associated with the colour 'red', and with such emotions as 'love' or 'passion'. Synonyms show clearly the presence of connotation: *nigger* has a pejorative ring compared to its more neutral counterpart *negro*; *steed* is archaic and poetic, whereas *horse* is relatively unmarked. These connotative attributes result from the way we habitually attach certain qualities to what is represented by the word, and our perception is influenced or conditioned by factors such as culture, experience, genre, period and the society we live in. Such factors provide the conventions for interpreting the connotations, so that, to some extent, a certain degree of predictability may be expected of the connotations of certain words under certain circumstances. In fact, Eco (1976: 56) in his semiotic approach considers that the difference between denotation and connotation is due only to a coding convention.[4] But, generally, connotative meaning is subjective: it is apt to vary from individual to individual, from period to period, or from community to community. This makes it too unstable and open-ended to constitute a major factor in ambiguity. Any part that connotation plays in a study of ambiguity is indirect in that, being so pervasive and crucial in poetic language, it inevitably affects the overall (or macro-) meaning which may, in itself, be ambiguous (see Chapter 8).

Connotation often contributes to the interpretation of figurative language. But even in metaphor, it is not the connotative meaning which contributes to the identification of any ambiguity present. Take the figure of speech *a human elephant* which has various interpretations at two levels:[5] at one level which concerns denotative rather than connotative meaning, two readings are engendered depending on which word is seen as figurative – if *elephant* is figurative, we get the reading 'a human being like an elephant', and if *human* is figurative, then *elephant* becomes the subject (or tenor) in the reading 'an elephant like a human being'; at another level, the readings generated depend on the connotations of the figurative component (or vehicle) – for the figure *elephant* (first reading at level one), the possible connotations are 'clumsiness', 'long memory', 'huge size', and so on, while the connotations for the second reading at level one are 'human behaviour', 'ability to speak', 'understanding', and so on. Ambiguity occurs at level one where the readings are distinct and mutually exclusive, rather than at level two, where the features of the readings can be compatible.

The figurative meaning is often held to be suggested by the literal meaning. In fact, Rimmon considers that the literal and figurative meanings of most expressions are not mutually exclusive: 'Had they been mutually exclusive, the literal would have been incapable of suggesting the figurative' (1977: 23). For instance, the word *candid* in 'candid flowers', from a poem analysed by Nowottny (1962: 161), carries the literal (etymological) meaning of 'white' and the figurative one of 'frank'. Rimmon observes that these two meanings can coexist without any incompatibility in the poem. Phrased differently, there is a basic meaning with other secondary meanings superimposed on it, as captured in Nowottny's term 'extralocution' which refers to 'having extra meaning or leaving extra meaning in' (1962: 156). In accordance with Rimmon's view that the literal and figurative meanings are not mutually exclusive, the 'extra meaning' (also the figurative meaning in this case) may be interpreted as a form of secondary meaning that is suggested by the basic, primary meaning (also the literal meaning in this case), and because they are so closely related, it would seem that they cannot qualify as disjunctive, as is required for the analysis of ambiguous items. Although it is undeniable that there is some kind of similarity (and compatibility) between the literal and figurative meanings, especially when the latter is derived from the former (for example, *mind's eye* where *eye* shares the same function as the bodily organ of sight), there is also present an underlying opposition. The literal *eye* has the semantic feature +CONCRETE in contrast to the metaphoric *eye* which is marked by −CONCRETE; similarly, the example *candid* has the contradictory properties of +CONCRETE (for the meaning 'white') and −CONCRETE (for 'frank'). Viewed this way, it is possible for ambiguity to occur in a word with a literal–figurative pair of meanings. (Chapter 7, sections

7.2 and 7.3 explore in greater depth this important source of ambiguity from the interaction between literal and figurative meanings.)

The different kinds of meaning discussed above, denotative and connotative, literal and figurative, all contribute to significance as defined earlier, i.e. everything that is communicated by a word, phrase, sentence, or poem (Leech 1969: 40). In poetry, denotative meaning may, in some cases, account for only a small part of the significance of a particular poem, but it is, nevertheless, an indispensable aspect that must be considered. It provides a more objective basis for arguing about the validity and tenability of interpretations. Thus, it is more sensible to anchor the issue of ambiguity on this kind of meaning which is more readily verifiable, than on 'significance' which, because it embraces types of meaning that allow subjectiveness and open-endedness, will render the concept of ambiguity more nebulous. Many literary accounts of ambiguity are of the latter kind, so that there is often the confusion of ambiguity with multiple significance (seen, for instance, in Empson 1961, discussed in the previous chapter). A look at another type of meaning, the affective (Leech 1981), will further show up this confusion.

Affective meaning concerns the feelings and attitudes of the poet towards his subject or reader, and may be conveyed explicitly (e.g. satire and sarcasm) or implicitly (e.g. irony). Many literary studies of ambiguity are concerned with the ambiguity in the author's attitude which is seen to determine or contribute to the overall interpretation of the work. Affective meaning is certainly important in literature, but like connotative meaning, elusive to pin down. It seems more reasonable to restrict ambiguity to the denotative type of meaning, and to consider multiple effects derived from affective meaning as ambivalence. Leech (1981) describes affective meaning as 'parasitic' on the denotative and connotative types of meaning, as it is expressed through them. Thus, ambiguity may be a potential source that a poet can exploit to create affective ambivalence as part of the significance of his text.

Denotation and reference

Useful in the eventual analysis of ambiguity is Lyons's distinction between denotation and reference: the former is not bound to particular occurrences of utterances whereas the latter is (1977: 208). The entity referred to is individually identified within a context. In other words, 'referential meaning is based on the relation between the lexical unit and the referent' (Nida 1975: 25), but the referent does not constitute the meaning.[6] Rather, meaning consists of the set of conceptual features for a lexical unit, which we have described above in association with denotation. This set of features enables us to identify the referent. There is, thus, a close connection between denotation and reference: the former is the part of a language system that determines the referential meaning. Further, for Lyons, reference and denotation depend on 'the axiom of existence', i.e. what is denoted or referred to must exist. This constraint of existence will not, however, be taken into account in the use of the term 'denotation' in this study; rather, it will be used in a more general sense that includes concepts which have no external actualizations in the real world, such as 'unicorn'. This has the advantage of circumventing the problem of deciding whether an entity exists, especially in the fictional world of literature.

Ambiguity can occur at the denotative as well as the referential levels. In the example: 'The soldiers took the port at night', the word *port* can mean 'harbour' or 'a kind of alcoholic beverage'. Ambiguity of this kind arises from the word having two or more possible denotations. Referential ambiguity, on the other hand, comes about not from double or multiple senses, but simply from uncertainty regarding the referent intended. A literary example from Hopkins's 'Henry Purcell' will serve as an illustration:

> Not mood in him nor meaning, proud fire or sacred fear,
> Or love, or pity, or all that sweet notes not his might nursle:
> It is the forged feature finds me; it is the rehearsal
> Of own, of abrupt self there so thrusts on, so throngs the ear.

In the stanza quoted, *self* shows that referential ambiguity can occur without denotative ambiguity. It can refer to the self of Purcell, the poet's own self, or the more generic self of all men. This kind of referential uncertainty is not uncommon in poetry, affecting the interpretation of the significance of the text. Ambiguity by denotation can be said to be a form of inherent ambiguity, while the referential uncertainty a form of non-inherent ambiguity. (Chapter 7, section 7.4 discusses the latter kind of ambiguity in more detail.)

2.1.2 'Lexical ambiguity'

In *De Sophisticis Elenchis* (165ff), Aristotle listed lexical ambiguity as one of six types of ambiguity, and he clearly differentiated ambiguity located in words from that found in sentences (see Kooij 1971: 2–3 and Edlow 1975: 427). Thus, as early as Aristotle (and the Stoics), there was an indication of the importance of considering lexical ambiguity as a class by itself. More recently, this importance of lexical ambiguity is recognized by Katz and Fodor (1964: 497) in their claim that 'a necessary condition on the semantic ambiguity of a sentence is that it contain an ambiguous lexical item'.

In naming a type of ambiguity as lexical, we implicitly assume a notion of 'word-sense', an assumption that underlies lexicography. Dictionaries set out for each word entry its sense or senses. In relation to such a notion, Wilks (1988: vi)[7] makes the following observation:

> The point can be put most clearly with the suggestion that there never was any lexical ambiguity until dictionaries were written in roughly the form we now have them, and that lexical ambiguity is no more or less than a product of scholarship: a social product, in other words . . . . If any reader finds this position bizarre, even as a discussion point, let them ask what empirical evidence they have that there were word senses before the publication of dictionaries.

The above quotation challenges the status of lexical ambiguity, suggesting it is something created by a lexicographer's arbitrary segmentation of words and their senses. It is difficult to argue for or against such a position, although the fact that Aristotle recognized lexical ambiguity before the known existence of dictionaries itself calls Wilks's view into question. A lexicographer abstracts from concrete uses of word-tokens the abstract type-meaning (see section 2.2.1); from this point of view, dictionaries do not bring about word senses, but record them. This implies that word senses exist with or without the publication of dictionaries. As a consequence of cultural and conventional as well as innovative usages of words, lexical ambiguity is a reality, a 'social product' in this sense. On the other hand, as Zgusta (1971: 54) notes, 'the lexicographer's picture of what he considers to be the system exerts a certain influence upon the actual occurrences: . . . the lexicographer's influence upon the usage is if not strong yet appreciable and in some respects important'. The latter view would support the suggestion found in the quotation from Wilks above (see also the discussion on semantic distance in note 12, this chapter). Holding the second view in exclusion of the first would mean that any theory of lexical ambiguity can be based on lexicography, which is not very satisfactory. Rather, we incline towards the belief in the ontological status of lexical ambiguity, which gives the basis for taking the examination of the phenomenon beyond the boundary of the semantic system of the lexicon. Nevertheless, the quotation from Wilks above reminds us that, for our study, it is reasonable to take into account the way dictionaries record word senses.

Before proceding further, it is pertinent to consider what is meant by 'lexical'. This adjective covers, in particular, two nominals which should be clarified in relation to our study of lexical ambiguity. They are 'lexeme' and 'lexical item (or unit)'. Cruse (1986: 24) defines lexical units as 'the smallest parts which satisfy the following two criteria: (i) a lexical unit must be at least one semantic constituent [and] (ii) a lexical unit must be at least one word.' Thus, *black* is a lexical unit in the phrase *black bird*, but in the compound *blackbird* it is not a lexical unit as it does not fulfill the two criteria listed. These criteria also admit as lexical items expressions which are idioms (e.g. *to kick the bucket*), irreversible binomials (e.g. *fish and chips*), and frozen or dead metaphors (e.g. *to leave no stone unturned*).[8] Most of such phrasal lexical items have specific single meanings, but some are capable of becoming ambiguous. For example, *to give a hand* can mean 'applaud' or 'lend assistance'. In addition, our consideration of lexical ambiguity will include lexemes, which are 'the items listed in the lexicon, or "ideal dictionary", of a language' (Cruse 1986: 49). Lexemes represent a finite set although a lexeme can have an indefinite number of senses. For instance, in the example 'We went to the bank', the word *bank* is a lexeme with the different senses of 'financial institution' and 'side of river', so there are two lexical units corresponding to these two different senses.

Lexical units and lexemes are usually studied in relation to a form-meaning dichotomy. Cruse (1986: 76–7) notes that his definition of lexical unit is based on the assumption that a word form is associated with a single sense, but he qualifies this by stating that there is only one lexical unit for words formed from attaching inflectional affixes to a stem (e.g. *obey*, *obeys* and *obeyed*) but derived words constitute different lexical units from their bases (e.g. *true : untrue; kind : kindness*). We can add to Cruse's account by pointing out that derivation results in one or both of the following: a change in the grammatical class of the base word (e.g. the noun *kindness* is derived from the adjective *kind*); and/or, a shift of semantic features (for instance, *untrue* clearly contrasts semantically with *true*). Lexical units which belong to the same grammatical class come under the same lexeme if (a) the sense of one lexical unit predicts the sense of the other; or (b) the senses of the lexical units belong to the same sense-spectrum (Cruse 1986: 77–9). By making use of Cruse's definitions of 'lexical unit' and 'lexeme', we can describe the two important sources of lexical ambiguity, polysemy and homonymy, in the following way: polysemy refers to a lexeme consisting of different lexical units; homonymy has different lexical units which belong to different lexemes.[9]

The lexical items and lexemes considered so far are 'full words'

(Sweet, in Bolton and Crystal, 1969: 12). A full word is a word that has a full stress, that has 'a minimum free form' (Bloomfield 1935: 178) and that can stand as an independent, meaningful unit. There is another class of words which grammarians call function words, such as *and*, *the*, *is* and so on. Often, whereas full words are held to 'mean something when in isolation, like "apple", "gramophone", "tulip" ' (Burgess 1969: 298), function words are seen to be meaningless by themselves. This is not entirely correct, as is seen in examples such as the auxiliary *can* which signals 'ability', 'permission' or 'possibility'; the article *a* which can indicate 'some' or 'every' (cf. 'A beer is in my refrigerator' and 'A beer is a drink'); and so on. In addition, there is the problem of some words which fall on the borderline between the two categories of full words and function words. This is seen, in particular, in the case of prepositions (often manifestly ambiguous) which are the most 'lexical' of the function words.

A number of instances where ambiguity arises from a play with function words are found in Hopkins's poetry. An example can be seen in the following lines from one of his sonnets:

> Thou art indeed just, Lord, if I contend
> With thee; but, sir, so what I plead is just.
> Why do sinners' ways prosper? and why must
> Disappointment all I endeavour end?

The word *so* in the second line can be seen as adverb meaning 'likewise', or, according to Milward (1969: 137), it can carry the archaic sense of 'provided that'. Choice of either or both readings will influence the way we see the argument forwarded in the poem: *so* with the 'likewise' sense would undercut the assertion that the Lord is just as He allows sinners' ways to prosper, and so on; with the second (archaic) reading of *so*, the reader is invited to examine whether the poet's plea is just. This example indicates that it is sensible to include function words in our study of lexical ambiguity as they are capable of being ambiguous and, thus, of enriching a text.

Having shown what is included under the adjective 'lexical', we shall make a similar attempt with 'lexical ambiguity'. One way to do so is to differentiate lexical ambiguity from syntactic ambiguity, which is commonly represented in the following manner:

> A sentence is *lexically ambiguous* if its ambiguity results from at least one of its words having two meanings (admitting of paraphrases that are not paraphrases of one another), even if that word is isolated from its containing sentence . . . . On the other hand, a sentence is *syntactically ambiguous* if its ambiguity is due to its structure or syntax, rather than to one of its words having more than one sense . . . .
>
> (Edlow 1975: 427)

Such a view is problematic if we consider instances such as 'His will be done'[10] where it is not easy to draw the line between ambiguity that is lexical and that which is syntactic. Syntactically, the sentence can have the structure of (a) Pronoun (*His*) + Noun (*will*) + Copula (*be*) + Verb (*done*); or (b) Pronoun (*His*) + Ellipted Noun (0) + Auxiliary (*will*) + Copula (*be*) + Verb (*done*). Integrated with this 'constructional homonymy' (Chomsky's term) is the ambiguity that is centred on one lexeme, *will*, which can be, grammatically, either an auxiliary or a noun. For our purpose, the latter may be considered to be an instance of lexical ambiguity, but of a different kind from lexically ambiguous items such as *bank* (as indicated in our previous discussion of function words). The alternatives for *will* belong to different grammatical categories. There are, thus, two kinds of lexical ambiguity: the latter kind we shall call 'categorial lexical ambiguity', and for the type exemplified by *bank*, we shall use the term 'pure lexical ambiguity'.[11]

Categorial lexical ambiguity

As already noted, this kind of ambiguity refers to ambiguity of category, such as is found in *fish*, which can be noun or verb. Many lexemes possess different grammatical categories and, in a favourable environment, the ambiguity generated involves alternation between such categories. For instance, in 'I whirled out wings that spell' (Hopkins, 'The Wreck of the Deutschland', stanza 3) the word *spell* can be a noun or a verb (see section 6.4 which analyses this).

Categorial lexical ambiguity is different from, yet can co-occur with, structural ambiguity which arises when there is more than one phrase structure tree assigned to the sentence concerned, as seen in the example, 'He hit the man with the umbrella', where in one structural description, 'with the umbrella' modifies *man*, and in another, it does not. Ambiguities of this kind will not be of much concern to our study except when they provide the context for the occurrence of a lexical ambiguity, such as, in the example given, directing attention to the item *with*, which is ambiguous between the different readings of 'instrument' and 'accompaniment' (but *with*, in itself, is not categorially ambiguous). Similarly, for our purpose, the structural ambiguity of a sentence such as 'They are flying planes' is worth noting only in so far as it highlights *flying* as capable of being a present participle (as verb) and an adjective (modifying *planes*), and *are* as capable of being an auxiliary as well as a full verb. Here, structural ambiguity and categorial lexical ambiguity coincide, and the categorial ambiguity of *flying* does not entail a major difference of meaning (and hardly any for *are*).

The potential for the occurrence of categorial lexical ambiguity in the English language is extensively exploited by Hopkins: 'Hopkins, of course, took such a positive joy in these ambiguous placings of words that the habit must be counted as one of the guiding principles of his art' (Milroy 1977: 9). Milroy, in fact, devotes one section of his book (1977: 220–9) to the way Hopkins manipulates parts of speech for ambiguous effects. One passage from 'That Nature is a Heraclitean Fire and of the comfort of the Resurrection' is particularly effective in showing a concentration of this type of ambiguity (italics mine):

> Delightfully the bright wind boisterous ropes, wrestles, beats earth bare
> Of yestertempest's creases; in pool and rutpeel *parches*
> Squandering ooze to squeezed dough, crust, dust; *stanches, starches*
> Squadroned *masks* and *manmarks* treadmire toil there
> Footfretted in it.

The italicized words can be nouns or verbs, and the uncertainty caused by the high incidence of categorial lexical ambiguity in the quoted part of the poem above is one of the causes of its difficulty. However, there is a justification for the presence of this type of ambiguity, which, according to Milroy (1977: 223), is the suggestion that '*parches, stanches, starches* are things as well as acts', i.e. a form of double-vision. From this interpretation, we can observe here that, although categorial lexical ambiguity involves mainly the matter of grammatical categories, it is not devoid of semantic implications. This applies even to the less exciting example given earlier: *flying* bears a semantic contrast between 'activity' (when seen as a verb) and 'attribute' (when seen as an adjective).

Pure lexical ambiguity: polysemy and homonymy

Pure lexical ambiguity occurs when lexical entries with two or more readings differ in their semantic components, without necessarily involving different grammatical categories. There are, then, three types of ambiguity considered so far:

(a) Pure lexical ambiguity: this is concerned mainly with semantics (and reference); it occurs when different senses or references of the same word apply (e.g. 'He has gone to the bank').

(b) Categorial lexical ambiguity: this is concerned mainly with grammar; it occurs when different grammatical categories of the same word form apply (e.g. 'They are flying planes').

(c) Structural ambiguity: any ambiguity due to different assignments of syntactic structures (e.g. 'Old men and women have to leave the city').

Types (a) and (b) can be subsumed under the label 'lexical ambiguity' and, in principle, are not necessarily mutually exclusive. In practice, very often there are no grammatical differences associated with the different senses of (a) type of ambiguity because of the built-in structural clues in the English language (e.g. a determiner signals a following noun, a certain affix signals a certain word-class, and so on). But this does not preclude the possibility of (a) and (b) co-occurring when the context is vague enough to permit it. The following example from Hopkins's 'The Wreck of the Deutschland' (stanza 22) illustrates this point (italics mine):

Five! the finding and sake
And cipher of suffering Christ.
Mark, the mark is of man's make

Mark can function as a noun or verb, and each class carries a sense that is distinct and different from the other: the noun form refers to Christ's wound in the context, while the verb form calls for the reader to take notice. Type (c) can co-occur with (a) and/or (b): 'He hit the man with the umbrella' is an example of the (a) and (c) combination; 'His will be done' illustrates the (b) and (c) combination. Structural ambiguity will not be taken into account in this study, except incidentally, when it co-occurs with the other two types of ambiguity.

Pure lexical ambiguity derives mainly from two sources: polysemy and homonymy. They were distinguished one from the other in section 2.1.2 by means of the form-meaning dichotomy. To recapitulate in slightly different terms, homonyms are different words which have the same form and sound but different, unrelated meanings (e.g. *ball* for 'a spherical object' and for 'a social function for dancing'), whilst polysemous words have different but related meanings for the same word (e.g. *mouth* for 'opening of river' and for 'opening through which food is taken'). In practice, the distinction is not always easy to make, as will be discussed below.

The key distinguishing feature between homonymy and polysemy, that is, relatedness or unrelatedness of meaning for a lexeme, is not as unproblematic as it seems at first glance. There are some examples of lexemes which have been considered to be clearly homonymous, especially in cases where the senses are opposite, such as *cleave* ('part asunder') and *cleave* ('unite'), or are disparate and incompatible, such as *mail* ('armour') and *mail* ('post'), or *cape* ('garment') and *cape* ('promontory'). The distinctness or unconnectedness of meaning points to homonyms as a favourable source of potential lexical ambiguity.

Polysemy is illustrated by *position* ('rank', 'location in space'): the two senses are clearly related, having an underlying relation of 'place with respect to something'. Many studies of polysemy concentrate on the element of semantic similarity, but the conventional notion of polysemy as applicable to a word with several meanings implies the presence of a semantic difference as well. Regarding their relevance to lexical ambiguity, polysemous items are interesting more for their semantic difference than for their semantic similarity.

Semantic relatedness and semantic unrelatedness

Far from constituting a clear-cut dichotomy, semantic relatedness and unrelatedness occupy two ends of a continuum. Polysemous words vary in their degrees of semantic relatedness and, conversely, in their semantic difference; what is of relevance to a study of ambiguity is to decide whether the meanings diverge far enough to enable us to recognize the characteristic coexistence of distinct images or impressions which is associated with ambiguity. In practice, deciding on semantic similarity or difference is not easy, which is the underlying reason for the difficulty of distinguishing between homonymy and polysemy. This distinction is, in fact, of interest to us only in so far as it isolates the cases of homonymy, which form a clearer source of ambiguity. Apart from this, we shall not worry too much over the distinction, especially when studies on these phenomena usually end up despairing of the possibility of any clear-cut frontier. What is more important, making the distinction does not seem to have any theoretically significant function in the study of literature, although it may have a role in the construction of dictionary entries or the performance of psycholinguistic tasks (Kempson 1977: 103; Lehrer 1974: 38).

Palmer (1981: 100) points to the difficulty of determining whether two meanings are the same or not. He illustrates this matter with the verb *eat*, which has the senses 'take food', 'use up' and 'corrode'. Although the last two meanings are related to the first through being metaphorically derived from it, the three senses may be treated as different. On the other hand, according to Palmer, a puzzle arises when we compare 'eating meat' and 'eating soup', where in the latter one sense of *eat* corresponds to *drink*. Palmer poses the problem of whether to consider this a distinct meaning of *eat* or whether to view it as a semantic overlap with *drink*. As we see it, this example does not pose any problem in distinguishing the meanings: the literal and derived senses of 'take food', 'use up' and 'corrode' denote different processes and are used in different contexts, whereas 'eating meat' and 'eating soup' differ only in what is being eaten and how the food is eaten: the core meaning remains unchanged. Semantic overlap is also found in the classic example of *dog* which has been much debated over by linguists dealing with lexical ambiguity. Some (e.g. Zwicky and Sadock 1975: 7) consider it is ambiguous between a general ('canine') and specific ('male canine') reading. Others (e.g. Kempson 1979: 12) argue that it is not ambiguous as one entails the other. We agree with the latter view since, like *eat* (in 'eating meat/ soup'), the core meaning for *dog* is unchanged, whether it is applied to the more general or more specific reading.

It would seem, then, that the notion of a common core meaning can be used to cast doubt on the distinctness of meanings. Although to a large extent, core meaning is a valid notion, a note of reservation should be sounded, in that the central (or core) meaning 'often turns out to be a historical abstraction, a matter of common etymology, rather than a fact of the present-day language' (Waldron 1967: 68). As language changes over time, etymological information is not the best means of deciding on semantic relatedness or unrelatedness. An example from Lyons (1977: 551) serves to illustrate this: *port*[a] ('harbour') is derived from the Latin 'portus', and *port*[b] ('a kind of wine') is derived from the name of a city in Portugal called Oporto. However, the origin of *port*[b], Oporto, is itself derived from 'o porto' which has the same meaning as *port*[a], i.e. 'harbour'. 'Porto', in fact, shares the same Latin origin as that of *port*[a]. If etymology is used to establish relatedness of meaning, then *port*[a] and *port*[b] must be seen to be polysemous. But it is doubtful if a present-day user of the language would argue against their disparateness. A psychological element is implied as well in deciding between polysemy and homonymy, as borne out in Zgusta's (1971: 74) observation: 'the category of homonymy [and polysemy, we may add] is founded on the way the speakers understand and interpret the meaning or the senses of identical forms'. Thus, common etymology is not entirely reliable as a criterion for establishing core meaning, although this does not mean that etymological information is not relevant in the analysis of particular texts (see Chapter 6, section 6.5). On the other hand, there is a strong likelihood that meanings which do not share the same etymological origin do not share a core meaning and, hence, are different and unrelated.

Merely establishing the presence of semantic difference is not adequate for identifying polysemy as a source of ambiguity, but it is the first step. In addition, we need to consider the degree of difference. As Caramazza and Grober (1976: 202) observe: 'It would be a basic principle in the theory that the semantic distance between any pair of acceptable senses generated from a single core meaning (polysemy) will always be smaller than the distance between any pair of senses generated from different core meanings (homonyms).' The wider the gap between the senses of a polysemous item, the more akin it is to homonymy and, hence, the greater the likelihood of its being a source of ambiguity. Putting it another way, whereas homonymy is a clear-cut phenomenon, polysemy is not: 'polysemous words can differ very considerably according to the degrees of relatedness and difference which their meanings display, and . . . homonymy (total distinctness of the meanings of identical forms) is properly seen as the end-point of a continuum' (Cowie 1982: 51). This view is shared by many studies on polysemy. In fact, Caramazza and Grober talk in terms of 'degree of polysemy' (1976: 197).[12]

The distinction between polysemy and homonymy above was made with reference to pure lexical ambiguity, but it can also be applied to categorial lexical ambiguity. A polysemous word can be a member of different categories, such as *ship* (noun) and *ship* (verb); homonyms can also be in different categories: for example, *bear* (noun) and *bear* (verb). In these and many cases of categorial lexical ambiguity, grammar interacts with semantics. By extension, we could note that the two types of lexical ambiguity, one based mainly on grammatical classes and the other on semantics alone, can go hand in hand (see the example *mark* discussed at the beginning of the sub-section on pure lexical ambiguity). Thus, 'lexical ambiguity' is used in this study to refer to lexical items which are homonymous or polysemous, involving the semantic components of word-senses, word-forms and/or word-classes.

Finally, it should be noted that a semantic treatment only deals with *potential* lexical ambiguity; for lexical ambiguity to become actual it has to be realized in context by a perceiving consciousness (see section 2.2.2 and Chapters 4 and 5).

2.2 Some useful related notions

Having looked at some terms which are essential to the concept of lexical ambiguity in section 2.1, we shall now examine some notions which are deemed to be useful in furthering our understanding of the phenomenon.

2.2.1 Type-token distinction

The distinction between type and token is now widely employed in semantics and semiotics. Lyons (1977: 14) describes the difference between type and token in the following manner: 'Tokens are unique physical entities, located at a particular place in space or time. They are identified as tokens of the same type by virtue of their similarity with other unique physical entities and by virtue of their conformity to the type that they instantiate.'

When the same word occurs more than once in the same sentence or in different sentences, it is identified as a token in its particular occurrences, and the tokens seen collectively constitute a type. For instance, a computer print-out of all distinct words in a text lists the word-types, whilst a frequency count of words involves counting tokens per type. Thus, the expression 'The cat sat on the mat' contains six word tokens, but five distinct word types (since *the* occurs twice). Type, then, occurs at a higher level of abstraction; in fact, according to C. S. Peirce (1960: 423) who introduced the terms, the word as type 'is not a single thing or single event. It does not exist; it only determines things that do exist.'

The meanings at the level of type is what a competent user of the language will grasp in order to determine what is expressed in a token. On the other hand, the token, because it is identified with reference to a particular context, has a context-dependent interpretation. This means there are different interpretations on different occasions for the same polysemous expression (type). Multiplicity of lexical meaning, then, can occur at two levels: the more abstract and theoretical level of the type, and the particularized level of token.

Since linguistics deals with the language system, it is not surprising that linguists investigate ambiguity at type level (e.g. Kooij 1971; Cruse 1982). Token-ambiguity involves taking into account contextual and situational factors which, according to Kooij (1971: 6), 'would make the description of the ambiguity of sentences themselves virtually impossible, since their ambiguity would then vary with every situation where they are used'. However, while it is no doubt indispensable to have a linguistic understanding of type-ambiguity, it is not realistic, especially in literature, to dismiss token-ambiguity. The literary text provides a context in which ambiguity of particular occurrences of words or sentences is considered in the light of its contribution to the significance of the text. Limiting our study to the type level would amount to giving emphasis to potential ambiguity, whereas what is of more concern in literary texts is realized ambiguity (see section 2.2.2).

In addition, considering ambiguity at token-level allows a recognition of the creative element of literary language. Eco (1976: 245) describes the type as 'a set of properties that have been singled out as pertinent' and the token as a set which is 'obtained by mapping out the elements of the original set in terms of those of the token set'. The token set contains elements which are pertinent properties of the type, as well as elements which are non-pertinent and variable (Eco 1976: 246). As the token is context-dependent, it is possible that some semantic elements in the token set are 'created' by the context and so will not be found in the type. The significance of this observation is that it further highlights the importance of considering ambiguity at the token-level, which takes into account the variables that a creative work such as a poem can generate. Ready examples are found in tropes which serve as a rich source of ambiguity at the token-level (see Chapter 7, sections 7.1 and 7.2). For instance, *rock* in Hopkins's 'Andromeda' carries the literal type-meaning of 'big stone', but the allegorical nature of the poem invites the reader to go beyond dictionary ambiguities and to interpret *rock* as referring to the biblical figure of 'Peter' as well (see section 7.2.3 for a more detailed analysis of this). In this way, a dual structure is set up, creating a favourable environment for ambiguity to occur. Such phenomena could not be explained if one were to adhere strictly to analysing ambiguity only at the type-level.

At this point, it is useful to distinguish between two kinds of tokens. The notion of token, according to Lyons (1977) and Peirce (1960), is that if there are a thousand copies of the same text (poem, passage, etc.), then there is the same number of tokens for a given occurrence of a word. For example, there would be a thousand tokens of the word *plead* in a thousand reprints of Hopkins's lines beginning with 'Thou art indeed just, Lord', quoted earlier. Such tokens may be termed 'copy-tokens'. Tokens of a second kind are defined in relation to their occurrence in a text. Any number of reprints of the lines mentioned will yield only one such token of the word *plead*. However, if there are two or more occurrences of this word within the same text, then there are two or more such tokens of this word. This kind of token may be called a 'text-token'. A simple diagram which summarizes the structure of the type–token relation is given in Figure 2.1.

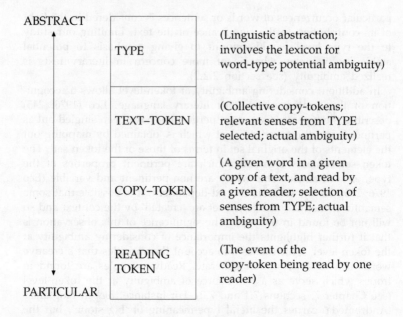

ABSTRACT

TYPE — (Linguistic abstraction; involves the lexicon for word-type; potential ambiguity)

TEXT–TOKEN — (Collective copy-tokens; relevant senses from TYPE selected; actual ambiguity)

COPY–TOKEN — (A given word in a given copy of a text, and read by a given reader; selection of senses from TYPE; actual ambiguity)

READING TOKEN — (The event of the copy-token being read by one reader)

PARTICULAR

Figure 2.1

The obvious difference between copy-token and text-token is the feature of exact replication both of the word and its context for copy-token, which, thus, renders the copy-token sense unnecessarily repetitive to be useful. A further, more pertinent, reason for making the distinction between the two kinds of token is that we are able to distinguish ambiguity as a phenomenon of a text from ambiguity as a phenomenon of a single reading of a (copy of a) given text. Our primary concern is with text-token, as we wish to see how the literary text provides a context in which ambiguity of particular occurrences of words or sentences may be considered in the light of its contribution to the significance of the text itself, leaving aside (at least for the present) the reader's role in determining significance.

2.2.2 Actual and potential ambiguity

The type–token notion is closely related to the actual or potential existence of ambiguity in a given text (see Figure 2.1 above). Like 'type', the *potential* ambiguity occurs at a level of abstraction from the text, whilst the *actual* ambiguity, like 'token', is a form of concrete realization of ambiguity. The senses of a type-word are encoded in dictionaries and thus correspond to *dictionary meaning*. But, since a token is an 'instantiation', it carries what may be called *contextual meaning*. The distinction between these two kinds of meaning corresponds to the distinction between actual and potential ambiguity: dictionary meaning consists of conventionally accepted meanings and forms the basis of potential ambiguity; contextual meaning is a particularized occurrence and provides the environment for realized ambiguity. For instance, the type word *man*, being polysemous, has a range of potentially applicable meanings. But we seldom ponder on these once we have selected the appropriate meaning under the given circumstances (e.g. *'man* the lifeboats!'). However, ambiguity arises once a word (or linguistic expression) offers a number of alternative meanings any of which would fit the context. Potential ambiguity is generally not perceived when context clearly points to a certain interpretation, while an absence of such contextual clues will lead to realized ambiguity. Literary analysis is concerned with realized ambiguity, so our concept of ambiguity must be viewed in terms relative to context.

2.2.3   *Context, reader and relevance*

The notions of 'type/token' and 'actual/potential' are linked to three other notions: 'context', 'reader' and 'relevance'; the latter three are integral to a deeper insight into the concept of ambiguity. The interrelation between all the preceding notions can be placed within the framework of the simplest form of (written) communication:

Author <—> Text <—> Reader.

The text is the medium through which the author communicates his message and through which the reader understands (or interprets or perceives) the author's message. In one sense, the arrows should be unidirectional as the reader may not be able to get feedback from the author. However, the double-headed arrows may be explained by taking the view that, on the one hand, the author creates his text partly through assumptions about the knowledge, attitudes, and so on, of possible readers, and on the other hand, the reader falls back upon these assumptions when he interprets the text by reconstructing what the author could have meant by it. (The reader, therefore, is not a passive mental vessel into which is poured the original shape of the author's thought.) The communication between author and reader can take place because they share certain knowledge (linguistic as well as non-linguistic). Awareness of both parties having this knowledge permits certain assumptions to be made. One assumption is that, on a purely linguistic level, members of the same linguistic community have a basic competence which assures the author that some kind of transmission of his message will be effected. This takes us back to the 'type' idea: a competent reader recognizes that a certain word-type has a range of potentially applicable meanings. He selects from this potential range for the word-token he encounters in a text, guided by what the context determines as relevant.

The notion of 'context' is complicated and will be dealt with in Chapter 4. Here, it can be described as a communicative situation which consists of factors that, 'by virtue of their influence upon the participants in the language-event, systematically determine the form, the appropriateness or the meaning of utterances' (Lyons 1977: 572). This quotation shows up the interrelation between the notions of 'context', 'reader' and 'relevance'. This interrelationship is so important that it will pervade a large part of this thesis in the course of its examination of the concept of ambiguity. For the present, it will be baldly stated here that there is an intricate and complex interplay between them in turning type-ambiguity into token-ambiguity, and potential ambiguity into realized ambiguity. 'Context' and 'reader' will be studied in greater detail in Chapters 4 and 5 respectively, whilst the principle of relevance will be discussed in section 3.3.2 of Chapter 3.

Our discussion so far, in clarifying 'meaning' and relating 'context', 'reader' and 'relevance' to ambiguity, points in the direction of a dual approach to the explication of ambiguity, one which is to be based on both semantics and pragmatics. We turn to this in our next chapter.

Notes

1. A possible objection to this might be a structural or a purely phonetic argument. An example such as 'Old men and women must leave the city' can be parsed as having two readings, the first with *old* modifying *men* only, and the second with *old* modifying *men* as well as *women*. This kind of structural ambiguity may be discussed without reference to the semantics of the sentence, but it does not take very close scrutiny to tell that the two structures also reflect two different meanings. Thus, there is in effect no running away from the semantic issue, which is made even more significant when ambiguity is studied in the poetic context, since this involves the whole question of interpretation, and perhaps, value

judgement as well. A similar argument can be made concerning the phonetic treatment of ambiguity, seen, for instance, in the homophony of /led/ (*lead, led*), which corresponds to two distinct meanings as well as two distinct word forms.

2. Quoted in Katz and Fodor (1964: 480).

3. See Lyons (1977, section 9.9) for a fuller description of this approach to the meaning of words.

4. More specifically: 'a denotation is a cultural unit or semantic property of a given sememe which is at the same time a culturally recognized property of its possible referents; a connotation is a cultural unit or semantic property of a given sememe conveyed by its denotation and not necessarily corresponding to a culturally recognized property of the possible referent' (Eco 1976: 86).

5. This example is borrowed from Leech (1969: 147).

6. For instance, proper names are only referential, and do not, at least theoretically, contain any meaning, although in practice many proper names carry certain types of meaning pertaining to gender, animacy, and so on. In poetry, proper names are often given the referential as well as denotative qualities. For example, the two parts of the name *Felix Randal* (also the title of one of Hopkins's poems) have meanings: *Felix* is Latin for 'happy' or 'blessed' and *Randal* has an etymological sense of 'sandal' (Mariani 1970: 170). Both meanings are appropriate in the context of the poem about a farrier (sandal being a type of horse-shoe) who has found spiritual comfort before his death.

7. In his preface to Small et al. (1988).

8. It should be noted that the diverse types of phrases can often make the task of deciding whether or not a phrase constitutes a lexical unit a complex one (see Nida, Louw and Smith 1977: 155).

9. It will be seen, in a discussion later on pure lexical ambiguity, that this terminological description of homonymy and polysemy does not resolve some problems associated with their distinction.

10. This example is borrowed from Small, Cottrell and Tanenhaus (1988: 5), who call this kind of ambiguity 'syntactic lexical ambiguity'. As it is easy to confuse this with 'syntactic ambiguity', our label 'categorial lexical ambiguity' (see the following subsection) will be safer. This is a matter of terminological convenience, and we do not deny that this type of lexical ambiguity is inevitably accompanied by syntactic ambiguity. However, our term also calls attention to the underlying source of this type of ambiguity, which is the existence of alternative grammatical categories for a single word.

11. See note 10 above. Small, Cottrell and Tanenhaus use the label 'semantic lexical ambiguity' (1988: 5), but, in order to avoid the possibility of confusing this with the more general 'semantic ambiguity' (Cruse 1982: 74) that can be found in sentences as well as words (and, even more specifically, categorial lexical ambiguity), and also to simplify matters, we consider it better to use the term 'pure lexical ambiguity' for ambiguity between senses.

12. Lehrer (1974) devised certain tests which were meant essentially to measure semantic similarity, but which could also be used to determine the degree of semantic difference. The tests made use of native speakers' intuition, and the results showed that judgements were more stable for meanings which were very different or very similar, i.e. for words with meanings occupying both ends of a continuum on sense relations. The unclear cases fall in-between these extremes. Lehrer used the scaling method to determine which meanings are more similar and thus, conversely, less different, and vice versa, but this method is far from being decisive. The reason is that there is variability not only for different speakers, but for the same speaker at different times (Lehrer 1974: 36). This implies an element of arbitrariness will be present when deciding on the distance between two or more meanings (see the earlier discussion on the dictionary in section 2.1.2).

CHAPTER THREE

A semantic–pragmatic approach to ambiguity

Lexical ambiguity has been characterized as a linguistic (i.e. grammatical, semantic) phenomenon. The stand taken here is that it is primarily a pragmatic phenomenon; by this is meant that it is realized in context and through contextual interpretation. Semantically, a word with different senses is polysemous or homonymous, not ambiguous. Such words have a potential of becoming ambiguous, but actual ambiguity results only when a certain relation is set up between the senses, and this happens when the word is:

(a) placed in context: linguistic and/or non-linguistic;
(b) interpreted as having disparate and alternative senses which are both (or all) tenable or relevant in the context.

Thus, lexical ambiguity (and, more generally, ambiguity itself) occurs in language use, which calls for a pragmatic method of explication.

A pragmatic view of (lexical) ambiguity serves three functions:

(a) it encompasses (or is interrelated with) a semantic characterization of the phenomenon;
(b) it captures the cognitive conceptualization (the psychological dimension) of the phenomenon;
(c) it identifies ambiguity as an aspect of communication.

To understand the concept of ambiguity, we need to start with (a), which is an essential component of the phenomenon. For this reason, and, secondarily, to acknowledge the important contribution of semantic studies to the phenomenon, our approach is called a semantic–pragmatic approach.

3.1   Distinctions between semantics and pragmatics

The division between semantics and pragmatics was initially made by philosophers such as Peirce and Morris. Morris (1938: 60) defined pragmatics in terms of 'the relations of signs to interpreters' and semantics in terms of 'the relations of signs to the objects to which the signs are applicable'. The two fields are concerned with meaning, but whereas semantics studies meaning as a property of language, pragmatics considers meaning in terms of language use. The former is rule-governed, and is conceived of as a theory that deals with the meaning aspect of language as a system.[1] It characterizes and explains the systematic relations between words and between sentences, and is thus able to predict the ambiguous forms of words or sentences which occur in isolation. We can call this 'system ambiguity', which occurs at the abstract level of *type* rather than of *token*.

Pragmatics, on the other hand, treats meaning not at an abstract level of the system but at the concrete level of use. It deals with meaning in terms of speaker's intention, hearer's interpretation, context and performance or 'action' (see Leech 1981: 320). Because of its concern with use, pragmatics is especially relevant for studying actual token-ambiguity.

Another useful distinction made by Leech (1983: 30) is that between 'sense' (the semantic meaning which we discussed in Chapter 2, section 2.1.1) and 'force' (the pragmatically determined meaning which includes sense). Theoretically, the former does not require locating lexically ambiguous items in context although, in practice, semantic studies of sense often use at least a minimal 'unit' of context in the form of the immediate surrounding syntax, extending often to the sentence. What is important to note is that the target of the semantic approach is to *identify* the senses of an ambiguous word. Pragmatics, on the other hand, is concerned with *interpreting* the meaning or force, and it usually does so by involving reference to not only the conventional sense but any other relevant factors (e.g. linguistic or non-linguistic contextual knowledge).

As stated at the beginning of this chapter, the pragmatic approach to ambiguity involves a semantic characterization of the phenomenon. It would, therefore, be pertinent to carry out a semantic examination of the concept of ambiguity before moving on to a pragmatic one. For the former, the emphasis is on the sense-relations of lexical items (cf. the issue of 'meaning' which has been treated as central to ambiguity in section 2.1.1), whilst for the latter, attention is given to such pragmatic factors as the Cooperative Principle, implicatures and the principle of relevance.

3.2   A semantic approach to ambiguity

3.2.1   Sense relations

In section 2.1.1 of the previous chapter, we showed that, as 'meaning' is an essential component in the notion of ambiguity, an examination of some aspects of meaning will help us to understand better what constitutes ambiguity. We can take this further by looking at the relations between senses of words in order to explicate the concept of ambiguity.

In our discussion on homonymy and polysemy in Chapter 2, section 2.1.2, we mentioned two basic kinds of semantic relations: sameness and difference, and we noted that ambiguity is concerned with the latter. Semantic difference can be further specified in terms of *hyponymy*, or meaning inclusion and *incompatibility*, or meaning exclusion (Leech 1981: 92–4). It is suggested here that hyponymy does not give rise to ambiguity: consider the *dog* example mentioned earlier (section 2.1.2) in which *dog* ('male canine'), like *bitch*, is a hyponym of *dog* ('canine species'). Some linguists accept hyponymy as a relation that contributes to ambiguity,[2] but to do so gives rise to the problem of distinguishing ambiguity from lack of specification or vagueness (see Chapter 6, section 6.3). A more important objection is that implicit in hyponymy is the relation of entailment, which undermines the criterion that the senses of an ambiguous lexical item are distinct and separate.

On the other hand, the second kind of semantic difference, incompatibility, is more obviously relevant to ambiguity. It is generally considered to be equivalent to 'meaning exclusion' (Leech 1981: 92): 'We may say that two componential formulae, or the meanings they express, are *incompatible* if the one contains at least one feature contrasting with a feature in the other. Thus the meaning of *woman* is incompatible with that of *child* because of the clash between +ADULT and −ADULT.'

Incompatibility underlies the idea of 'mutual exclusiveness' which is central to Rimmon's (1982: 21) definition of ambiguity as 'a conjunction of exclusive disjuncts'. Rimmon specifies the relation between the disjuncts in terms of contradiction and contrariness,[3] both of which are constituents of incompatibility, and which are, according to Rimmon (1977: 9), necessary conditions for ambiguity: 'ambiguity can be the coexistence of contraries (mutually exclusive but not exhaustive) or the coexistence of contradictories (mutually exclusive and exhaustive)'. There is no doubt that ambiguity is most obvious in cases where the two or more senses of a word are incompatible (i.e. contradictory or contrary), *but* reducing ambiguity to a matter of incompatibility can be too limiting, as we shall argue below.

Contradiction involves the idea of opposition which is one of the most important principles underlying the language system. As Wildgen (1983: 338) observes, 'Semantic bi-polarity is a fundamental principle in the organization of the lexicon.' Many terms in the vocabulary of the English language have an opposite counterpart. Of the different kinds of opposites, those that are complementary are most clearly relevant to contradiction.[4] Complementaries are two-member sets of ungradable opposites (i.e. opposites which do not involve degrees along a scale, such as *male/female*, *married/single*, and *alive/dead*). In logical terms, 'Two propositions are *contradictories* if one is the denial of the other, that is, if they cannot both be true *and* they cannot both be false' (Copi 1961: 142–3).[5] It follows that contradiction is based on binary contrast, with an absolute division between an affirmative and a negative value. Consequently, the occurrence of one proposition implies its negation, and vice versa. Thus, to say that 'The rat is dead' is to imply that it is not alive. Contradiction arises when a proposition and its negation coexist: 'The rat is dead' : 'The rat is not dead'; or when the propositions are related by implicit negation: 'The rat is dead' : 'The rat is alive.'

The logical specification for *contraries* is that the two propositions cannot both be true, but they may both be false. The propositions may be in the form of opposites or non-opposites: e.g. 'The coffee is hot' : 'The coffee is cold', or 'The dress is white' : 'The dress is red' (see Lyons 1977: 272). The opposites in contraries differ from those in contradictories in being gradable, i.e. measurable in terms of degree and comparison. The feature of incompatibility remains important. In logical symbols, Rimmon (1977: 9) formulates contradictories as a and $\bar{a}$ (a and not-a) and contraries as a and b. Contradictories are strictly binary, whereas contraries involve a range of alternatives. From the above descriptions of contradiction and contrariness, it is clear that these forms of incompatibility are useful for characterizing the phenomenon of ambiguity. However, it is arguable that they do not constitute necessary conditions, as can be gathered from examining the following lines from Blake:[6]

Never seek to tell thy love,
Love that never told can be.

Love in the first line is ambiguous between the senses referring to 'state' and 'person'. These senses are incompatible in at least one underlying feature: +ANIMATE (for 'person') and −ANIMATE (for 'state'); i.e. the binary contrast indicates an inherent contradictoriness between the senses for *love*. However, this does not make incompatibility (or contradiction here) a necessary condition for the occurrence of ambiguity. The two senses for *love*, in fact, can be compatible, as one can tell one's love (person) about one's love (state of emotion). *Told* in the second line above provides us with another example: it can have the sense of (a) 'communicated', 'disclosed' or (b) 'counted', 'measured'. These are alternative senses in the context, but they are not incompatible. Similarly, *light* in 'He wore a *light* suit' is ambiguous not because its senses of 'weight' and 'brightness' are contradictory but because they are just unrelated. The context may even allow the two senses to apply simultaneously, which then results in a pun. What the last two examples indicate is that *difference between senses which are distinct and disparate* is a sufficient condition for ambiguity to occur.

As in the case of contradictoriness, senses of an ambiguous item may be contrary, but they do not necessarily have to be so. Despite their semantic difference, contrary senses have an underlying relatedness in belonging to the same semantic field; on the other hand, many ambiguous words, especially those which derive from homonyms, have entirely divergent senses. This is illustrated by examples such as *light* (given earlier), *ball* ('spherical object', 'dance function') and *mole* ('animal', 'spot on skin'). Thus, although an understanding of contradictory and contrary relations helps to explicate the nature of the alternatives present in ambiguity, such relations are not necessary for ambiguity. At the semantic level, the potential for ambiguity is generated when there is the criterion of distinctness of senses, which serves as the basis for an 'either–or' interpretation. This is a weakened form of mutual exclusiveness which does not insist that the alternatives be perfectly balanced as incompatibles (cf. Rimmon's use of 'mutual exclusiveness' discussed earlier in this and the first chapters). The following (very rough) diagram may be useful in picturing the sense-relations involved in the semantic aspect of ambiguity (only the unshaded area is relevant):

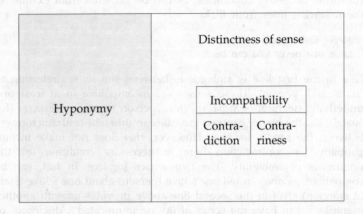

Figure 3.1

The semantic view given so far deals with ambiguity at the level of type or system. This remains an abstract treatment of ambiguity until it is placed within a pragmatic framework, which is our concern next.

3.3   A pragmatic approach to ambiguity

Words are essentially tools which are used by a human subject to refer to entities (concrete or abstract). We have attributed to words the function (among others) of denoting; in reality, it is more accurate to say that the writer uses the word to denote something. As Zgusta (1971: 47) observes,

> Words do not have an abstract existence of their own as some unalterably defined units of a system, but they are used. The distinction is so very important that it is useful to discern even terminologically the meaning of a word as a part of the system . . . and its signification, or actual signification when it occurs in a text.

'Signification' occurs at the token-level when the context in which the word is located particularizes the reference made by the word, or disambiguates it by eliminating other possible senses of the word than that in which it is applied, or performs both operations. Our study of ambiguity must thus be placed in the context of language use, which, in turn, points us in the direction of pragmatics.

Leech (1980: 2) defines pragmatics as 'the study of the relation between the abstract meaning or sense of linguistic expressions, and the communicative force which they have for speakers and hearers in given utterance situations'. As our focus is on *lexical* ambiguity, it is pertinent here to establish the relation between force and word. Word-senses are quite clearly identifiable; force is, however, spoken of in terms of utterance. An utterance, usually expressed in the form of a sentence, is a verbal act or product of a verbal act (Leech 1983: 14). For instance, 'Have you got something to drink?'[7] is ambiguous between a request and an offer; the ambiguity arises from the utterance corresponding to more than one (illocutionary) force or speech act, and is not based on lexical ambiguity. Pragmatic ambiguity of this kind, which has little to do with lexical ambiguity, is outside the scope of this study. However, it should be noted that ambiguity between speech acts or forces can be found in Hopkins's poetry as well. For instance, the question asked in the first stanza of 'The Lantern Out of Doors' may be a genuine request for information, or a rhetorical question that expresses the poet's pensive mood:

Sometimes a lantern moves along the night.
That interests our eyes. And who goes there?
I think; . . .

The problem is to determine how a word in an utterance can contribute to different forces, possibly resulting in pragmatic ambiguity.[8] One way is to consider force as speaker's (or author's) meaning, so that a word occurring in an utterance is ambiguous because the reader is unable to decide which of two or more senses or references is intended by the author. For example, a pronoun which is referentially opaque is an instance of pragmatic ambiguity in that the reader has to interpret or locate the reference intended by the author in a given context. Other obvious linguistic items which depend on context for interpretation are deictic forms such as *here, now, this, that*, and so on. Similarly, when the reader remains uncertain which sense is intended in a polysemous or homonymous word because of insufficient contextual clues, then ambiguity is generated at the pragmatic level. In this respect, pragmatics is important to the concept of ambiguity because it contextualizes, and therefore, actualizes, potential ambiguity which is inherent (e.g. homonyms) or non-inherent (referential uncertainty) in words.[9]

Many pragmatic studies deal with conversation or other forms of direct interaction between speaker and hearer, so that there is some likelihood of being certain about the speaker's intention, as the hearer is able to verify the intended meaning with the speaker. In written discourse, there is an absence of face-to-face interaction, feedback mechanisms and paralinguistic clues, thus rendering the author's intention less directly accessible or certain. It seems more reasonable, therefore, to approach the issue of pragmatic ambiguity from the perspective of the reader's interpretation, or, putting it another way, to study speaker's meaning as 'a REFLEXIVE INTENTION, i.e. an intention whose fulfilment consists in its recognition by [hearer]' (Leech 1983: 34–5).

Thus, our pragmatic approach to ambiguity involves a consideration of the two important issues of context and reader interpretation (see Chapters 4 and 5 respectively). Their interaction gives rise to two notions which are useful for explicating the concept of ambiguity from a pragmatic viewpoint: these are implicature and relevance. The former can be examined in conjunction with the Cooperative Principle.

3.3.1 Implicature and the cooperative principle

The meaning of an utterance is not always explicit; on the contrary, 'Virtually every utterance conveys implicit information whose recovery may be crucial to the interpretation process' (Wilson and Sperber 1986: 2). This implicit content is also termed 'implicature', which it is the task of pragmatics to recover, or explain how it is recovered. For instance, the utterance 'Have you got something to drink?' (given earlier) may implicate (a) my reason for asking this is that, if not, I wish to offer you a drink; or (b) my reason for asking this is that I am thirsty and I need a drink. The two implicatures (a) and (b) set up an ambiguity in terms of force, i.e. between an offer and a request respectively.

The notion of implicature was first developed by Grice in his 'Logic and Conversation' (1975). According to him, the use of language in communication is governed by an underlying principle of cooperation, called the Cooperative Principle. He expresses this principle in the following manner: 'Make your conversational contribution such as is required, at the stage at which it occurs, by the accepted purpose or direction of the talk exchange in which you are engaged' (1975· 45).

Although Grice talks in terms of conversation, his principle applies to any communicative situation of interaction, and, thus, is relevant to poetry. Specifically, following the Cooperative Principle (henceforth CP), the reader establishes the significance of the poem and uses that to provide the general direction in which to interpret ambiguity or to infer that ambiguity is intended. Within Grice's intentionalist theory of meaning, significance may be equated with inferring the author's intended meaning, as far as is possible, from the text.[10] This communicative goal, or what Grice calls 'the accepted purpose or direction of the talk exchange' (see above quotation), performs two functions: (a) it helps to actualize potential ambiguity in that it provides the general frame which admits the tenability of the two or more senses of a word in the context; and (b) it governs the meaningful interpretation of ambiguity in terms of its poetic value (see Chapter 8). For instance, Hopkins's sonnet beginning with the line 'I wake and feel the fell of dark, not day', is about the despair of a self alienated from God. One reading for the word *fell* is 'descend' as found in expressions such as 'dark (or night) falls'. However, the word is semantically capable of other senses, such as: (a) 'to cut or knock down', as in felling a tree, (b) 'a single hasty action or occurrence'; (c) 'an animal skin or hide'; and (d) 'a mountain hill or moor'.[11] The metaphorical nature of 'feel the fell of dark' allows, in principle, any of the senses listed to be applicable. These senses are apparently violations of the CP because of the literal falsehood of the proposition containing them. But the assumption that the poet is observing the CP leads the reader to work out through implicature that the senses listed are relevant because they help to concretize the abstract *dark*, making it, for example, tactile and claustrophobic (as suggested by sense (c)), and intensifying the poet's experience of alienation.

Grice (1975: 45–6) identifies four maxims subsumed under his Cooperative Principle; of these, the Maxim of Manner is of particular interest to us. Unlike the three maxims of Quantity, Quality and Relation, the Maxim of Manner relates not so much to what is said as to how something is said. Leech (1983: 100) suggests this maxim belongs as much to Textual Rhetoric as to Interpersonal Rhetoric, which makes it highly appropriate to be considered in any stylistic study. Grice (1975: 46) formulates this maxim in the words 'Be perspicuous' and suggests one way to promote perspicuity is to avoid ambiguity. The purpose of perspicuity is to convey the intended communicative goal in the clearest and most direct way possible. This maxim is, without doubt, frequently flouted in poetry through, among other means, introducing ambiguity into the poem. Going by the CP, the flouting draws the reader's attention to the seemingly deliberate ambiguity in the text, and makes us seek its relevance to the poem. That is, the reader looks for (what he thinks might be) the poet's underlying intention. Semantically, there are two or more explicit meanings which are applicable to the ambiguous item, but the implicit significance of the use of ambiguity has to be inferred through implicature by the reader.

There is another angle from which to view how the notion of implicature contributes to the concept of ambiguity. Grice differentiates what is said from what is implied, since he uses the term implicature 'to account for what a speaker can imply, suggest, or mean, as distinct from what the speaker literally says' (Brown and Yule 1983: 31). This means that there are essentially two layers of meaning: the said and the implied. It is possible, for example, in the phenomena of irony and metaphor, that these two layers are distinct and disparate one from the other, but both being tenable interpretations, they give rise to ambiguity (see Chapter 7). This can be seen, for instance, in some metaphors where what is said makes good sense on a literal plane, and where the implied (or figurative) interpretation is, so to speak, an optional extension of it. Furthermore, ambiguities may arise, purely on the pragmatic level, from the coexistence of more than one implied meaning. As Pilkington (1989: 129) observes, 'there is no cut-off point that allows us to say that so many implicatures are communicated and no more'. To illustrate, Sperber and Wilson (1986: 236) use a line from Flaubert in his comment on the poet Leconte de Lisle: 'His ink is pale. (Son encre est pale.)' The literal interpretation refers to the colour of the ink, but the implicatures derived range from 'Leconte de Lisle's character is weak' to 'Leconte de Lisle's writing may fade.'[12] Sperber and Wilson (1986: 236) state that 'the wider the range of potential implicatures and the greater the hearer's responsibility for constructing them, the more poetic the effect, the more creative the metaphor', and, we would add, the greater the possibility for ambiguity.

3.3.2 The notion of relevance

Working hand-in-glove with the notion of implicature is that of relevance: firstly, implicatures are generated because an utterance is seemingly irrelevant in a given context; i.e. when the Maxim of Relation, 'Be relevant' (Grice 1975: 46) is flouted (in fact, the flouting of any of the maxims will cause implicatures to be made); and secondly, in compliance with the Cooperative Principle, the reader works out implicatures that will be interpreted as relevant to the communicative goal of the situation at hand. The notion of relevance here may be formulated in terms of the 'goal-oriented' definition given by Leech (1983: 94), which applies, not just to speech, but to written (literary) discourse as well: 'An utterance U is relevant to a speech situation if U can be interpreted as contributing to the conversational goal(s) of s[peaker] or h[earer].' Defined in this manner, the notion of relevance can show how ambiguity is actualized through the interaction between context and interpretation. More specifically, (a) it can explain the ideas of tenability and choice, and (b) it can make evident three ways in which ambiguity can occur. However, before we proceed to examine ambiguity by means of relevance, a selective overview of the principle of relevance as developed by Sperber and Wilson (1986) will first be given, if only to sound a cautionary note that their principle cannot be adopted unquestioningly for our purpose.

Sperber and Wilson (1986)

Sperber and Wilson expand the Maxim of Relation into what they call the Principle of Relevance, which they describe in the following way: the greater the contextual effects (this term is explained below) yielded with as little as possible processing effort involved, the greater the relevance (1986: 125). The two factors of effect and effort relate respectively to the two important notions of context and reader which we have indicated are integral to the concept of ambiguity (see section 2.2.3). Although 'effect' and 'effort' are useful in our discussion of pragmatic ambiguity, they should be viewed critically, as we shall do below.

For Sperber and Wilson (1986: 15), 'context' consists of 'the set of premises used in interpreting an utterance . . . [it] is a psychological construct, a subset of the hearer's assumptions about the world'. A contribution to these assumptions which affects interpretation is information, and old and new information interact to give contextual effects. The notion of contextual effect, then, is a dynamic one in which new information can add to or strengthen old information, or change it by providing contradictory evidence (Sperber and Wilson 1986: 109). It would seem, then, that relevance has to do with newness of information within a previously established context; thus, implicatures count as contextual effects. Ambiguity which arises from the contrast between what is said and what is implied (discussed earlier) may be placed within this effect account of relevance. However, what has not been addressed so far is the relational nature of relevance (i.e. relevant to what? and to whom?). It would be more complete to include in the description of relevance the usefulness new information may have for the reader's or author's purpose.[13] This view of relevance will, for our purpose of explicating ambiguity, be more functional than that of limiting relevance to newness of information, in that it can help to explain the factors of tenability and choice (see discussion in the section on the actualization of ambiguity).

The other axis on which Sperber and Wilson's principle of relevance turns is that of effort. This is seen to be negative, in that the greater the processing effort required, the smaller the relevance. In order to minimize effort, ambiguity should be avoided, since 'the communicator should have used a stimulus which would have saved the addressee the effort of first accessing two hypotheses consistent with the principle of relevance, and then having to choose between them' (Sperber and Wilson 1986: 168). This assertion is in accord with the hypothesis of economizing effort for relevance, but it wrongly assumes that all acts of communication have only a single intended interpretation: it denies that the communicator (or author) can intend ambiguity. What is excluded is the possibility of several tenable interpretations for a given utterance in a given context. Minimizing processing costs also means that the speaker will try to make 'the required contextual assumptions . . . easily accessible to hearers' (Blakemore 1987: 713). This is not necessarily the case with poetry, which is known to be often deliberately obscure, requiring readers to work out the meaning of the poem at a high processing cost. Some poets, including Hopkins, overtly declare the virtue of obscurity in their poetry (see Chapter 6, section 6.4). Introducing ambiguity into poetry as one device to make readers 'work' is evidence that the hypothesis of minimal processing effort for interpreting a text should be viewed critically.

In relation to ambiguity, a more serious issue concerns Sperber and Wilson's (1986: 169) claim that 'it is the first interpretation to occur to the addressee that is the one the communicator intended to convey'. No doubt this is, again, consistent with the minimal processing effort hypothesis, but it renders ambiguity and various forms of indirect speech act impossible, and certainly does not explain the multiple interpretations and reinterpretations demanded by literary texts. The most accessible interpretation, being the one requiring least effort, is not necessarily the most relevant.

It is, thus, with some reservation that we apply Sperber and Wilson's principle of relevance to the concept of ambiguity; but the notion of relevance, especially when related to the communicative goal between interactants, is itself of utmost relevance for our study. Therefore, we disagree when Wilson and Sperber (1981: 172–3) consider unresolved ambiguity to violate the principle of relevance: 'It is only in the rare cases where two senses of an utterance would be equally relevant that semantic ambiguity is accompanied by pragmatic equivocation. Equivocation . . . violates the principle of relevance . . . .' Violation is present only if we unquestioningly adopt Sperber and Wilson's hypothesis that this principle works on a single-interpretation basis. We have argued against this; for us, the principle or (to avoid a confusing identity with Sperber and Wilson's principle) the notion of relevance still applies in the case of ambiguity, as will be argued in the following section.

The actualization of ambiguity

Ambiguity is actualized or realized when interpreted in context. Interwoven in this are the two factors of tenability and choice: that is, ambiguity occurs when two or more distinct meanings or readings are tenable in a given context, rendering choice between the alternatives an uncertain one.

A reading is tenable, that is, 'capable of being held' (*OED*), when it has relevance to the assumed communicative goal of a particular situation. To a large extent, tenability serves to regulate the variation found in the process of interpretation. A reader may interpret an item differently on different occasions, or different readers may interpret differently; each interpretation taken on its own may not yield any reading of ambiguity, but viewing interpretations collectively, the item may be considered to be ambiguous. This collective reading corresponds to the more clear-cut case of the perception of ambiguity when a single reader has simultaneously different interpretations of an item on a single occasion of reading.[14] Whether it is from the perspective of collective reading or the different readings of one reader, the underlying important factor is tenability. Moreover, interpretation may, in part, be a subjective process, yet it is far from being arbitrary because it is guided by the notion of relevance.

A reader's interpretation of ambiguity is closely bound up with the question of choice. According to Rimmon (1977: 9), the impulse to choose is arrested by 'the equitenability of mutual exclusives'. It is arguable that the alternatives[15] need not be equally or perfectly balanced in terms of tenability for ambiguity to occur, and such an argument can be forwarded by using the notion of relevance. Relevance is, in fact, of crucial importance as it directs a meaningful exercise of choice, as will be explicated below.

Let us take, for example, a certain expression x which has several possible meanings at the semantic level. In a stylistic (or any practical) study of ambiguity, what is important is the pragmatic level where a meaning is, or meanings are, selected according to what is interpreted as appropriate or intended within the context in which the expression occurs. The governing principle for this process of selection is relevance. This works within the framework of the two levels of semantics and pragmatics, which interact to give three distinct ways in which ambiguity can occur, thereby also showing that the nature of choice between ambiguous readings is not necessarily an impossible one.

(1) A common form of ambiguity occurs in what are called 'garden-path' sentences, where the structure in which x occurs suggests, initially, more than one possible meaning for x. More linguistic clues further on in the structure will determine the appropriate meaning; i.e. backtracking and re-analysis in the light of later evidence result in disambiguation. Alternatively, the obvious reading suggests itself first but will be abandoned if it fails to be relevant.[16] For example, in 'The bench was requested to stop drinking in the courtroom', the word *bench* is initially ambiguous between an animate and an inanimate reference, but may be parsed as the latter. This is, however, reinterpreted as the former in the light of the rest of the sentence. (Similarly, *to stop drinking* may be disambiguated with more clues given.) This understanding of structural garden-path ambiguity is captured by Milne (1983: 38) who defines it in terms of sentences 'which have perfectly acceptable syntactic structures, yet which many readers initially attempt to analyse as some other sort of construction, i.e. sentences which lead the reader "down the garden path".' However, for our purpose, we may take a *broader* view, to include any case where the reader, after being led to interpret one way, is later compelled to reinterpret in a different way. Such garden-path ambiguity is, thus, temporary, although its effect may not be.

(2) The second form of ambiguity is the ambiguity with perfectly balanced disjuncts postulated by Rimmon. The semantic meanings of x which are pragmatically relevant are 'equally basic' (Rimmon 1977: 24), which implies that there is the same degree of relevance for the disjuncts in the context. This is an 'ideal' form of ambiguity, as the alternatives are so perfectly balanced that the act of selection, according to Rimmon (1977: 83), perpetually oscillates between one and the other. Hopkins's 'The Wreck of the Deutschland' is largely pervaded with the ambiguity of God's role in the shipwreck, i.e. God as Saviour or God as Destroyer. This ambiguity culminates in the word *doom* at the end of stanza 28:

> But how shall I . . . make me room there:
> Reach me a . . . Fancy, come faster –
> Strike you the sight of it? look at it loom there,

> Thing that she . . . There then! the Master,
> *Ipse*, the only one, Christ, King, Head:
> He was to cure the extremity where he had cast her;
>   Do, deal, lord it with living and dead;
> Let him ride, her pride, in his triumph, despatch and have
>   done with his doom there.

Doom bears the senses of 'judgement' and 'destruction', which both seem to be equally relevant: line 6 'He was to cure the extremity where he had cast her' encourages the first more favourable interpretation of God's role in the shipwreck, but in the environment of words such as 'despatch' and 'have done with his doom there', the less favourable interpretation of 'destruction' is very plausible, so that *his triumph* may strike the worldbound reader as callous. This example seems to illustrate ambiguity which involves perfectly balanced disjuncts; however, a reader's preference should not be discounted, which can often lead to the third type of ambiguity: MacKenzie (1981: 49), for instance, is aware of the relevance of the two senses of *doom*, but prefers the reading of 'judgement'.[17]

(3) In the third form of ambiguity, the two or more meanings are applicable, but they are imperfectly balanced in that one is more relevant than the others. Selection of the preferred meaning is quite clear, but the other relevant, though (sometimes) less obvious, meanings are kept in view. Again, an example from Hopkins's 'The Wreck of the Deutschland' illustrates this:

> Sister, a sister calling
> A master, her master and mine! –

In the context of the poem, *sister* here takes on the obvious meaning of 'nun' but it also coexists with the other sense of 'woman fellow member (or 'kin') of the church'. In 'how he [the falcon] rung upon the rein of a wimpling wing' ('The Windhover'), *rung* is a falconry term that describes an upward spiralling movement, but also present is the less obvious but still relevant reference to a horse-riding metaphor to mean 'check on the end of a long rein' (Richards 1969: 11); similarly, *wimpling* carries the sense of 'quivering', but the word can also be seen as a derivation from 'nun's wimple'.

These three forms of ambiguity are represented diagrammatically in Figure 3.2 (for simplicity, only two senses or readings, A and B, are given).

1. *Garden-path ambiguity*
(e.g. 'The *bench* was requested to stop drinking in the courtroom.')

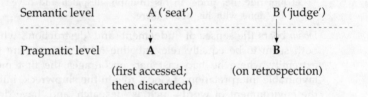

Semantic level	A ('seat')	B ('judge')

| Pragmatic level | **A** | **B** |

(first accessed; then discarded)   (on retrospection)

2. *Ambiguity with perfectly balanced alternatives*
(e.g. 'Let him . . . have done with his *doom* there')

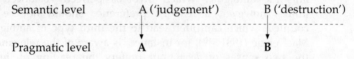

Semantic level	A ('judgement')	B ('destruction')

| Pragmatic level | **A** | **B** |

(equal tenability; choice rendered impossible)

3. *Ambiguity with imperfectly balanced alternatives*
(e.g. '*Sister*, a *sister* calling / A master')

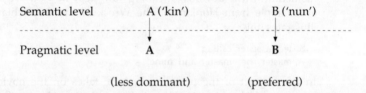

Semantic level	A ('kin')	B ('nun')

| Pragmatic level | **A** | **B** |

(less dominant)   (preferred)

Figure 3.2

All the above three forms of ambiguity hinge on selection based on the principle of relevance. The first kind is the least interesting as there is no longer any ambiguity once disambiguation takes place. The second kind is theoretically possible, but, in practice, is not at all as likely to occur as the third kind which can be safely considered to be the most common form of ambiguity that is of significance in a stylistic study. In addition, ambiguity is a dynamic phenomenon, so, for instance, the second and third types of ambiguity may become the first type if there are strong contextual clues that call for disambiguation at some later point in the text. In this, the notion of relevance has an influence as well, as new information that unfolds in the linear progression of a text is processed with the aim of arriving at the intended meaning.

3.4 A redefinition of ambiguity

Having examined ambiguity by means of a semantic–pragmatic approach, we can now propose that the phenomenon can be more clearly conceived when defined in the following manner:

An item is ambiguous when the two conditions below are fulfilled:
  (a) semantically, it is capable of having two or more distinctly different meanings (senses or references), *and*
  (b) pragmatically, the different meanings of (a) can be interpreted as being tenable in a given context.
Conditions (a) and (b) must both obtain for ambiguity to occur.

Notes

1. Leech (1983: (Chapter 2)5) gives a detailed comparison of the two fields of semantics and pragmatics.
2. Zwicky and Sadock (1975: 6) call senses which stand in hyponymous relation 'privative opposites'. They, among other semanticists (e.g. Cruse 1982; 1986), put forward some tests for detecting ambiguity. However, either such tests are not real tests but mere listing or selection of dictionary meanings (e.g. synonymy test) or, where they are promising (e.g. the conjunction reduction test, or the zeugma or pun test), they are not universally applicable (i.e. some tests apply to some expressions or constructions but not to others). Above all, the semantic tests become even less important in the light of the pragmatic view taken towards ambiguity in this study. Hence, it is considered unnecessary here to take them into account.
3. These are really logical distinctions for propositions and, therefore, they apply to sentence meanings rather than to word-meanings. Nevertheless, we can make use of them, as Lyons does, in talking about lexical sense relations.
4. See Lyons (1977: 270–80) and Palmer (1981: 94–100) for a fuller treatment of

'opposition'. In addition, it ought to be noted that a simplified version of complementaries which captures the essential properties is adopted here; a more complicated version is discussed in the sources just quoted.

5. Quoted in Rimmon (1977: 7). See also note 3.

6. Quoted in Grice (1975: 54).

7. This example is borrowed from Thomas (1985: 9).

8. According to Horn (1985: 135), the term 'pragmatic ambiguity' was coined by Donnellan (1966) to describe the two understandings found in a sentence such as 'Smith's murderer is insane', which can be attributive ('Whoever it may have been who murdered Smith . . .') or referential (a specific individual referred to). Pragmatic ambiguity is also applied to modals such as *should* which can be epistemic or deontic, and to scalar predications found in examples such as '*Some* men are chauvinists' and 'It is *possible* that it will rain tomorrow' (Horn 1985: 136).

9. For inherent or non-inherent lexical ambiguity, see Chapter 2, section 2.1.1.

10. See especially Grice (1957).

11. *The Collins English Dictionary* was consulted for these senses. See also Herman's (1986) analysis of this poem.

12. See Sperber and Wilson (1986: 237) and Pilkington (1989: 128–9).

13. Morgan and Green (1987: 726); they specify the purpose as nonlinguistic, but bearing in mind the poetic function of literary discourse, the communicative purpose is just as relevant. Consider also Leech's (1983: 94) definition given in the previous section on the notion of relevance.

14. Chapter 5 gives a detailed study of the various ways of reading, which are related to the notions of type and token discussed in section 2.2.1.

15. This term 'alternatives' is preferred here to Rimmon's 'mutual exclusives' as the latter is often understood to mean 'incompatibility'. See section 3.2.1 which argues against restricting the notion of ambiguity to the sense-relation of incompatibility.

16. Cf. Sperber and Wilson's theory that the 'least effort-consuming, and therefore potentially the most relevant interpretation, should be considered first (although it should be abandoned if it fails to yield the expected effect)' (1987: 705).

17. Also, see note 9 of Chapter 1.

CHAPTER FOUR

The role of context in ambiguity

It was briefly indicated in Chapter 2, section 2.2.3 that context has an important role to play in the concept of ambiguity. This role will be examined more closely from the linguistic and literary views described in section 4.1 below. For our purpose, the notion of context is given a functional definition in section 4.2, and this functional perspective can be seen to be useful in actualizing ambiguity in the poetic text, which is discussed in 4.3.

4.1 The importance of context in a study of ambiguity

In Chapter 1 we noted that our study of the phenomenon of ambiguity is carried out within the framework of stylistics, the latter being defined in the following manner by Leech (1985: 39):

> In its broadest sense, stylistics is the study of STYLE; of how language use varies according to varying circumstances: e.g. circumstances of period, discourse situation or authorship. A style X is the sum of linguistic features associated with texts or textual samples defined by some set of contextual parameters, Y [such as formality, medium and communicative function].[1]

The usefulness of this definition is in its emphasis on the contextual factor, and since stylistics involves the two disciplines of linguistics and literary criticism or theory, it is pertinent to look at the treatment of context by these disciplines.

4.1.1 *Linguistic views on context*

As pointed out in the previous chapter, our semantic–pragmatic approach to ambiguity calls for serious consideration to be given to context, which is here taken broadly to refer to linguistic as well as situational contexts (the notion of context will be explicated in section 4.2). The concern of pragmatics with language use deals with the contextual determination of meanings for utterances. In comparison, traditional semantic (and linguistic) approaches to language, including ambiguous language, have tended to bypass context (see Lyons 1968: 410), and one usual justification given for doing so (against which we shall argue later) is that a sentence or word cannot have readings in a setting which it does not have in isolation. This neglect of context is explicit in a linguistic observation made by Katz and Fodor (1964: 484):

> Grammars seek to describe the structure of a sentence [or other linguistic forms such as a phrase or a word] *in isolation from its possible settings in linguistic discourse (written or verbal) or in non-linguistic contexts (social or physical)* . . . . Every facet of the fluent speaker's linguistic ability which a grammar reconstructs can be exercised independently of information about settings: this is true not only of the ability to produce and recognize sentences but also of the ability to determine syntactic relations between sentence types, to implicitly analyze the syntactic structure of sentences, and to detect grammatical ambiguities.

It should first be noted that although Katz and Fodor's focus here is on the sentence, their observation can be generalized to embrace other linguistic forms including the word. Their example of an ambiguous sentence, 'The bill is large', has ambiguity that is, in fact, contained in a lexical item, *bill*, which occurs in a syntactic structure that fails to reduce the entire expression to a single reading. Hence the parenthesis in square brackets.

In a negative way, Katz and Fodor recognize the importance of context for any linguistic structure. They acknowledge that a theory which considers how settings control the understanding of utterances is more powerful in principle than a theory of the semantic interpretation of sentences in isolation, but, nevertheless, in constructing their semantic theory, they argue for the exclusion of setting on the basis that 'the readings that a speaker attributes to a sentence in a setting are a selection from among those that sentence has in isolation' (1964: 488).

The implication behind Katz and Fodor's stance is that a linguistic structure has a predetermined, complete set of meanings (for words, these meanings are encoded in the dictionary). To some extent, meaning must be determinate, or, more precisely, be consensually determined by the linguistic community, in order that communication is possible at all. Words cannot mean anything; on the other hand, they are not limited in their range of application by just their dictionary definitions. The implication that meaning is fixed and given denies language its flexibility and creativity in context, as seen, for instance, in tropes. Katz and Fodor's stand can only be acceptable for language treated at the abstract level of type (rather than token) where the established meanings of words form part of the system of language. At this level, we conceive of a word as being *potentially* ambiguous because it has a *possible* array of given meanings (see section 2.2.2 and the quotation from Zgusta given in section 3.3). But a poem is an instance of language use, which makes a type-approach inadequate since it is possible, and likely, for a word in a poetic discourse to have meanings it does not have in isolation (section 2.2.1 discusses creativity at token-level). In other words, considering ambiguity as ambiguity of token rather than type necessitates locating utterances in particular surroundings, linguistic as well as non-linguistic.

A further examination of Katz and Fodor's statement also reveals that it is not entirely free of contextual considerations: the process of selection must be determined by some overall governing factor, and one such crucial factor is context. This context may be provided by the immediate linguistic environment surrounding the word, as in 'The stuff is light enough to carry' (Katz and Fodor 1964: 497), where, out of the senses of 'colour' and 'weight' for *light*, the latter is chosen on account of its coherence with the expression 'enough to carry'. Where it is not possible to specify which meaning of a word is operative within the sentential context, as in 'The soldiers took the port at night', we look to context outside of the sentence for the selection of the appropriate meaning. Occurring in a textual or real-world environment about destruction in a war, this sentence will mean that the soldiers conquered the harbour. Here, we see the importance of context as a means for disambiguation; it sometimes serves as the prior setting which determines access of only one meaning, so that the potential ambiguity may not even be perceived.

In addition, the act of selecting indicates that meaning is not entirely contained within language, but is also attributed by a human consciousness.[2] This selection process is not, as implied by Katz and Fodor, a passive activity of choosing from a given, fixed set of meanings, but rather, it involves an active interaction between the human mind and the text (i.e. any stretch of verbal discourse), and a juggling with diverse factors such as language, knowledge and context. It can even be said that meaning is not selected but constructed out of various relevant factors which interact within a given context. Constructing meaningful representations of verbal utterances requires, apart from linguistic comprehension, general background knowledge. For instance, in order to understand an utterance such as 'The two cars collided' as (typically) referring to an accident, we need to know what accidents entail. Similarly, background knowledge comes in useful as a way to explain why an ambiguous statement, such as 'The soldiers took the port at night', is more likely (in isolation) to be interpreted one way (e.g. 'harbour' for *port*) than another (e.g. 'drink' for *port*, because soldiers are more likely to favour other kinds of drink).

Like Katz and Fodor, Kooij (1971) does not take into account the contextual factor in his study of ambiguity as a purely linguistic matter that is separate from ambiguity as a communicative device. However, he acknowledges that the phenomenon 'is still connected with various aspects of language *use* that can*not* be disregarded so easily' (1971: 4), and emphasizes the inseparability of context from language:

> Even under the assumption that a linguistic study of ambiguity should start by restricting itself to the study of the inherent ambiguity of sentences and should as much as possible free itself from contextual and situational variables at that stage of the investigation, it cannot be overlooked that one is dealing with a system which is essentially a system for communication. Losing sight of this one runs a heavy risk of giving a distorted picture of what the problem is.
>
> (Kooij 1971: 5)

In spite of recognizing the importance of context, Kooij excludes it in his study of ambiguity for the reason that there are too many variables in a situation of utterance (1971: 6). Admittedly, variability poses a difficulty for a study interested in establishing regularities in the description of ambiguity. The specificities of context are variable, but context in itself is always present in any form of language use. Kooij's excuse is all the more impermissible in this study, which is concerned with ambiguity not only of type but also of token, that is, with ambiguity in actual use.

4.1.2   Literary views on context
Unlike the linguists discussed above, literary critics and students of style have generally paid more attention to context. It is pertinent to make an observation here about New Criticism which dominated the critical scene for three or four decades. It would seem that the

insistence of New Criticism on the autonomy of the individual literary text to the exclusion of moral, historical or biographical frameworks or backgrounds is an implicit declaration of the dispensability of (non-linguistic) context. Whatever their theoretical orientation, in practice the New Critics, as Harris (1988: 31) puts it, 'smuggled in reality by silently depending on common experience'. Harris also points out Bateson's comment in his *English Poetry: A Critical Introduction*, that all sorts of contextual information 'provide the spectacles through which the poems can be read. Without their assistance a poem's central point may be missed, the grammar may be misconstrued, the allusions may be misunderstood, and instead of a clear-cut, sharply focused experience the reader may only register a semantic blur, an emotional haze' (quoted in Harris 1988: 31).

Empson, who was well known for his strategy of close verbal analysis as exemplified in his *Seven Types of Ambiguity*, has been accused by some critics of reading ambiguous meanings into texts with no awareness of the controlling context in which the local ambiguity appears. No doubt some of Empson's readings are ingenious, but he is not unaware of the importance of seeing a word as part of a larger whole in his comment on the need to observe 'the context implied by the statement, the person to whom it seems to be addressed, and the purpose for which it seems to be addressed to him' (1961: 19–20). He continues to note that

> the literary critic is much concerned with implications of this last sort [i.e. of making statements designed for a purpose, context and person], and must regard them as a main part of the meaning. There is a difference . . . between the fact stated and the circumstance of the statement, but very often you cannot know one without knowing the other, and an apprehension of the sentence involves both without distinguishing between them.
> (1961: 20)

An important observation made in the quotation above is of the integral relation between meaning and context, even though, basically, the two are not the same. This is because every utterance carries what Leech (1969: 183) calls 'IMPLICATIONS OF CONTEXT; that is, it conveys information about the kind of situation in which it would occur.' It follows from this that a verbal ambiguity is fundamentally dependent on the context that is implicit in the linguistic structure. This is further borne out by Nowottny's observation (her use of the term 'ambiguity' here can be understood to refer to actual or token ambiguity):

> . . . ambiguity has a peculiarity of its own that makes it even less susceptible of an atomistic approach. For if we are right in positing that

ambiguity lies in the relations of a locution to its context, it will follow that a group of words in itself and by itself has no existence as an ambiguity; the question of ambiguity will not even arise until the relation of the words to some context or contexts is brought into question.

(1962: 151)

Context is, thus, of inevitable importance for our study of ambiguity, but what, in fact, constitutes context? We examine this in the following section.

4.2 The nature of context

'Context' is often understood by referring to the 'relevant' factors which influence interpretation. Thus: 'The context of any bearer of meaning includes all those factors in the setting of that bearer which significantly affect the eventual determination of the meaning' (Hill 1974: 61). What 'those factors' are is further specified in Hirsch's (1967: 86–7) definition of the term

> by which we normally mean a very complex and undifferentiated set of relevant factors, starting with the words that surround the crux and expanding to the entire physical, psychological, social and historical milieu in which the utterance occurs. We mean the traditions and conventions that the speaker relies on, his attitudes, purposes, kind of vocabulary, relation to his audience, and we may mean a great many other things besides.

Considering the variety of factors and the risk of arbitrariness in deciding which are involved, the term 'context' seems to act as a ragbag for anything which gives an utterance meaning. The factors named include those which are readily observable (e.g. the surrounding text, the physical setting), as well as those which are not so readily observable (e.g. the relationship between interactants). Implicit in Hirsch's description is the suggestion that the contextual elements can be arranged into a series of concentric circles structured on a principle of immediacy: e.g., the surrounding linguistic environment within the sentence in which an ambiguous word is located forms the most immediate context, and the least immediate is that which is spatially and temporally removed from the situation of utterance, such as the historical milieu. If we incorporate the basic

'Author(A) – Text(T) – Reader(R)' form of written communication (see section 2.2.3), the contextual framework could be represented in the following manner:

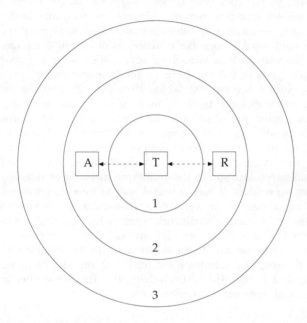

Figure 4.1

1: Most immediate context, which includes the surrounding linguistic environment (from phrase and sentence to the entire poem as a linguistic construct), and the subject matter or topic of the text.
2: Immediate context of act of communication, which includes situational factors such as, among others, author–reader relationship, and physical and social milieu.
3: Least immediate context, which includes circumstances of authorship, culture and tradition, and various historical factors. (Context can be conveniently divided into linguistic and non-linguistic settings, with the former more likely to occur within the innermost circle and the latter outside of it. See the discussion on linguistic and non-linguistic contexts in section 4.3.2.)

In making use of context to resolve an ambiguous word or

expression, the reader *tends* to move from the innermost ring to the outermost. Consider Brown and Yule's *principle of local interpretation* which 'instructs the hearer not to construct a context any larger than he needs to arrive at an interpretation' (1983: 59). However, as suggested by the concentric circles' image, the factors falling within the outermost ring may exert an influence on those contained within ring 1 or 2, so there is, in effect, a complex interaction between the various contextual factors. For instance, to determine the referent of, say, a pronoun such as *thou*, the reader will consider any anaphoric reference given in the text (ring 1), the interactants engaged in the communication and their social standing (ring 2), and the fact that *thou* is conventionally used as an address to God (ring 3). It is, perhaps, even the case that all these factors are considered simultaneously (hence the emphasis on 'tends' earlier on) – but tracing the cognitive process of comprehension is not the issue here. What is of interest is that the contextual factors interact within a communicative situation to determine the meaning or reference of a word or expression. In fact, a useful way to come to terms with the notion of 'context' is to see it as a communicative construct which provides an interactive framework within which particular meanings of particular utterances are determined. This conception is, in essence, functional: any factor contributing to the framework which fulfills the role of determining the form and appropriate meaning of an utterance is contextual.[3] Underlying this functional view are the requisites of relevance and coherence.

4.2.1 Coherence and relevance

Coming to grips with what makes up the context for a particular occurrence reduces itself to considering the specific contextual factors. Here, it is pertinent to take note of van Dijk's observation that a communicative situation is 'an empirically real part of the real world in which a great number of facts exist which have no SYSTEMATIC connection with the utterance (either as an object or as an act), such as the temperature, the height of the speaker, or whether grass is growing' (1977: 191), thus admitting '*ad hoc* features of concrete "situation tokens" ' (1976: 29). Context, on the other hand, abstracts from situation those facts which systematically determine the structure and meaning of utterances.[4] This it carries out under the governing goal for coherence: contextual factors interact in a way to give a coherent whole (see discussion on textual features of the linguistic context in section 4.3.2). Inseparable from the goal of coherence is the notion of relevance, and elements become part of the context if they are relevant to, or if they cohere with, a consistent pattern of thought found within a text.

Take, for instance, a passage quoted in Green (1989: 104): 'One afternoon last fall I found myself unable to leave my car when I arrived at the grocery store. On "All Things Considered" there was an excerpt from a series called "Breakdown and Back," the story of a mental breakdown as experienced by one woman, Annie.' On the face of it, the two sentences in the quotation do not have an immediately obvious connection. However, in accordance with the Cooperative Principle, an assumption can be made that these sentences are intended to be relevant in contributing to the writer's communicative objective. In order to make sense of the text, the reader seeks out contextual factors which cohere in a way that allows him to reconstruct (or interpret) the writer's intended meaning. One factor which is relevant is the radio and TV guide magazine that the above text appears in, which explains the writer taking for granted that the reader will recognize 'All Things Considered' as the name of a radio programme. The reader may infer that the writer was listening to the programme over his/her car radio. Supposing there is another contextual factor regarding the status of the writer; say, a housewife who has experienced a breakdown herself. This would add to the previous information, suggesting, perhaps, that the writer is unable to leave her car because she is paralysed by her recall of her own experience when she hears the story over the car radio. The reader goes on drawing upon other contextual elements which will 'build up' a coherent picture of the text. The context for a particular occurrence is, therefore, closely tied up with the notions of coherence and relevance.

The notions of coherence and relevance in relation to context can be further captured in what may be called 'core context' and 'peripheral context'. The former is most obviously determined by contexts which are most relevant, such as the linguistic context and other 'givens' (Hirsch 1967: 87) which are (usually) consensually agreed upon as significant in determining the meaning of the utterance. Core context is likely to overlap with the inner rings of Figure 4.1. The latter, on the other hand, is more likely to coincide with the outer ring consisting of factors more distant from the immediate situation of interaction. There is, however, no strict correspondence between the contexts arranged on the basis of immediacy and those which are considered for their coherence and relevance. Frequent overlaps may, nevertheless, be expected.

The idea of core and peripheral contexts may be one means to handle what we initially (at beginning of section 4.2) noted to be the variety and risk of possible arbitrariness of contextual factors. Furthermore, these factors vary from situation to situation. However, by making use of core and peripheral contexts, or alternatively, the notions of coherence, relevance and immediacy, the nature of context can be seen to be flexible enough to accommodate variety and variability, and at the same time specific enough to refer to only relevant factors which cohere between one another, ultimately determining the meaning of an utterance or a text.

4.2.2 *Context and reader*

So far, the description of context projects it as an external and objective framework consisting of components which are appropriate for a coherent interpretation of a given utterance or text. This picture is incomplete without considering the consciousness which constructs, selects or supplies the different contexts demanded by different utterances. This was indicated in the previous chapter where Sperber and Wilson (1986: 15) define context as 'a psychological construct'. Similarly, de Beaugrande (1980: 12) sees context as a 'situation of occurrence, in which a constellation of strategies, expectations, and knowledge is active'. This cognitive aspect is clearly stated in Leech's (1983: 13) definition: 'Context has been understood in various ways, for example to include "relevant" aspects of the physical or social setting of an utterance. I shall consider context to be any background knowledge assumed to be shared by s [speaker] and h [hearer] and which contributes to h's interpretation of what s means by a given utterance.' Leech's 'background knowledge' is also variously known as 'mutual knowledge' (Smith 1982), 'horizon' (Husserl, cited in Hirsch 1967: 221) and 'common ground' (Werth 1984). The distinctive feature is the assumption that such knowledge is shared between the interactants, as pointed out by Leech above.

The reader's assumptions form the basis for his 'strategy' of understanding an utterance by means of inferences. Consider an example from Sperber and Wilson (1986: 56):

Peter: Do you want some coffee?
Mary: Coffee would keep me awake.

Mary's answer can be interpreted in two contrasting ways, one as a refusal and the other as a wish to accept. If Mary is tired and ready to go to bed, Peter will infer the 'refusal' sense, given the shared knowledge that if Mary wants to go to bed, then she will want to sleep, she will not want to be kept awake, and, since coffee is a stimulant, she will not want coffee. But if Peter knows that she has to stay up in order to complete a piece of work, the second answer would be correct, and a process of inference similar to the previous one could be spelt out.

Similarly, background knowledge comes into play when resolving ambiguity at word-level:

Peter: Do you want some coffee?
Mary: Yes, please.

If we take 'coffee' to be ambiguous in its reference to a packet of coffee beans or to a drink, the appropriate reference is selected when the question is asked when Peter and Mary are shopping in a supermarket. Here, again, the interpretation is based on the assumption that we shop not for coffee drinks but for coffee beans or powder to make the drink.

This psychological dimension will be integrated into the discussion on context in the rest of this chapter, and in particular, in the section that discusses the non-linguistic context. Moreover, the next chapter will consider the reader's role in determining meaning. Thus, for the present, the point of concern here is to emphasize that context is not merely an external construct but it involves a cognitive aspect as well.

4.3   Context and ambiguity in the poetic text

Some linguistic treatments of ambiguity assume a null context by looking at words and structures as isolated instances, when the introduction of context will easily disambiguate many of the ambiguities. We argued in the first section (4.1) that every form of language use carries with it contextual implications, which makes an idea such as 'null context' a theoretical but not a practical construct. The next section (4.2) then examined the nature of context as a communicative construct comprising of factors which function to determine the meaning of given expressions or utterances. In this, the notions of relevance and coherence, and the part played by the reader, were pointed out as significant. The next step is to provide a more direct link between context and ambiguity, which will be 'contextualized' more particularly within the poetic text.

4.3.1   Context and ambiguity

There are two ways in which context relates to the concept of ambiguity: the first has to do with contextual cues and the second with plurality of contexts for a given word or utterance.

Contextual cues

Context is usually cast as a means for resolving ambiguity, and it is able to do so only if it contains sufficient specifications which guide the selection of one meaning over another for a homonymous or polysemantic word. In fact, it often happens that context sets the frame which determines access to only one meaning, so that potential ambiguity is not activated and may not even be perceived. For instance, in a classroom setting, a word such as *sheet* will immediately bring to mind 'paper', even though the word has other meanings. Conversely, insufficient contextual specification permits homonymous or polysemous meanings to apply at the same time, thus giving rise to ambiguity. An example is *wading* in the first stanza from Hopkins's 'The Lantern Out of Doors':

> Sometimes a lantern moves along the night,
> That interests our eyes. And who goes there?
> I think; where from and bound, I wonder, where,
> With, all down darkness wide, his *wading* light?

The dictionary meaning of *wade* is 'to walk with feet immersed in water' (*Collins English Dictionary*), which does not seem to make sense in the collocation *wading light*, unless it is interpreted figuratively. Apart from a metaphorical reading, a literal interpretation is possible if we see the word as having been used in a dialect form (this makes use of the reader's background knowledge of Hopkins's interest in dialect usage).[5] The *English Dialect Dictionary* reveals that the word was used in a number of regional dialects of nineteenth-century England, and the dialectal senses listed are applicable to the poem (McCarthy 1979: 12): (a) 'endurance, power of lasting'; (b) 'of the sun or moon: to gleam intermittently through clouds of mist'; and (c) 'to diminish gradually, to cause to diminish'. Senses (a) and (b) are derived from the noun form of *wade*, and (c) from the verb form. All these senses can be incorporated into the V-*ing* form of the word. The linguistic and nonlinguistic context in the stanza above, as well as in the whole poem, does not provide strong enough cues which will select one of the senses (a)–(c), thus permitting all of them to be tenable. Note especially the sense of permanence in (a) which is absent in (c), thus setting up an incompatibility, so that the coexistence of these two senses, in particular, indicates that *wading* is ambiguous.

An alternative way of describing contextual cues in relation to the actualization of ambiguity is to consider how strongly constraining a context is. The context may be neutral, weakly biasing or strongly biasing, as illustrated below (Gildea 1983: 14):

a. Neutral context: 'We had trouble keeping track of the *count.*'
b. Weak context biasing towards the atypical interpretation: 'The king kept losing track of the *count.*'
c. Strong context biasing towards the typical interpretation: 'The musician kept losing track of the final *count.*'
d. Strong context biasing towards the atypical interpretation: 'The vampire was disguised as a *count.*'

Gildea reports that, from experiments carried out, contexts (a) and (b) encourage a multiple reading where two or more meanings are active; this is less so in contexts (c) and (d). The 'typical interpretation' in the above quotation refers to the usual or conventional sense that occurs most readily and frequently to the language users. Gildea (1983: 10) describes psycholinguistic experiments which show that some words are interpreted equally often in their various senses (e.g. *bark* in its 'tree' or 'dog' senses), but some others are more frequently interpreted in one sense than in another (e.g. *bank* is more often given the 'money' sense than the 'river-side' sense). This factor of accessibility of meaning is, to some extent, subjective, as different people perceive different meanings more readily for certain expressions. Nevertheless, some words and expressions are generally more readily interpreted in one way than in another. An effect of this is that, if the atypical sense of an ambiguity is appropriate to the context, other more typical senses will be accessed. Consider the following example:

Babies have little religion, other than
Categorical imperatives and feast days,
And no politics, apart from the *arms race*,
Chronic inflation and minor *uprisings*.
They move in mysterious ways.

(D. J. Enright, 'Babies', in Sail 1988)

The italicized expressions are somewhat surprising because they have been given atypical, literal senses instead of their more usual, figurative uses. Gildea's category (d) applies here, so that the literal readings which cohere with the rest of the text are quite obvious. However, these expressions also carry implications of another context in which their typical senses occur, i.e. the context of politics and economics. This *covert* context coheres with the adult world that is consistently referred to throughout the whole poem. It contrasts with the *overt* one about babies, and the coexistence of these two disparate contexts generates the ambiguity found in the lexical items concerned, in that the atypical as well as the typical senses are accessed. This illustration, in fact, indicates the second way in which the notion of context is related to ambiguity, i.e. through the plurality of contexts for a given expression.

Plurality of contexts

A given text may be interpreted with the assistance of a range of contexts. For instance, the contexts that can be called upon in a poem such as Hopkins's 'The Wreck of the Deutschland' may be historical (knowledge of the shipwreck off the coast of England which drew so much attention and which affected the poet emotionally), biographical (knowledge of the poet as priest, his personality, etc.), poetic (knowledge of the poetic conventions and norms: prosody, structure, etc.), and so on. These different contexts may be interconnected to produce a consistent overall interpretation of the poem. On the other hand, there may be clashes between what is meant in one context and what in another, although both contexts are deemed appropriate and relevant. In such instances, ambiguity occurs. Lexical ambiguity exists when the same word form relates to more than one different context. For example, this occurs, in poetic texts, because of the coexistence of what may be known as the actual and fictional worlds, and the possibility that more than one fictional world may be evoked.

Actual and fictional worlds

According to Leech (1969: 187), 'Poetry is virtually free from the contextual constraints which determine other uses of language, and so the poet is able – in fact, compelled – to make imaginative use of implications of context to *create* situations within his poems.' Considering that all language is used in context, and that poetry is one form of language use, we need to clarify the statement 'poetry is virtually free from . . . contextual constraints'. Language used in a typical communicative situation (such as conversation or ordinary prose writing) varies according to such contextual factors as the relations and roles of participants, the physical setting, the degree of formality of the occasion, the kind of topic or subject discussed, the medium used (spoken or written), and other parameters. Poetry, like any discourse, is not free of such contextual factors: a poet who wishes to be published writes ultimately with a reader or audience in mind; his writing is carried out at an actual place and time; the kind of subject he writes about determines the words and structures he chooses; and poetry is usually found in the written medium (even recitals are seldom from the head but usually from the page). But, paradoxically, such factors are not *binding* in poetry the way they are in other discourses: for instance, a letter applying for a job cannot (appropriately) mix formal language with colloquialism, but descriptive verse in poetry can suddenly introduce informal conversation (such as found in 'A Game of Chess' in T. S. Eliot's *The Waste Land*).[6]

The paradox may be explained by the presence of two worlds in many poems: the actual and the fictional (or what Leech (1969: 187) calls the 'given' and 'inferred' situations; also applicable here is Werth's (1984: 92) definition of 'world': 'A state-of-affairs, real, imaginary, or stipulated, consisting of a triple of situation, time, and location. The situation includes objects, events, states, and relationships which may themselves be complex combinations of the same elements.'). Poetry can be fiction and not bound to any real context. In such a case, the reader has to construct a context within the poem in order to make sense of what is said, i.e. what is created is a 'world within the poem' (Leech 1969: 189) which is a non-actual world. This does not, of course, mean that the fictional world is so far removed from the actual world that it becomes incredible (although this may occur in some poems or stories).[7] Traugott and Pratt (1980: 256) comment that 'the usual connections between words and the world are severed' in fictional discourse. On the other hand, as we have noted in section 4.1.2, every form of language use carries implications of context which have connection with what usually occurs in the real world. This is particularly the case in the light of what Whorf points out in *Language, Thought, and Reality* (1956: 61): 'every language contains terms that have come to attain cosmic scope of reference that crystallize in themselves the basic postulates of our unformulated philosophy, in which is couched the thought of a people, a culture, a civilization, even of an era'. Thus, for an utterance such as 'Down, Fido' (Leech 1969: 183), the situation conjured would be likely to be that of a command given to a dog. A fictional text containing such an utterance may not have an actual referent for 'Fido', or the name may be used to refer to, say, a child in the text, but there remains, nevertheless, a suggestion that 'Fido' is a doggy name, and reference to a dog is therefore evoked. The point is that the actual and fictional worlds are not entirely divorced from each other; rather, the actual world is often evoked in the fictional world, with the difference that the appropriateness conditions which govern utterances in a real situation are suspended in a poem.

In ordinary discourse, the participants are usually directly involved; i.e. the hearer or reader is the one addressed, and the speaker or writer is also the first person 'I' in the text. In poetry, the interactant relationship is much more complicated in that the 'I' and the 'you' of the poem may or may not (usually the latter) be equivalent to the poet and reader respectively.[8] A corollary of this is that the spatio-temporal references (such as are found in deictic expressions) in poetry may have addresser–addressee orientations that are different from those of ordinary discourse. Such a variable is a potential source of ambiguity. For instance, many of Hopkins's poems contain first and second person address, and critics tend to identify the 'I' with the poet. Even though many of such poems, especially the sonnets, are considered to be autobiographical (Carroll 1949: 4–5), the fundamental assumption underlying poetry that it belongs to the fictional discourse makes it more sensible to speak of the 'I' as a persona rather than as the poet himself (although such a distinction is sometimes not important for the interpretation of some poems). As Herman (1989: 213) points out, the danger of conflating the first-person subject with the real-world author is that it obscures the fact that the subject within a poem is a linguistic and fictional construct, and hence, that it involves a text–reader interaction which may result in multifaceted interpretations. Thus, embedded within the persona may be incompatible roles, such as the roles of advocate and supplicant for the speaker in Hopkins's sonnet beginning with 'Thou art indeed just, Lord . . .'.[9] The two roles undercut one another, generating in the reader's mind an ambiguous presentation of the character.

The actual world which consists of the setting (historical period or culture) of the poem, or the place and time it was written, creates certain expectations which set up biases in the processing of ambiguity. A very simple example is the word *thou* which appears as the first word of the sonnet mentioned above. There are two ways in which this pronoun is used: one is the archaic reference to the addressee, or the dialectal equivalent to 'you' for someone close and familiar, and the other is the address to God during prayer. When the reader first encounters the word, he will very likely access the latter sense and not the first at all, given that he knows that the poem was written in the nineteenth century when the *thou* form as a second person pronoun is obsolete, that the poet is a Jesuit priest, that his poems are religious in nature (this presumes knowledge of an intertextual kind), and so on. Thus, any potential ambiguity in this instance is not actualized because of the disambiguating context provided by the real-world knowledge. In principle, this could be reversed by the fictional world if the poet should, contrary to expectation, decide to write a love sonnet to his lady following the court tradition of the sixteenth or seventeenth century. Or the poet might decide to integrate his 'old' and 'new' themes, giving rise to a third possibility where the pronoun could be kept ambiguous. What this shows is the complex interplay between two or more worlds, which creates different or overlapping contexts. Contrasts between the worlds giving rise to alternative visions often result in ambiguity.

The actual and fictional worlds that we have been discussing so far are, respectively, presupposed and created by the text. Even extraneous information such as biographical or historical details must be related back to the text if they are to be relevant. Thus, the text is ultimately the entity we start from and return to in considering context and ambiguity.

4.3.2 *Text and context*

Text and context are complementary in that the one presupposes the other: 'any text can be regarded as a constituent of a context of situation' (Firth, quoted in Lyons 1981: 195), and 'context can be situational, temporal, geographic, cultural, but it is always mediated by the context of the individual speaker's symbolic system, especially his language' (Friedrich 1979: 451). A text is a product of its context, and at the same time, context is shaped and reshaped by the text produced in a particular situation. Thus, ambiguity considered in the text must take into account the context (situational and linguistic) and, similarly, ambiguity defined in relation to different contexts needs to be concretized by taking into account the text.

The term 'text' is used in this study to refer to a stretch of coherent written or (transcribed) spoken language. Also relevant is van Peer's (1989: 274) characterization of the text as being transportable from an original time-and-space situation to another time-and-space con-figuration.[10] It is this feature of transportability that makes it possible at all to study written texts. Further, there is a concept of the text as a kind of super-sentence (such as is found in Katz and Fodor 1964), but the text is more than just a unit that is larger than, though essentially similar to, a sentence. Whereas the sentence is a grammatical structure, the text is a semantic one. It is realized by strings of sentences, but is not constituted by them (Halliday 1977: 194). Its decisive trait is its occurrence in communication (de Beaugrande 1980: 2), which means that words or linguistic units of which a text is composed must be connected in some contextually appropriate or coherent way. In discourses such as conversation, the text is indeterminate in the sense that it is difficult to specify its beginning and ending, but in writing, the text is a discrete unit (which, in literature, may take the form of a novel, short story, poem, or play).

According to Halliday (1977: 199), the text is not only a semantic unit but also, 'a text is an instance of social meaning in a particular context of situation. We shall therefore expect to find the situation embodied or enshrined in the text not piecemeal, but in a way which reflects the systematic relation between the semantic structure and the social environment'. This dual view of the text as a semantic unit and as a 'sociological event' (Halliday 1977: 197) provides a conveniently broad semantic–pragmatic frame within which to discuss ambiguity in relation to context and poetic text. In addition, such a view corresponds to the usual practice of dividing context into linguistic and non-linguistic types. However, it should be borne in mind that there is interdependence and interplay between these two types of context, so that often, in discussing one, it will be inevitable that the other will also be considered.

The linguistic context

The linguistic context refers to the verbal surround of a given word, phrase or sentence, i.e. the grammatical and semantic relations it contracts with other elements of the text. The most immediate contextual environment is the sentence in which the potentially ambiguous word is located. (The word *potential* is pertinent here: 'The most a linguistic description can achieve . . . is to indicate the conditions under which a sentence is *potentially* ambiguous inasfar [sic] as its grammatical structure is involved' (Kooij 1971: 115)). To interpret the word within this context, we note not only the semantic but also the syntactic relationships within the sentence. For instance, when we see a noun phrase preceding a dynamic verb, our first response is that the noun phrase is the subject of the verb, subjects of cognitive or emotive verbs being usually assigned the feature [+human] or [+animate]. Poets play around with this kind of immediate contextual environment to bring to ready attention the possibility of the presence of ambiguity, such as the ambiguous class membership of words found in Hopkins's sonnet 'Spring':

> The glassy peartree *leaves* and *blooms*, they brush
> The descending blue;

where *leaves* and *blooms* can be nouns or verbs, although within the line the following *they* anaphorically strengthens the 'noun' reading. Very often, because word-order in poetry tends to be much less conventional than that in ordinary discourse, the syntactic context may leave the uncertainty over the part-of-speech of the word unresolved. A particularly effective example is:

> Not, I'll not, carrion comfort, *Despair*, not feast on
>   thee;

Despair can be interpreted as a verb ('I'll not despair') or as an apposite noun of 'carrion comfort'. The capitalization of *Despair* may argue for a preference of the latter reading, which, on the one hand, will help to explain the paradox in the preceding noun phrase and, on the other hand, will propagate the antithesis between 'comfort' and 'despair' (see section 7.2.4 for a fuller treatment of this paradox). But there is a strong case for retaining the 'verb' reading which coheres with the sense of the persona's strong resolve (note the textual structure in the triple repetition of *not* within one line, and the full stress on each occurrence).

What the above two examples show is that the immediate syntactic context can be functional in resolving garden-path ambiguity (see previous chapter) as well as in actualizing the potential for ambiguity that is inherent in so many English words. A third effect that can be brought about by context is to generate ambiguity where none would ordinarily have existed. A clear illustration of this is a prose example given in Harris (1988: 18):

> Early in *Vanity Fair* Becky Sharp and Rawdon Crawley are returning one night to Crawley Hall: '. . . the walk over the Rectory fields and in at the little park wicket, and through the dark plantation, and up the checkered avenue to Queen's Crawley, was charming in the moonlight to two such lovers of the picturesque as the Captain and Miss Rebecca'.

The word *lovers* first suggests that Becky and the Captain share a romantic relationship with one another, but on completing the sentence, the reader realizes that the intended meaning is that they love, not one another, but the picturesque (i.e. a form of garden-path ambiguity is effected). It should be pointed out that the syntax plays a significant role in arousing the first reading, as well as suggestive collocates such as *walk, charming, moonlight*. A cultural context is also evoked in which these words are commonly associated with romance (cf. 'implications of context' discussed earlier). Thus, in this particular instance, it can be seen that, although we talk about an immediate syntactic context, in practice, a complex of a set of different contexts is evoked in the eventual perception and interpretation of the essentially uncomplicated word *lovers* (note the plural form also helps to suggest the first reading of two people involved in a love affair). In the immediate context, the ambiguity, being of a 'garden-path' nature, is temporary and eventually resolved; but in the remoter context, the interplay of the different contexts sets up an ambiguity that is retained in the mind of the reader, and turns out to be relevant in the wider context of the story when it is revealed that Becky and the Captain become lovers (the ambiguity here may be seen to function as some kind of foreshadowing).

So far, the focus has been on the immediate syntactic context surrounding a given word. An obvious feature is that the ambiguous word interacts semantically with other words within the sentence. This interaction is not limited to the immediate sentence but can be extended to words in neighbouring sentences or structures, i.e. to the wider textual environment which may be a stanza or an entire poem. (Sometimes a stanza or a whole poem can be made up of only one sentence, thus our use of the sentence here should be regarded as an approximate rather than a precise representation of the immediate syntactic context.) The following section explores this wider text in terms of its properties or features of sequencing, coherence and semantic constraint.

Textual features of the linguistic context

The interaction between words is structured sequentially, but it may also be conceptualized non-linearly. In linear sequencing, earlier words and sentences exclude certain possible meanings from subsequent words and leave certain other possibilities open. But reading is not restricted to the sequential order; there is much 'back and forth' movement which sets up relations between words which do not follow one another in order, but which are scattered in different parts of the text. Linear sequencing and non-linearity in the text create respectively chronological context and cross-referring contexts, giving a complex interplay of perceived meaning at one point which may be reversed or contradicted or alternated at another point, so that the total effect may be one of irony, paradox, or (garden-path) ambiguity.

The relations between words (e.g. lexical collocation) or parts of the text which are derived from the linear or non-linear sequencing are guided by the textual property of coherence. Coherence 'requires a consistent pattern of thought' (Harris 1988: 52) which makes for the unity of the text. It depends on certain conventional patterns as well as on specific knowledge, as can be gathered from Harris's description and Fass's definition of coherence:

> Discourse requires . . . internal coherence in which the content of the sentences which make up the discourse is related according to patterns of organization and facts of experience that are conventional or at least deducible. But internal coherence is in fact inseparable from intelligible relationships to external patterns of organization and sets of experientially understood relationships.
>
> (Harris 1988: 53)

> We define coherence as the synergism of knowledge, where synergism is the interaction of two or more discrete agencies to achieve an effect of which none is individually capable. In our account, semantic relations and metonymy are instances of coherence and coherence is also used in resolving lexical ambiguity.
>
> (Fass 1988: 151)

An important feature in the notion of coherence for lexical ambiguity resolution is semantic constraint. According to Oden (1978: 26), 'Intuitively, a semantic constraint is a relationship between two parts of a proposition such that the meaning of one part constrains what the other part may be, or in other words, it is a limitation on the ways in which particular semantic elements may be sensibly related.' Being a feature that is integral to coherence, semantic constraint is not limited only to linguistic considerations, but, like coherence, includes background knowledge as well, i.e. 'that which is believed to be true simply because things happen to be that way' (Oden 1978: 27). The text in fact identifies the world being spoken of; i.e. persons, objects, places, events, and so on. Further, it establishes the thematic motifs which also serve as a constraint in interpretation.

An illustration of the linguistic context described so far as involving the various related textual features of linear and non-linear sequencing, coherence and semantic constraints may be found in some selected (potentially) ambiguous words in the poem 'In the Valley of the Elwy' by Hopkins:

> I remember a house where all were good
>   To me, God knows, deserving no such thing:
>   Comforting smell breathed at very entering,
> Fetched fresh, as I suppose, off some sweet wood.
> That cordial air made those kind people a hood
>   All over, as a bevy of eggs the mothering wing
>   Will, or mild nights the new morsels of Spring:

Why, it seemed of course; seemed of right it should.

Lovely the woods, waters, meadows, combes, vales,
All the air things wear that build this world of Wales;
   Only the inmate does not correspond:

God, lover of souls, swaying considerate scales,
Complete thy creature dear O where it fails,
   Being mighty a master, being a father and fond.

At least three instances of lexical ambiguity will show the influence of the linguistic context on interpretation. *House* in the first line can refer to a building or to the people in it. The former sense coheres with the adverbial of place which follows ('where'), and reinforced by the word 'entering' two lines later which suggests the presence of a physical entity. However, the anaphoric reference in 'those kind people' (line 5) suggests that the second sense is also present. The literal (first) and the metonymic (second) senses are both clearly intended in the context of the poet's description of the hospitality he receives. In the two cases, the double readings are triggered by the feature of linear progression which leads to an acceptance of both meanings.

   Linguistic context continues to be important for interpreting *morsels*; in this instance, context functions to disambiguate. The typical reading of 'small mouthfuls of food' gives way to the atypical reading 'tender growing things'[11] in the context of other lexical collocates such as 'new', 'Spring', 'eggs' (which carries not so much the connotation of food as that of birth or the young) and 'mothering'. In addition, the ellipted clause 'mild nights [will make a hood over] the new morsels of Spring' echoes the theme of protection and providing shelter in 'as a bevy of eggs the mothering wing / Will [make a hood over]'. These two lines are even more closely linked together as analogues for the theme of shelter given in the fifth line. The close textual cohesion between these three lines is marked by *as* and *or*, as well as by the common ellipted phrase 'make a hood over' which is filled in by the reader for lines 6 and 7. All these are textual features which set up semantic constraints for disambiguation.

   Perhaps the most interesting and significant instance of ambiguity is that triggered by the word *inmate* in the sestet. This lexical item is not in itself ambiguous, but in the context of the poem, it takes on ambiguity in its reference. The ambiguity generated here stems not from different senses inherent in the word, but rather from a contextual cause: i.e. it is a form of ambiguity that is contributed to not only by the linguistic context but also by factors such as background knowledge which the reader brings to the situation described in the text. In examining *inmate*, then, we shall be looking at more than just the linguistic context.

Inmate usually refers to one who dwells in or is confined to an institution. In the poem, there is uncertainty in the reference:

(a) Following the immediately preceding mention of 'this world of Wales', *inmate* could refer to the Welsh. This inference from the textual context is strengthened by the extra-textual information provided by one of Hopkins's letters to Bridges which states: 'As the sweet smell to those kind people so the Welsh landscape is NOT to the Welsh' (Abbott 1935: 76).

(b) The persona 'I' being the subject of the poem could also be the one referred to, especially in the light of line 2, which is semantically cohesive with the sense contained in line 11. This is reinforced if we consider the older sense of *inmate* which is defined in the *Oxford English Dictionary* as 'one not originally or properly belonging to the place where he dwells; a foreigner, a stranger', a description which also fits in with the background knowledge of Hopkins as a sojourner, so to speak, in a place not his own. (For this bit of information to be relevant, an underlying assumption that the poem is autobiographical, thus equating the persona with the poet, is made.)

(c) Milward and Schoder (1975: 26–7) suggest reference could also be made to the Jesuit community since *inmate* is usually used in association with an institution – this interpretation is dependent on our knowledge of Hopkins as a Jesuit priest.

(d) A more general reference to mankind may be possible (Gardner 1969: 261, vol. 2), but this is more difficult to justify contextually, except perhaps to advance the rather weak argument that the unspecific nature in the use of the word, and later, a similar unspecificity in 'thy creature' (line 13) suggests a general reference to man. Yet, this interpretation is found in many readings of the poem (e.g. McChesney 1968: 61), so that what seems to be indicated is that context (linguistic or non-linguistic) is not the sole factor for interpreting ambiguity; it is probable that the tendency to generalize that literature is concerned with mankind and human condition may contribute to such a reading.[12]

From the various readings (a)–(d), it can be seen that use is made, not only of the linguistic context together with the attendant textual features of sequencing, coherence and cohesion, but also of background knowledge which contributes to the non-linguistic context.

The referential ambiguity of *inmate* is significant in that the various readings give different perspectives to the interpretation of the poem in general. For instance, (a) calls attention to the direct contrast between the beauty of the Welsh landscape and the imperfection of its inhabitants, with the result that the poem 'gives the impression that the Welsh are less righteous than other peoples' (Gardner 1969: 261, vol. II); while (b) casts the poem as an expression of a personal experience (compare other sonnets of this nature, especially the 'dark' sonnets); and (c) seems to be a much less acceptable interpretation than the others, as there does not appear to be substantial textual support for it. The same could be said of (d), except that the literary genre creates an expectation that literature or poetry relates to the human condition and life in general. It is, of course, entirely possible for a combination of any or all of these readings to hold at the same time.

Foregrounding

Related to the linguistic context is a feature which deserves mention, i.e. that of foregrounding (Leech 1969, Chapter 4). The term applies to any linguistic or semantic pattern, word usage or creation, or any aspect of the language which has been thrust into prominence so that the reader's attention is attracted to that aspect of language or language use. Foregrounding, which is especially evident in the compact form of poetry, results from linguistic deviation and/or parallelism. Hopkins, in fact, considered parallelism to be integral to poetry: 'The structure of poetry is that of continuous parallelism' (House and Storey 1959: 84). Ambiguity can be a kind of foregrounding or it can be foregrounded itself. Going by Grice's Cooperative Principle and the submaxim of Manner which advocates avoiding ambiguity (see Chapter 3), we can consider ambiguity (particularly of the more obvious 'punning' kind) to be a form of deviation, and hence, an aid to foregrounding. For instance, in a narrative about a shipwreck, the word *shrouds* in 'To the shrouds they took' (Hopkins's 'The Wreck of the Deutschland', stanza 15) is foregrounded because it puns on the two meanings of 'rigging' and 'winding-sheets'.

The foregrounded parts of a poem are the most arresting, and foregrounding presupposes latent significance: 'A question-mark accompanies each foregrounded feature; consciously or unconsciously, we ask: "What is the point?" Of course, there may be no point at all; but the appreciative reader, by act of faith, assumes that there is one, or at least tends to give the poet the benefit of the doubt' (Leech 1969: 58–9). Thus, when an ambiguous word is foregrounded, the ambiguity is, presumably, significant. Or, to put it the other way round, significant ambiguity (i.e. which affects the interpretation of the poem in part or whole) is generally foregrounded. Even where the ambiguity itself is unobtrusive, it may receive prominence through its participation in the foregrounding of deviation or parallelism. For instance, in the lines

> Generations have trod, have trod, have trod
> And all is seared with trade

foregrounding is effected in the repetition of the verb phrase 'have trod' and in the pararhyme (Leech 1969: 89) between 'trod' and 'trade'. *Trade* has the meaning of 'commerce', but the connection set up with the word 'trod' through the sound parallelism calls attention to their etymological relation, where *trade* (as defined in Richardson's *New Dictionary of the English Language*) also means 'A way or course trodden, and retrodden, passed and repassed' (MacKenzie 1981: 65). The effect of monotony and heaviness suggested by the repetition of 'have trod' is reflected on to *trade* which, with its other meaning of 'commerce' and its collocation with 'seared', takes on further connotations of unpleasantness. The interpretation described here points towards a reaching after unity in the text, which, as Leech (1985: 56) tells us, 'is arrived at through the interpreter's search for maximum coherence in the artistic features of the work, which in a poem means maximum coherence of foregrounding'.

The non-linguistic context

The non-linguistic context here can be taken to refer to the more immediate context of situation as well as to the broader context of culture. The expression 'context of situation' is most often associated with the name of J. R. Firth[13] who regarded meaning as an essentially social phenomenon and, thus, as something that cannot be dissociated from the social context in which the utterance is embedded (1957: 226). According to him,

> 'context of situation' is best used as a suitable schematic construct to apply to language events . . . . A context of situation for linguistic work brings into relation the following categories:
> A. The relevant features of participants: persons, personalities.
>   (i) The verbal action of the participants.
>   (ii) The non-verbal action of the participants.
> B. The relevant objects.
> C. The effect of the verbal action.
>   (Firth 1957: 182)

Category A(i) may be said to correspond to the linguistic context that we have discussed. Category (A), in particular, relates to the immediate context of situation, but what is overlooked are the cultural and cognitive dimensions of context. Further, as Werth (1984: 37) noted, if (i) and (ii) are meant to be exhaustive subcategories of A, then the only information given about the situational context concerns actions: there is no mention, in categories A or C, of the events that lead up to the action. What constitutes the relevant objects of B and the relevant features of A also needs to be made more explicit. Despite these shortcomings, Firth's schema may be said to be the precursor of later approaches to the study of the contextual role in interpretation (see Brown and Yule 1983: 37 and Werth 1984: 37–8).

The notion of 'context of situation' is best illustrated with an example which is borrowed from Werth (1984: 41):

WEST'S BID FAILS

Given that this is a headline found in a newspaper, the sequence of words will vary in meaning according to the situation reported upon. If the situation concerns international relations, *West* is usually taken to refer to the Western world, and *bid* will read as 'attempt'; in a card-game, *West* refers to the immediate right of the dealer, and *bid* to the number of tricks one expects to make; and in an auction, *West* might be the name of a dealer or company, while *bid* will mean 'offer'. Such ambiguity, which frequently occurs in the block language found in newspapers, indicates the importance of knowing what situation is referred to in order that an unambiguous reading is arrived at.

It is difficult to specify all the elements of a given situation which make up the context of an utterance: according to Sinclair and Coulthard (1975), situation may be said to include 'all relevant factors in the environment, social conventions and the shared experience of the participants' (quoted in Werth 1984: 38). This is a broad description, but like Firth, we can first pick out the participants involved in a communicative situation for consideration.

There are different levels on which we can place the participants, their relationship and roles. The actual, material world of the poetic text involves a real poet and a real reader who are usually separated in time and place. This level of participant consideration is often regarded to be of secondary importance by advocates of close textual analysis, such as the New Critics who uphold textual autonomy and an objective method of criticism.[14] Ultimately, there is no running away from these real 'persons', as a text has to be physically produced by someone and read by someone, and the environment in the course of the process of production or reception may influence the form or perception of the text. The serious disadvantage is, of course, that it is impossible to determine such situational elements with absolute certainty. Nevertheless, having information about aspects of a poet's life or the period in which he wrote may, in cases of ambiguity (and other forms of plural readings), bias interpretation or, in fact, invite a reading of ambiguity into what would usually be taken to be unambiguous instances of language use. For instance, if one knows of Hopkins's deep religious involvement and his training as a Jesuit (though at a later date than that when the following poem was written), the title 'The Habit of Perfection' of one of his poems immediately registers the double meaning of 'regular practice' (more typical reading) and 'apparel of nun or monk' (less usual reading which is also metaphorical here).

As for the reader, if he lives in the twentieth century and is reading a sixteenth-century poem, he may either miss out on certain specific meanings peculiar to the period in which the poem was written or he may introduce additional meanings found in modern use of language. What is important to note about the reader's role in connection with the situational context is that he brings with him certain background knowledge which must be taken into account in interpretation (see the quotation from Leech 1983: 13 given in section 4.2.2). This, essentially, takes us beyond the immediate context of situation to the context of culture. Consider the following definition:

> The context of the utterance must be held to include, not only relevant external objects and actions taking place at the time, but the knowledge shared by speaker and hearer of all that has gone before. More 'abstractly', it must be held to comprehend all the conventions and presuppositions accepted in the society in which the participants live, insofar as these are relevant to the understanding of the utterance.
>
> (Lyons 1963: 83)

The definition above takes context beyond the particular social situation, and emphasizes the shared knowledge which is derived, in part, from the social conventions and norms which may be summed up in the term 'culture'.[15] It may be considered that the context of situation is embedded in the context of culture.

Often, when we look at the participants, whether at the 'actual world' level or at other discoursal levels, both contexts of situation and culture affect interpretation. This is exemplified in Herman's (1989) analysis of the terms of address in Hopkins's sonnet 'Thou art indeed just, Lord . . .'. The second-person address takes the various forms of *Thou, Lord, Sir, Lord of Life, my friend*, which variously indicate formality and familiarity, distance and closeness. They also set up different social domains: *Thou* signals a religious context (but see an earlier discussion of this pronoun in this chapter); *Lord* both religious and feudal contexts; and *Sir* a secular context. Through the social and situational contexts in which these address forms are used, the addressee within the poem is placed in a position of power, while the speaker is placed in the opposite position of deference and smallness. Herman notes that this unbalanced relationship between the two participants in the poem is suddenly upset when *my friend* is introduced, at which point the speaker takes on a role of equality. She concludes that 'God is consequently known in two contradictory roles in this poem – the one in majesty and power, in lordship over the persona; the other, within the trust and closeness of friendship' (1989: 220). What is interesting is that the ambiguous status of God is arrived at by an examination of just the contextual implications of the forms of address. In the process, there is a dependence on cultural norms to generate the interpretations arrived at. It could also be noted, in conjunction with the linguistic context of the previous section, that Herman's interpretation could be further supported by the foregrounding of *my friend* in its central placing within the poem, which thus draws attention to a possible contrast with the other forms of address. In addition, *my friend* is juxtaposed with *my enemy* in the same line, which further foregrounds the antithetical roles attributed to God, the addressee. There is, thus, not only use of the non-linguistic context, but also of the linguistic context.

4.4 Conclusion

What has been demonstrated in this chapter is the indispensability of context for a study of (lexical) ambiguity. Put in another way, ambiguity is a pragmatic phenomenon, as pointed out in Chapter 2. In the course of our discussion on context, much emphasis has been given to the reader who is closely interconnected with context in a pragmatic exposition of the phenomenon of ambiguity. The next chapter examines the reader's role in greater detail.

Notes

1. Leech (1985: 41) is aware that defining style as the correlation between language variation and situational parameters carries the assumption that

literature is a special kind of language distinct from others. But, as he observes, it is futile to differentiate literary from non-literary language; the former is more profitably considered on functional grounds in that the artistic function receives greater priority than any other function such as propaganda or biography.

2. As Firth (1964: 111) comments, ' "meaning" is a property of the mutually relevant people, things, events in the situation . . . as much . . . as of the noises made'. Firth's position is the opposite of Katz and Fodor's. For Firth, the complete meaning of a word is always contextual: 'an isolated word which does not function in a context of experience has little that can be called meaning' (1964; both quotations cited in Phillips 1985: 14). This is veering to the other extreme of denying any intrinsic semantic content to words.

3. Cf. the definition given by Lyons (1977: 572) in section 2.2.3.

4. For an earlier treatment of the difference between 'context' and 'situation' along similar lines, see Ellis (1966: 79–95).

5. See Milroy (1977, Chapter 3) who gives an account of the period of interest in English dialect research which coincided with Hopkins's lifetime. Hopkins himself made many notes on dialect words in his Journal, and even contributed to Wright's *English Dialect Dictionary* (Milroy 1977: 80).

6. See Leech (1969: 188–9) for a further comparison of the contextual factors found in ordinary discourse and those found in poetic discourse.

7. See Werth (1984: 46–50) for an account of the actual and non-actual worlds.

8. Of relevance is the discussion in Leech and Short (1981, Chapter 8) of the different levels of discourse with the different addressers and addressees in literary prose. Related to this discoursal perspective is the fact that language in literature can be both exophoric and anaphoric in reference, in the sense that 'exophoric references are those references that are directed outside of text toward the audience and toward the world that exists beyond the text. Anaphoric references are references that direct our attention in the text to things that have preceded a particular utterance' (Amante 1980: 17).

9. See Herman (1989) for an analysis of the subject in this sonnet.

10. The reader is referred to van Peer's (1989) article for an analysis of five common notions of 'text'.

11. This meaning is found in Milward and Schoder (1975: 25), MacKenzie (1981: 72–3) and McChesney (1968: 61), among others.

12. This takes us back to the previous mention of context as a psychological construct, so that, in the words of Sperber and Wilson (1986: 15–16): 'A context in this sense is not limited to information about the immediate physical environment or the immediately preceding utterances: expectations about the future, scientific hypotheses or religious beliefs, anecdotal memories, general cultural assumptions, beliefs about the mental state of the speaker, may all play a role in interpretation.'

13. The other name that is often mentioned in connection with 'context of situation' is B. Malinowski. In fact, Firth is indebted to Malinowski for the origin of this concept (Palmer 1981: 53).

14. This stand is represented in particular by Wimsatt and Beardsley in their treatises on the intentional and affective fallacies (see Wimsatt 1954: 3–39).
15. A definition of 'culture' is provided by Bartsch (1987: 294): 'A *culture* is the sum of repetitive, relevant, and deliberate actions, activities, and products produced by a population. This sum is reproduced and preserved by systems of norms practised in the population.'

CHAPTER FIVE

The role of the reader in ambiguity

The previous chapter integrated a discussion of the reader with that of context and ambiguity from a pragmatic angle. Complementary to this is reader-response criticism which we will draw upon in our study of the reader's role in ambiguity in this chapter. The first section, therefore, takes a brief look at what reader-response criticism is. This is followed by a section (5.2) which maps out the relevance of the reader in a study of ambiguity, with sub-sections given to the issues that are of concern to reader-response criticism: who the reader is (5.2.1) and what his relation to the text is (5.2.2). In an attempt to deal with reader-relativity, the notions of type-reading and token-reading are introduced in section 5.3.

5.1 Reader-response criticism

'Reader-response criticism' is an umbrella term used by many literary theorists to refer to an area of investigation that is centrally concerned with the reader, the reading process and response. Precursors of this form of criticism include classical rhetoric concerning affect and reception, Renaissance and Augustan poetics centred on the audience, and seventeenth-century aesthetics which focused on subjective perception (Hobbes and Locke). Even the 'fathers' of New Criticism, Richards and Empson, attributed an importance to the reader (see discussion on Empson in Chapter 1 and, also, Freund 1987: 41), although, ironically, the reader-response movement arises as a reaction against the New Critical exclusion of the psychological effects a text has on its reader (see Tompkins 1980: ix). In fact, trends

LEXICAL AMBIGUITY IN POETRY

in literary theory and criticism have moved beyond the 'objective' paradigm where the text is the autonomous object that determines literary meaning, to the 'subjective' paradigm where interpretation and even the nature of the work itself are seen to necessarily involve a subject's consciousness.[1] Any study which concerns itself with interpretation (and this is, without doubt, involved in a stylistic study on ambiguity) would be incomplete if it did not take into account this significant movement. However, a caveat is in order here: whilst reader-response theories are useful in highlighting and illuminating the role of the reader and reading, some centralize the reader to the extent that the text 'vanishes'. For us, the importance of the reader is acknowledged, but so is the constitutive role of the text (see section 5.2.2). Reader-response criticism embraces a number of different reader-oriented theories, which include Iser's phenomeno-logical criticism, Culler's structuralist poetics, Fish's affective stylis-tics, Holland's transactive criticism, and many others.[2] Common to these various theories is the view that the reader plays an active role in formulating the meaning of a text. With such a central focus on the reader, it is to be expected that reader-response criticism will take up, *inter alia*, issues such as who the reader is, what happens during the process of reading, what the relation is between the reader and the text, and what the criteria are for deciding on the validity (as opposed to correctness) of readings. These issues will also be examined in this chapter, but, obviously, only in terms of their relevance to our study of ambiguity. Hence, many of the complexities connected with their discussion will necessarily be left out.

5.2 The reader and ambiguity

Rimmon makes a distinction between what Stanford calls 'unes-capable ambiguity' and what she refers to as 'ambiguity proper' (1977: 12). The first type 'is mainly a function of what the reader brings into the verbal structure, whereas ambiguity is located in the verbal structure itself' (1977: 17–18). Rimmon considers Stanford's 'unescapable ambiguity' to be really a matter of 'multiplicity of subjective interpretations' rather than a real case of ambiguity which she conceives of as 'a fact in the text' (1977: 12). We have indicated in Chapter 4, section 4.2.2 that it would be incomplete to see ambiguity only in terms of the text without also taking into account the cognitive aspect of the reader.

The reader was a big cornerstone of Empson's conceptualization of ambiguity (see Chapter 1), to the extent that, in the words of Freund (1987: 48) in discussing Empson, 'ambiguity was a condition of the reader's response – "not knowing which of them to hold most clearly in mind" '. In addition, a consideration of ambiguity in its potential and actual states reveals that the reader should not be dismissed as one formative factor of the phenomenon (see Chapters 2 and 3). Along with context, an obvious contribution of the reader lies in actualizing potential ambiguity. This corresponds to the reader-response view that the realization of meaning (and hence, ambiguity) is accomplished by the reader. The reader has a mediating, constructive role to play, as can be shown through a simple illustration.

Consider the indeterminate lines which appear on the screen of calculators.[3] For instance, the shape 5 is a poor approximation, but is seen as the digit '5'; in an electronic display of words, the same form will appear to the eye as a letter 'S'. As we saw in the previous chapter, context plays an important role in determining the selection of meaning, and it is precisely the notion of *selection* which indicates that context is not the only factor which makes possible the successful communication of the figure or letter. The reader, or, in the case of the example given, the viewer himself, plays an active role in constructing meaning out of an arrangement of lines. He does this by drawing on his real world knowledge (in this case, the numerical and alphabetical systems) and his tendency, as well as ability, to make sense of what is given by selecting that which is relevant and ignoring that which is not – even to the extent of imagining or projecting on to a picture what is in fact not there. To quote Gombrich (1977: 204): 'Any picture, by its very nature, remains an appeal to the visual imagination; it must be supplemented in order to be understood.' In a similar way, it is the reader who sifts the linguistic clues contained in a poem, while, at the same time, supplementing from his own experience, in order to arrive at plausible interpretations. Meanings are selected or rejected according to whether they are consistent with what the reader understands to be the communicative goal.

The reader's actualization of ambiguity occurs only when there is 'uptake'. This term is Austin's (1976: 117), and is used to refer to securing an effect by 'bringing about the understanding of the meaning and of the force of the locution'. In speech-act theory, there is successful uptake when the hearer recognizes the speaker's intention behind the latter's utterance. We could transpose this to the literary situation with some modification. That is, rather than considering uptake in terms of the author's intention, which we have established is problematic in written discourse (Chapter 3, section 3.3),[4] we could regard uptake to have occurred when the reader recognizes and responds to an ambiguous item in a given text (e.g. in the form of a pun). At first glance, this seems to run the danger of arbitrariness, but it should be remembered that interpretation, as dealt with so far, occurs in context and is thus subject to certain constraints. So far as ambiguity is concerned, the reader's uptake assumes the form of choosing to regard the different meanings as tenable in a given text (see the more detailed discussion in Chapter 3, section 3.3.2 on the relation between choice and the three ways ambiguity can occur).

The view that ambiguity is realized when interpreted in context implies that there is interaction between the reader and the text. This will be discussed in section 5.2.2, but before we do so, it is as well to be clear about the two components: the text has been dealt with in the previous chapter (section 4.3.2); the reader, and the associated feature of subjectivity, will be discussed in the following section.

5.2.1 Subjectivity and the status of the reader

It was indicated in the previous section that the reader is not a mere passive recipient of a formulated meaning, but rather, he is an active agent in projecting an interpretation onto a given code. Further, it has been made clear so far in this study that ambiguity, as a pragmatic phenomenon, involves different but tenable interpretations of an item in a given context (see Chapter 3, section 3.4). Interpretation is a cognitive activity, and so, subject-dependent. The important role of the reader, then, makes it expedient for us to understand who he is.

Reader-response critics posit different kinds of readers, but they can generally be divided into two broad categories: real and hypothetical. The former category refers to the actual people, made up of complex personalities and prejudices. The specific identity of a reader which constitutes his individuality influences the way he reads and can result in a response that is different from another reader's. For instance, what is ambiguous to one person may not be so to another, and two persons who perceive ambiguity in a text may choose their preferred meaning differently. This variability underlies Hungerland's (1958: 165) assertion that ambiguity results from differences in perceptual experience. Such variability, which results from subjectivity in reading, poses a problem as it can give rise to arbitrary and idiosyncratic interpretations (see, for example, Chapter 8, note 4).

The play of subjectivity on the perception of ambiguity forms a substantial portion of psycholinguistic and psychological studies on the phenomenon, as a sample of titles indicates: 'Self-Perceived Creativity and Ambiguous Figure Reversal Rates' (Bergum and Bergum 1979),[5] 'Intolerance of Ambiguity as an Emotional and Perceptual Personality Variable' (Frenkel-Brunswick 1954), 'Bias, Individual Differences, and "Shared Knowledge" in Ambiguity' (Kess and Hoppe 1985), 'Student Performance in Recognizing and Interpreting Ambiguity in Poems and Paintings' (Weil 1985). The practice of criticism itself has revolved around and given credence to personal readings. For instance, theorists such as Holland (1975) and Bleich (1978) are interested in reading as an individual and subjective experience.

In empirical research, the individual real reader is indispensable for investigation into actual responses. However, reader-relativity could become a stumbling-block in a theory-oriented study. In order that a study of ambiguity as a phenomenon, and not just as particularized occurrences, is possible, it would be useful to have a hypothetical reader who is not subject to the vagaries of the real reader's responses.

The hypothetical reader is a construct of the critic, and a proliferation of terms has cropped up to embody him. He has been described as

(a) an *ideal reader* (Culler 1975: 124), who understands perfectly and concurs completely with the author, and is able to realize, exhaustively, the full meaning potential of a text (hence, he can only be a theoretical abstraction);

(b) a *mock reader*, who is 'a fictitious reader . . . whose mask and costume the individual takes on in order to experience the language' of a given text (Gibson, in Tompkins 1980: 2);

(c) a *super-reader* (Riffaterre, in Tompkins 1980: 37), who is the composite for a group of readers of different competence;

(d) an *informed reader* (Fish 1980b: 145), a hybrid between an abstraction and a real reader, and who is in possession of linguistic competence, semantic knowledge and literary competence;

(e) an *implied reader* (Iser 1978: 34), who 'embodies all those predispositions necessary for a literary work to exercise its effect – predispositions laid down, not by an empirical outside reality, but by the text itself';

(f) an *intended reader* (Wolff; see Holub 1984: 152), who is
presupposed by the author for his text.

Types (c)–(e) are drawn from a combination of real and ideal qualities
of a reader.

With such a long list (which can be further extended!), one can
become easily confused about the identity of the hypothetical reader.
However, many of these terms share similarities. In general, their
reader can be characterized in the following ways: (a) he is an
abstraction; and (b) he possesses all the desirable and expected
qualities of a 'good' (proficient, competent) reader. They differ,
depending on the orientation of the theorist, according to whether
they are located (a) in the text (such as Iser's implied reader), (b) in
the author (such as Wolff's intended reader), and (c) in the
community (such as Fish's informed reader). It is not clear that each
of the type of reader just listed should be considered separate and
distinct from the other in so far as the factors of authorial intention,
textual cues and communal values and conventions can all simultaneously affect the reader in a particular act of reading. For instance,
the hypothetical reader could take on the guise of Iser's implied
reader; however, his role is not dictated solely by the text as he also
lives in a certain period of time, society and culture, and is capable of
informing himself of the conventions of another period, society and
culture (thus, an incorporation of Fish's informed reader). In addition,
the text is produced by an author who writes with a purpose or
intention, which the reader tries to discover or reconstruct (thus, an
incorporation of Wolff's intended reader).

On the other hand, even this composite figure does not escape the
criticism Wales (1989: 390) levels at the figure of the hypothetical
reader in general:

> One problem with all these reader figures, apart from their vagueness, is
> that they seem much more static than seems credible; and rather imply that
> a response to a text is a straightforward process, that will be the same on re-
> reading; or for another reader; or for a reader who is not a critic; or for
> another generation.

By contrast, the actual reader and his act of reading are dynamic.
Moreover, in practice, there is ultimately no escape from the real
reader, which is perhaps the reason behind Suleiman's (1980: 26)
observation that the individual reader 'is often indistinguishable
from an abstract and generalized "reader" '.

An illustration of Wales's criticism is evident in Fish's claim that
'what happens to one informed reader of a work will happen, within

a range of inconsequential variation, to another' (1980a: 89). Fish's description of an optimal reader glosses over the fact that the responses of different informed readers can and do diverge widely. This can be seen from Kintgen's comparison of his response with Fish's to the same text that Fish uses (Kintgen 1977: 5–7). Kintgen concludes that 'the assumption that readers, informed readers, respond in the same way to linguistic configurations in texts, despite its initial plausibility, is not strikingly confirmed by any evidence' (1977: 7). Nonetheless, if we recognize that interpretations can vary with different hypothetical readers (whether they are conceived of as implied, intended, and so on), then a concept of this kind of reader can be useful as a means of reducing uncontrolled relativism. For the time being, general reference to the reader in this chapter will be taken to mean this hypothetical figure, unless otherwise specified. However, rather than relying on the notion of hypothetic reader, it is suggested that the problems of reader-relativity and reader-identity may be better circumvented by the notions of type-reading and token-reading (see section 5.3). These notions, as will be seen later, will allow us to deal with actual readers.

5.2.2 Interaction between reader and text

The logical assumption in a study of reader response is that the response must have been stimulated by an object (the text). The text is 'dead' until a consciousness brings it to life. Conversely, the text makes it possible for the role of the reader to be played, and the act of reading to be initiated. To consider the reader without the text (or vice versa), or to consider either as formed or complete before their 'encounter', is to misrecognize both entities. It is, as Iser (1974: 274) says, 'the convergence of text and reader [which] brings the literary work into existence'. Similarly, this convergence actualizes ambiguity which would, otherwise, remain potential, present in the text but not realized.

The above view of the relation between the text and reader, which is essentially held by reader-response critics, is also echoed from a pragmatic perspective. Thomas (1985: 3) points out that 'pragmatic force can no longer be thought of as *given*, but as something to be negotiated through interaction'. To 'get at' the meaning of a text involves a process of negotiation rather than mere discovery, and this takes place through the interaction between the reader and the text. It follows that, ultimately, analysis of a literary discourse orientates towards the relation between the meaning of the linguistic signs in a text and their communicative force for the reader.[6]

Any description of text interpretation or decoding would involve some notion of construing or (re)constructing meaning. Fillmore (1974: IV, 4) describes the interpretive act in the following manner:[7]

> A text induces its interpreter to construct an image, or maybe a set of alternative images. The image the interpreter creates early in the text guides his interpretation of successive portions of the text and these in turn induce him to enrich or modify that image. While the image-construction and image-revision is going on, the interpreter is also trying to figure out what the creator of the text is doing – what the nature of the communication situation is. And that, too, may have an influence on the image-creating process.

From the above quotation, we gather that (a) the text is the governing structure that directs the reader's interpretation; (b) interpretation is not a smooth, uninterrupted act of expanding an image, but is characterized by the 'back and forth' activities of formulation and modification (Rosenblatt's (1978: 66) term for this is 'backward flow'); and (c) the interpretive act is carried out within a pragmatic context (awareness of text being informed by an author's meaning and governed by a communicative goal). (Point (c) has been discussed in Chapter 3, section 3.3.1, and will not be dealt with here.)

Point (a) brings up the interesting and contentious question of: how much freedom does the text allow the reader? From Fillmore's description, the answer seems to be – little. Here, although the reader is allowed a (guided) role, it is the text which provides the ultimate control over meaning. Even Iser, a strong proponent of interaction between reader and text, answers the question in contradictory ways: on the one hand, he tips the scale of control towards the text when he says that 'The meaning is conditioned by the text itself, but only in a form that allows the reader himself to bring it out' (1974: 43). On the other hand, he tips the scale the other way in commenting that 'the literary text makes no objectively real demands on its readers, it opens up a freedom that everyone can interpret in his own way' (1974: 44). It is not certain, if possible at all, that the scale could be equally balanced. There are varying degrees of involvement of a reader or different readers in the text; and different texts vary in their demand on the reader.

A probable reason for the problem underlying the text-versus-reader issue above is that reader-based criticism was seen to be opposed to text-based criticism (as we noted earlier, the former arose as a reaction against the latter). But the formalist and reader-oriented approaches may complement rather than contradict one another.[8]

This is especially the case if we consider that the reader's experience must have been triggered by what he perceives in the text in the first place. It is also often the case that the reader will keep going back to the text (this happens especially for ambiguous and complex texts) for verification, confirmation, clarification, etc., of what he reads (i.e., understands, perceives, interprets, or evaluates). In doing so, there is constant interaction between the text kind of meaning and the reader kind of meaning. Thus, we see that text and reader are interdependent for a meaningful reading. In other words, the 'objective' (text) factor and the 'subjective' (reader) factor are both important in the study of ambiguity in poetry; in fact, in the study of literature itself.

Point (b) concerns the process of reading which the phenomenological approach defines as 'essentially a sense-making activity, consisting of the complementary activities of selection and organization, anticipation and retrospection, the formulation and modification of expectations in the course of the reading process' (Suleiman 1980: 23). The text is made up of sequences of sentences which link up to give a particular world-view. These sentences foreshadow what is to come, and thus create an expectation in the reader, but their interactions continually modify the expectation rather than fulfill it. The continual modification means that there is also a retrospective effect, giving the sentences which have been read a possibly different meaning from that they received when they were being read.

Underlying the idea of continual modification is the assumption that reading is guided by an expectation of consistency, which Halasz (1987: 16, note 10) translates as 'the effort aimed at balance, harmony, and the strengthening of the expected, of the familiar'. This expectation leads the reader to project on to the written parts of the text a consistency which may not be made manifest by the text itself: 'The text provokes certain expectations which in turn we project onto the text in such a way that we reduce the polysemantic possibilities to a single interpretation in keeping with the expectations aroused, thus extracting an individual configurative meaning' (Iser 1974: 284). In this quotation, Iser seems to exclude ambiguous readings. However, it is often the case that the text will also frustrate the reader's expectation: some elements in the text will resist being integrated into the pattern of consistency expected and sought by the reader. Alternatively, the reader may find himself caught in the act of balancing between components that fit into one pattern of consistency and those that fit into another. Either way, the consistency as described here is a matter of choosing from potential meanings of the text, and so, in a sense, it is to be found in the text.

One cause of the frustration of expectation described above is the polysemantic nature of the literary text, which may be expressed in the form of ambiguity in a text that encourages divergent readings. The reader's desire for consistency leads him to make selective decisions of the divergent meanings. Selection involves exclusion, and what is excluded is also a possibility for the selection, or, in Iser's words, it 'may take effect as a latent disturbance of the consistency established' (1974: 290), which, thus, gives rise to an uncertainty between alternative meanings.

Words and sentences are component parts, but not the sum total of the text itself (Iser 1974: 276); there are also gaps or blanks which occur when connections between segments of a text need to be made. At the simplest lexical level, these can be illustrated with compounds, which contain implicit relations between the components that have to be worked out by the reader. In the case of new compounds, in particular, there may be more than one way to do this. An example from Hopkins's 'That Nature is a Heraclitean Fire and of the Comfort of the Resurrection' is:

> wherever an elm arches,
> Shivelights and *shadowtackle* in long lashes lace, lance, and pair.

Shadowtackle, in the given context, may be seen to have a relation of material ('tackle made out of shadow') or cause ('tackle caused by shadow').[9] Communication is effected when the reader actualizes what is potentially meaningful in a text by constructing meaning as he fills in the blanks or gaps.

The crucial role of gaps is described in Iser's (1978: 16–19) words: 'The gaps function as a kind of pivot on which the whole text–reader relationship revolves. Hence the structured blanks of the text stimulate the process of ideation to be performed by the reader on terms set by the text.' The pivotal nature of the gap-filling is particularly evident in paradoxes, which are seemingly nonsensical and therefore require the reader to fill a sense gap for their resolution. This may be seen in the example *soundless wailing* from Eliot's *Four Quartets* (see Ching 1975: 59, 90). To resolve the apparent contradiction in the juxtaposition of antonymous items here, the reader draws upon his real-world experience where *wailing* is an expression of grief, so that the oxymoron can be interpreted as 'an expression of grief without sound'. The gap may be filled in an alternative way if the reader, drawing upon his lexical knowledge, sees *sound*(less) as having another sense of 'ground(less), (without) solid reasoning or logic'. Thus, the realization of potential ambiguity in this oxymoron can be explained in terms of the way the reader fills the gap.

Within the boundaries of textual constraints, the gaps can be filled in different ways. Gaps are markedly visible in the following line from Hopkins's 'The Starlight Night':

Buy then! bid then! – What? – Prayer, patience, alms, vows.

The disjointed syntax does not make clear the logical relations between the parts of the line quoted. The reader, in making the connections, may find the word *What?* ambiguous in its syntactic relations: is it a question of what to buy or bid, or *with* what to buy or bid? Added to these, Milroy (1977: 198) has a third reading: 'It may be Hopkins asking us *what* we have said in reply to his urging.' What this example illustrates is that the text 'sets the terms' which guide interpretation (cf. the flanking of *What?* with imperatives on one side and a series of nouns on the other), but at the same time it leaves some room for flexibility, making it possible for different readings to coexist. In other words, how gaps are filled in varies from reader to reader and even within a single reader at different times, which accounts for the differences in the perception and interpretation of ambiguity in a given text.

The gaps cause the reader to search for connections, and in doing so, he draws upon his preconceptions and presuppositions. This brings us back to the issue of subjectivity. In section 5.2.1, we noted that subjectivity is an inescapable factor because of the very nature of the reader and the process of reading. The subject-related factors such as personality, linguistic capability, real world knowledge, assumptions, experiences and vividness of imagination are not the same for all readers, so that there will be differences in perceptual experience. Critical works on individual texts or authors are filled with such personal responses; these works are invaluable in helping to illuminate the significance of particular occurrences of ambiguity (as a word or text), and in the process, to deepen our appreciation of that text. Ultimately, criticism and stylistics must work at this level of the particular, not only to explicate theories, but also to demonstrate their goal (stated or unstated) of a competent interpretation. At this level of the particular, different readings are not only accepted but welcomed, and they keep debates on even a much-discussed text on-going.

However, in a study on ambiguity, it is not sufficient to look only at the particular occurrences of ambiguous words in particular texts; it is also necessary to look at ambiguity as a phenomenon in itself. For this to be possible, there must be some way that will allow us to go beyond reader-relativity. One way is to consider what may be termed 'type-reading' as opposed to 'token-reading'.

5.3 Type-reading and token-reading

Essentially, the notions of type-reading and token-reading are an extension of the type–token distinction first made by Peirce. To recall briefly the description given in Chapter 2, section 2.2.1, type belongs to the language-system; it has no existence in itself since it occurs at a level of abstraction, but it determines things that do exist. Token is the counterpart of type: it is a physical entity which is instantiated as a particular occurrence. Tokens collectively are described as type.

The useful feature that can be extracted from this type–token notion is variability and its negative form, invariability. The act of reading always begins with a particular individual in a particular place and at a particular time. (The reader referred to here may be taken to be actual readers: the notions of type- and token-readings make it unnecessary to worry over the status of the reader.) The individual differences between different readers give rise to a diversity of readings conducted by given readers on given occasions. In fact, dissimilar readings are also possible from a single reader reading the same text on different occasions. Thus, there is no uniformity among these various readings, each of which is an act on its own. Each of these particular readings is a form of token-reading.

Although no two readers read in exactly the same way, the areas of agreement are probably wider and more solid than people imagine, because these areas are rarely thought of as contestable and therefore as unworthy of note.[10] In 'The Analysis of Compression in Poetry', Levin observes that 'it is not obvious to what extent intuitive responses would coincide even among those who might be said to have a competence in poetry. . . . informal tests, however, have indicated to me that agreement is in general forthcoming' (1971: 39; quoted in Kintgen 1977: 4). The use of a term such as 'token-reading' is preferable to expressions such as 'intuitive response' in this context, as it does not suggest as strongly that the interaction between reader and text is a purely idiosyncratic matter. Thus, Levin's observation, translated in our terms, means that a token-reading may be idiosyncratic or it may not be; more accurately, it may be similar or dissimilar in parts, or as a whole, from another token-reading. Taken collectively, token-readings can be said to be variant as well as invariant: in the midst of the variant multiple interpretations is an area of shared interpretations. This area constitutes type-reading which, in its incorporation of a communal consensus, is marked by a global character. This makes type-reading a possible means of circumventing reader-relativity in the study of ambiguity as a phenomenon, while token-readings are valuable as a source of data for actual readers' responses to actual occurrences of ambiguity.

A cautionary note concerning type-reading is in order here: it does not lay claim to correctness of interpretation, although it does amount to a claim for tenable, valid, or what Eaton (1970) calls 'good' interpretation. Logically speaking, two contradictory interpretations cannot both be correct at the same time, but they can both be valid or good. Eaton (1970) discusses the difference between good and correct interpretations in literary discourse. From a communicative point of view, the correct and best interpretation is the one intended by the addresser, but in literature, the interpretation which corresponds to the author's intention is correct but not necessarily the best. According to Eaton (1970: 231), 'the *best* interpretation is that which results in the most valuable work possible. Usually, I think, "most valuable" will be equivalent to "most aesthetically pleasing", whatever that is.' The vantage point for deciding on the 'best' or most valid interpretation is the reader. But, in view of the fact that an author's intention is usually difficult to access, and that the reader is seen to be actively involved in assigning meaning, it is more reasonable to look for validity in interpretation rather than correctness. Moreover, whereas 'correct' interpretation frequently suggests a fixed, given meaning, 'valid' interpretation is less likely to carry this suggestion but, instead, evokes a range of possible meanings (see the discussion on tenability in Chapter 3, section 3.3.2).

Thus, underlying type-reading is the notion of validity in interpretation. To examine the criteria which govern validity will, therefore, be relevant towards characterizing type-reading. Armstrong (1983) lists three tests.

(a) *Inclusiveness* According to this test, 'a hypothesis becomes more secure as it demonstrates its ability to account for parts without encountering anomaly and to undergo refinements and extensions without being abandoned' (1983: 346).

(b) *Intersubjectivity* '. . . our reading becomes more credible if others assent to it or at least regard it as reasonable. Conversely, the disagreement of others may signal that our interpretation is invalid because unsharable' (1983: 347).

(c) *Efficacy* 'The evaluation of a hypothesis or a presupposition on pragmatic grounds, to see whether it has the power to lead to new discoveries and continued comprehension' (1983: 347).

For each of the tests, Armstrong is careful to point out two matters: (i) each test on its own does not prove validity, but each can supplement and strengthen the stand of the other, and (ii) the tests acknowledge the credibility of alternative interpretations (and so, of possible ambiguity). The feature of plurality of readings that is implied in the word 'alternative' is applicable to type-reading, although the description for the latter as an area of shared interpretations seems to suggest more similarity than differences. The apparent contradiction of referring to type-reading as containing agreement as well as disagreement over a text can be disposed of by using Fish's concept of 'interpretive communities' (1980b: 182).

By 'interpretive communities' Fish refers to the groups of individuals who share interpretive strategies which shape the way they read. Members of the same community will hold a similar perception of the text, but members may move from one community to another as they change their strategy of interpretation, and, consequently, arrive at different interpretations which may be incompatible to those held by another community. Thus, by placing the feature of intersubjectivity in the context of interpretive communities, plural readings which are contradictory to one another can still be studied at the level of type-reading. In other words, there may be more than one type-reading for a text. This occurs when members of one community share one area of interpretation but differ in another which some of the members may share with members from another community. So some of the type-readings may contradict each other, but their characteristic feature is sharedness or consensus within a community or sub-community of interpreters. The term 'consensus' is used here to refer to agreement over the strategy of interpretation, as well as agreement over some interpretations. This ensures some form of validity which underlies all type-readings. The plurality of readings generated by shared as well as different interpretations, therefore, offers a rich ground for ambiguity, without the anxiety over the question of validity that would accompany readings considered only at the token-level.

If 'interpretive strategies are not natural or universal, but learned' (Fish 1980b: 183),[11] they are closely tied to conventions of reading. Culler calls this set of conventions 'literary competence', which is a form of an 'internalised' grammar of literature (1975: 114). These conventions include the 'rule of significance' ('read the poem as expressing a significant attitude to some problem concerning man and/or his relation to the universe', 1975: 115), metaphorical coherence ('attempt through semantic transformations to produce coherence on the levels of both tenor and vehicle', 1975: 115), and thematic unity (find a way of integrating elements in the poem with the rest of the text). Added to conventions are other forms of shared knowledge – of the real world, of language, social values, culture, history, and so on – which also influence the way we read. Fundamentally, (type-)reading is a socially institutionalized activity that relies on communal consensus for validity.

5.4 Conclusion

This chapter has shown that the reader plays a vital role in the actualization of ambiguity when he recognizes and responds to an ambiguous item in a given text. The subjectivity latent in such a cognitive activity can be dealt with in terms of type-reading and token-reading, where various and/or dissimilar readings arising from the latter can be, taken collectively, studied for shared interpretations which constitute type-reading. This way, type-reading, together with its underlying notion of validity, offers a possible solution to reader-relativity in the study of ambiguity.

Together with the previous chapter, this completes our exploration of ambiguity as a pragmatic phenomenon. This and the earlier chapters will form the basis for the further explication of the phenomenon in the following chapters.

Notes

1. Cf., for instance, Eagleton's (1983: 74) observation: 'One might very roughly periodize the history of modern literary theory in three stages: a preoccupation with the author (Romanticism and the nineteenth century); an exclusive concern with the text (New Criticism); and a marked shift of attention to the reader over recent years.'
2. Two collections which represent the variety of theoretical orientations under the banner of 'reader-response criticism' are Tompkins (1980) and Suleiman and Crosman (1980). Some, such as Holub (1984), have kept the term 'reader-response criticism' separate from 'reception theory'. For our purpose, this distinction is not important as our concern is with the reader who is central to the two terms.
3. This illustration is suggested by Selden (1985: 107).
4. Furthermore, to quote Culler (1980: 51), 'As a reader oneself, one can perform all the experiments one needs, and one has access to what numerous other readers have said about a given text, while the statements of its one author are few and problematical.'

5. From an experiment conducted on undergraduate architecture and business majors, the authors demonstrate that individuals who perceive themselves as more creative are more responsive to the ambiguous geometric figures shown to them.

6. This does not mean that the author's meaning is to be regarded as unimportant, irrelevant or invalid. As Varga (1976: 24) observes: 'It was already known and professed in the classical rhetoric of antiquity that the intentions of the speaker, the situation in which speech occurs, and finally the psychological effect the speech makes on the listener will all decisively influence the actual use of language and the choice of employing specific linguistic tools.'

7. Quoted in Pratt (1977: 153–4).

8. There is much similarity between my view and that held by Kintgen (1977: 4), although in the following quotation he is comparing the responses of different readers: 'empirical establishment of areas of agreement and disagreement should precede, or at least coincide with, formal linguistic explanations of these responses; otherwise those explanations might be for a purely idiosyncratic response'.

9. See Milroy (1977: 182–3).

10. An illustration of this can be found in Short and van Peer's (1989) experiment with 'Inversnaid', which reveals many overlaps between their individual readings.

11. There has been no absolute agreement in literary research so far that strategies or conventions of interpretation belong *only* to the 'nurture' position; some (such as the principle of coherence or consistency) may be reflexes of an innate tendency (cf. Gestalt theory).

CHAPTER SIX

Ambiguity and cognate phenomena

As we have seen in Chapter 1, literary critics have tended to use the term 'ambiguity' in a rather loose way to refer to expressions, utterances or narratives which have more than one meaning. Empson, who played a prominent role in highlighting this phenomenon in literature, was also responsible in propagating the use of 'ambiguity' as an umbrella term for many other related but dissimilar phenomena. This reduces the usefulness of the term as it lacks precision and clarity. In comparing 'ambiguity' with other cognate phenomena, it is assumed that all these phenomena are based on sets of relations, their differences lying in the differences between the relations or laws which govern each phenomenon. That is, a poem or word is not obscure, vague, or indeterminate by chance; as Sewell (1952: 5) noted in her discussion of 'nonsense', each phenomenon is 'a carefully limited world, controlled and directed by reason, a construction subject to its own laws'. These relations can be examined in terms of semantics and pragmatics, as we did for 'ambiguity'.

A useful starting point is Rimmon's (1974: 31) table which shows the differences between ambiguity and selected literary phenomena. Although Rimmon here concentrates on comparing cognates with narrative ambiguity, her table can be extended to verbal ambiguity as well. She describes the relations of meaning found within these phenomena in terms of the logical relations of (a) equivalence, which marks allegory; (b) conjunction, which marks double or multiple meaning; (c) exclusive disjunction, which marks irony; (d) conjunction of parts for 'mixture' (i.e. 'different parts of the totality', such as a character that is a mixture of bad and good; Rimmon 1977: 14–15); and (e) no necessary operation for 'open work' or 'infinite plurality' (this seems to be an admission that logical operators fall short of offering an adequate account for all literary phenomena).

As noted in Chapter 1, we should be cautious about an

unquestioning acceptance of Rimmon's (far too) logical theory of ambiguity, which is given in terms of the combined logical relations of conjunction and disjunction: 'a conjunction of exclusive disjuncts' (1977: 12) – the only phenomenon to have two logical relations in Rimmon's table. Naturally, this directs our attention to the phenomena which share these relations, i.e. (b) multiple meaning and (c) irony. It is suggested here that the three phenomena are different yet linked in some way; i.e. ambiguity should be distinguished from multiple meaning and irony, and yet not be 'divorced' from them. The view put forward here is that ambiguity is a category (or a manifestation) of multiple meaning (or, multiple meaning forms a broader category which embraces ambiguity), and irony can become ambiguous when all its disjuncts are interpreted as co-tenable, or ambiguity can be regarded as capable of generating irony. As such, irony will be more suitably examined in the next chapter (section 7.2.5) on sources of ambiguity.

In addition to multiple meaning, this chapter will compare ambiguity with other phenomena which are inherent in language and are often confused with ambiguity, such as vagueness, obscurity and indeterminacy (which is seen here to correspond to the 'infinite plurality' or 'open work' discussed by Rimmon 1977: 13). We shall also look at the pun, which is a sister cognate of ambiguity.

6.1 Double or multiple meaning

The relation between multiple meaning and ambiguity was touched upon in Chapter 1, section 1.2.2, where we saw that they were often taken to be interchangeable (see in particular the discussions on Empson, and Kris and Kaplan's 'integrative ambiguity'). However, for the sake of terminological clarity, it is useful to retain their distinct identity. The stand taken in this study is that multiple meaning is a more general phenomenon which embraces many other more differentiated phenomena, including ambiguity. This can be represented in a simplified manner as given in Figure 6.1.

(The dotted circles represent other phenomena, such as metaphor, symbolism, and other manifestations of the many-sidedness of language found particularly in poetry; some of these may overlap partially with ambiguity – for instance, when certain metaphors become ambiguous, as discussed in Chapter 7, section 7.1.) This view of the relation between ambiguity and multiple meaning contrasts

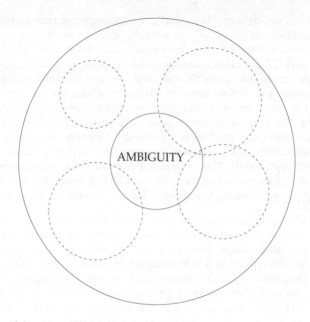

Figure 6.1

with that given in some earlier literature, which sees the two notions as either equivalent (e.g. Abrams and Empson; see below) or entirely separate and disjoint (e.g. Wheelwright and Rimmon, discussed below).

Conventional definitions of ambiguity refer to its property of having two or more meanings. For instance, much of Empson's *Seven Types of Ambiguity*, purportedly on ambiguity, actually analyses multiple meaning. Abrams (1981: 8–9) considers the terms 'ambiguity' and 'multiple meaning' or 'plurisignation' to be alternate terms for 'the use of a word or expression to signify two or more distinct references, or to express two or more diverse attitudes or feelings'. The only difference is that 'multiple meaning' and 'plurisignation' 'have the advantage of avoiding the pejorative aspect of the word "ambiguity" ' (Abrams 1981: 9).[1] Although Empson (1961: 11) at one point recognizes that the two phenomena need to be more clearly differentiated,[2] he, too, treats them as mutually transferable. As Wheelwright (1967: 252) points out, 'Mr William Empson in *Seven Types of Ambiguity* has made a survey of prominent types of plurisignation; unfortunately he has confused the matter by his misconception of ambiguity, which differs from plurisignation as

109

"either–or" differs from "both–and".' Wheelwright regards 'ambiguity' and 'multiple meaning' as two entirely separate phenomena which are differentiated by the 'either–or' and 'both–and' attributes. Rimmon (1977: 21) takes a similar stand in considering that, although both ambiguity and multiple meaning are based on the relation of conjunction, the former conjoins disjuncts (which are incompatible) while the latter conjoins 'conjoinables' (which are compatible). By keeping the two phenomena entirely separate, Wheelwright and Rimmon avoid the confusion typified by Empson. However, their characterization of the relation between the two phenomena has shortcomings as well. This becomes apparent from an examination of Rimmon's analysis, and in the process, we shall argue that ambiguity is a 'hyponym' of multiple meaning. Two arguments are given below.

(a) Plurisignation (used here as an alternate term for 'multiple meaning') is of different kinds, depending on the type of meaning which makes up the plurality of the sign; i.e., whether there is a simultaneous presence of (i) two or more denotations, (ii) denotative and connotative meanings, or (iii) just evocative meanings (Wheelwright 1967: 253–4). Only the first type, made up of denotations alone, forms the basis for possible ambiguity. Ambiguity, which Rimmon treats on a par with multiple meaning, should, therefore, really be subsumed as a subcategory of the latter (see Figure 6.1). It also follows that, when Rimmon (1977: 17) points out that the two phenomena share the property of having 'two or more distinct meanings operating in the given context', this should carry the qualification that the distinct and separate meanings for ambiguity are denotative, but multiple meaning may admit connotation and other types of associative meaning (see Leech 1981: 23). For instance, consider these lines from Eliot's poem 'Morning at the Window':

> I am aware of the damp souls of housemaids
> Sprouting despondently at area gates,

As Harris (1988: 21) analyses it, these lines carry at least two distinct connotations of futility from association with 'damp squib', 'damp powder', 'damp kindling', and of hiddenness from the association of dampness with darkness, 'damp cellars' and 'damp walls'. At this connotative level, there is plurisignation but not ambiguity. (There may, however, be a pun on *damp* in its echo of 'damn'.) Similarly, there is plurisignation in the example 'Dust hath closed Helen's eye' (a line from Nash's 'Summer's Last Will and Testament', quoted in Empson 1961: 45). *Dust* refers literally to external dirt, but in literature, it frequently carries the connotation of 'internal corruption' as well. These two meanings can be integrated into a form of multiple reading of the line, although if *dust* is taken to be a symbol, it can be ambiguous between its literal ('dirt') and figurative ('death, corruption') senses (see Chapter 7, section 7.2.2). On the other hand, in an example from Hopkins's 'Henry Purcell',

> . . . I'll
> Have an eye to the sakes of him, quaint moonmarks, to his
> *pelted* plumage under
> Wings:

the word *pelted* in the context given above is ambiguous between the diametric senses of (i) skinned (i.e., no feathers) and (ii) 'fixed in his skin like darts pelted at him' (Milward 1969; i.e., with feathers). It will help to avoid further confusion if we see multiple meaning as involving mainly 'significance', and ambiguity, 'meaning' (see Chapter 2, section 2.1.1 for the account on 'meaning' and 'significance').

(b) From the preceding argument (a), Rimmon's (1977: 17) proposition that multiple meaning and ambiguity share the property where the meanings 'are not reducible to each other or to some common denominator', is only partially correct. Plurisignation includes the disparate and distinct senses of ambiguity which exhibit the property mentioned, but it also admits meanings which are related in a way that violates this condition. Compare this with Rimmon's claim that ambiguity is distinguished from multiple meaning by the properties of mutual exclusion and choice.[3] As we see ambiguity as a manifestation of multiple meaning, it is arguable that these conditions separate ambiguity from other forms of multiple meaning rather than from 'multiple meaning' itself. This means that, in the case of the latter, it is possible for meanings to be superimposed on one another to become a univocal meaning, giving rise to a form of multiple meaning which we may call 'integrated multiple meaning' (cf. Kris and Kaplan's 'integrative ambiguity' in Chapter 1). An instance is the example given above, '*Dust* hath closed Helen's eye', where the literal sense ('dirt') and its connotation ('corruption') can combine to convey something undesirable. In addition, consider *build* in Hopkins's 'birds build – but not I build' (from the sonnet 'Thou art indeed just, Lord'), which Gardner (in Gardner and MacKenzie 1970: xxxii) interprets as having a material as well as a moral reading. This is an example of plurisignation but not ambiguity, as the meanings are reducible to the common idea of 'productivity'.

However, there is sometimes a choice between viewing an expression as an ambiguous or unambiguous plurisign. An illustration provided by Rimmon (1977: 21) is an idiom, *to count one's beads*, which can refer to prayers or rosary beads, but 'in which the difference between the two senses . . . does not affect the meaning of the utterance as a whole'. This expression may be classified under 'multiple meaning'. On the other hand, the two senses of prayers and rosary beads are not necessarily reducible to each other as the idiom can be used to express the activity of prayer without any literal reference to the counting of rosary beads, or conversely, the literal sense can be intended without any reference to its idiomatic meaning. Hence, depending on the context in which the expression is used, ambiguity can arise from its double senses. But there are two ways to understand the idiom as a plurisign: one in which the senses become integrated (i.e. Rimmon's reading), and the other in which the senses remain separate and potentially ambiguous.

6.2 Indeterminacy

Culler (1982: 189) describes indeterminacy as 'the impossibility or unjustifiability of choosing one meaning over another',[4] a description which contains the seed of confusion between ambiguity and indeterminacy in so far as the former involves an impossibility of choice as well. This possible confusion is made all the more significant in the light of what Bahti (1986) portrays as a shift in literary theory from the New Critics' 'ambiguity' to the 'indeterminacy' of more recent criticism. But whereas New Critics regard ambiguity as a textual phenomenon, Culler's notion of indeterminacy is an interpretive problem for the reader, a view that is echoed in some reader-response or reception theory. However, in our semantic–pragmatic approach, ambiguity has to do with interpretation as well. The feature of an 'absence of interpretive closure' (Bahti 1986: 216) which characterizes indeterminacy is also common to ambiguity. But in the case of indeterminacy, this absence of closure often comes about because of the gaps or blanks in the text that the reader must fill in from his personal knowledge or perceptions, so that 'The indeterminacy may always be "filled in" differently (both in subsequent readings, and in readings by different persons), and the horizon of such interpretive response to and completion of textual indeterminacy remains incomplete, for the text is never fully constituted, and the reading process could hypothetically go on forever' (Bahti 1986: 217).

There is a certain 'openness' to an indeterminate reading which is not found in an ambiguous one which plays with two or more determinate meanings. Consider the following example given in Empson (1961: 45):

Beauty is but a flower
Which wrinkles will devour.
Brightness falls from the air.
Queens have died young and fair.

(Nash, 'Summer's Last Will and Testament)

The third line is open to numerous interpretations: *brightness* can, in the first instance, be read with an abstract (i.e., referring to 'light') or concrete (i.e., referring to something bright) sense, giving rise to ambiguity. Further, the concrete reading can be extended to refer to lightning, meteorites, stars, and so on, as suggested by Empson (1961: 46). Here, the correctness of interpretation is beside the point. More significantly, what Empson considers to be ambiguity is, in fact, indeterminacy which is largely due to the vagueness of the word *brightness*. Thus, indeterminacy occurs because 'some aspects of poetic significance are indefinite, in that there is no finite number of possibilities to choose from' (Leech 1969: 215; Leech also gives sources of what he calls 'indeterminate significance'). Ambiguity, on the other hand, involves a definite and finite number of possibilities within a given context. In interpreting ambiguous words, a reader instinctively resorts to the exercise of choice which may or may not be frustrated. Indeterminacy, however, invites the reader to project an interpretation. This difference in the interpretative activities stems from the basic difference where one (ambiguity) frustrates the question of 'which is the intended meaning?' and the other (indeterminacy) frustrates the question of 'what is the intended meaning?' By analogy, it is a rabbit–duck representation versus a

Rorschach inkblot, the latter being an accidental shape which is capable of any number of possible interpretations.[5]

6.3 Vagueness

Compatible with the notion of indeterminacy is that of vagueness, in that both share a common characteristic of 'openness'. In fact, they are often treated as alternate terms (see Neustupny 1966: 39). But, whereas the former is an interpretative (i.e. pragmatic) matter (as we have seen in the previous section), the latter may be examined as a semantic attribute inherent in natural language.

In *The Collins English Dictionary*, ambiguity is defined as vagueness. The confusion between these two phenomena can be traced as far back as the classicists, as Stanford (1939: 139) notes in his comment on their study of ambiguity: 'In several cases it will be observed that the term ambiguity has been stretched to its widest limits to include vagueness and suggestiveness where they have appreciable dramatic force.' More recently, Norrman (1977: 6) insists that 'In literature . . . vagueness should be taken into account in a study of ambiguity'; what he calls 'vague ambiguity' is based on a dictionary definition of ambiguity: 'Doubtful, questionable; indistinct, obscure, not clearly defined', which he says 'could be summed up with the word "vagueness" ' (1977: 6). Not only is the confusion of the two terms perpetuated here, but vagueness and ambiguity are actually considered to be equivalent. While these two terms express cognate ideas, the difference between them can be made distinct:

> Although the same word can be *both* vague and ambiguous, vagueness and ambiguity are two quite different properties. A term is ambiguous in a given context when it has two distinct meanings and the context does not make clear which one is intended. On the other hand, a term is *vague* when there exist 'borderline cases' such that it cannot be determined whether the term applies to them or not. Most words are vague in the sense indicated.
> (Copi 1961: 92; quoted in Rimmon 1977: 20)

Similarly, Alston (1964: 84) notes that vagueness occurs 'if there are cases in which there is no definite answer as to whether the term applies'. This formulation highlights vagueness as a linguistic matter in that it is the 'term' that is vague, not the objects, situations, events or ideas to which the term is to apply or not apply. Between the two extremes of a term's clear applicability and non-applicability lies a grey area of unclarity. This grey area constitutes, in Black's terminology, a 'fringe' (1949: 28) or what can be called a 'periphery'. Black illustrates this with the word *chair* and shows that there are some structures which fall in the indeterminate case of being undecidable as 'chair' or 'non-chair' (1949: 32–3). A similar conclusion is reached by Labov (1973) in his empirical tests on what constitutes a cup. In effect, the meaning of most words can be said to have such a boundary of uncertainty since it is difficult to imagine that any word can specify all the detailed variations that can occur with things in the world.

The presence of a boundary of uncertainty, or, in Zadeh's (1972: 4) term, a 'fuzzy set' (i.e. 'a class in which transition from membership to non-membership is gradual rather than abrupt'),[6] provides a criterion to differentiate vagueness from ambiguity. This plays on the idea of word senses having criterial features which define the core meaning, and other features which are less crucial though recognizable as components that can contribute to the meaning of the word concerned. The potential for ambiguity is sited in the core area, whereas vagueness belongs to the fuzzy fringe (see Figure 6.2).

Whereas ambiguity is characterized by two or more denotations,

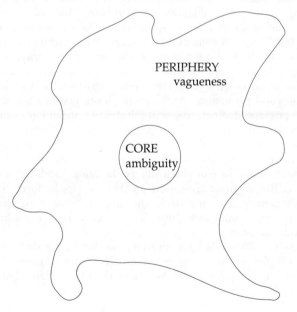

PERIPHERY
vagueness

CORE
ambiguity

Figure 6.2

vagueness is usually associated with one. The senses of an ambiguous word are multiple but distinct; vagueness does not enjoy such distinctness in its meaning, which is more appropriately described as a semantic nebula. For instance, an ambiguous use of *sage* will very likely play upon the 'plant' and 'person' references, involving disparate senses; vagueness creeps in, however, when there is referential uncertainty whether to consider a twenty-year-old wise person as a sage, age or 'oldness' being a variable defining component of *sage* and being subject to scalar value (see Leech 1976: 152). Vagueness is characterized by an uncertainty in deciding the applicability of a term to an object or referent; in comparison, uncertainty in the case of ambiguity lies in deciding between alternative senses within a context. Thus, the phenomena of ambiguity and vagueness are separate matters.

6.4 Obscurity

As in the case of vagueness, obscurity has often been used as a defining term for ambiguity; in particular, the adjectival form 'ambiguous' is almost always explained as 'obscure' (see, for instance, the *Oxford English Dictionary*). The most common feature that causes a confusion of the two phenomena is that of lack of clarity; however, ambiguity is more appropriately characterized by uncertainty. This becomes more evident if we turn once again to the two levels of semantics and pragmatics. At the former level, potentially ambiguous words possess distinct, disparate but *clear* meanings which are relevant as alternatives in a given context, although there is uncertainty which to select as more appropriate. Any lack of clarity lies at the pragmatic level where the intended meaning is not clear to the reader. In the case of obscurity, on the other hand, lack of clarity occurs at the semantic level itself, in that the words do not (at least initially) convey any intelligible meaning. Obscurity is, therefore, different from ambiguity, but it can provide the latitude for ambiguity to occur in.

In a sense, all words have meaning, so that to say that words are not intelligible seems to carry an inherent contradiction. Take an example from Hopkins's 'The Wreck of the Deutschland' (stanza 3):

I whirled out wings that spell
And fled with a fling of the heart to the heart of the Host

Every word in the lines above has at least one identifiable meaning;
but consider *spell* which usually refers to (i) a period of time, (ii) a
sort of magical force or fascination, or (iii) a certain arrangement of
letters, or as a verb, to write or say the correct order of the letters
which make up a word, or to indicate something (as in 'this spells
disaster'). In the context, none of these meanings applies in any
reasonable way, so that the reader is puzzled as to how to interpret
the word in its relation to the other words. McChesney (1968: 37)
interprets it as 'cry out on the holy name' which is really an attempt
to extend the meaning of *spell* as in 'spell (out) a word'; even then, the
reader has to make a leap in his imagination to associate McChesney's interpretation with the given denotative meaning. This
difficulty in identifying the meaning, which is fundamentally a
linguistic matter, is, then, characteristic of obscurity. At the pragmatic
level, the reader seeks to overcome the difficulty of understanding
caused by the obscurity by imputing his own interpretation, whether
with clues from the context (provided the context is quite clear, as in
the example above, which renders it possible to explain the obscurity
in some way), or with background information gathered from notes
appended by the poet (such as are found in *The Waste Land*), or with
knowledge of the poet's biography, ideology, and so on.

At the verbal level, we may distinguish three types of obscurity
which are based on: (i) the use of words in esoteric senses, (ii) the use
of recondite vocabulary, and (iii) the use of words which have an
irrational relation with one another. The nature of the meaning
harboured by obscurity of the first kind contrasts with that of
ambiguity. Whereas an ambiguous item usually contains meanings
that are 'standard' and denotative, the meaning or meanings of type
(i) is/are non-standard and evocative. Many poets, including Hopkins, introduce their own private allusions into familiar-looking
words. Unless the reader has access to such 'special' knowledge, he
will continue to be baffled by what appears to him to be obscure
words. Hopkins, who asserted that he 'was not over-desirous that the
meaning of all should be quite clear, at least unmistakable',[7]
sometimes provided explanations. An instance is *wind* in 'The
Lantern Out of Doors':

wind
What most I may eye after, be in at the end
I cannot, and out of sight is out of mind.

For the strange image of 'winding the eyes', Hopkins explained in one of his letters to Bridges (no. 66): '. . . I mean that the eye winds only in the sense that its focus or point of sight winds and that coincides with a point of the object and winds with that. For the object, a lantern passing further and further away and bearing now east, now west of one right line, is truly and properly described as winding.' Obscurity of this type, arising out of the use of words in an esoteric way, characterizes Hopkins's poetry: in fact, Milroy has a commentary numbering sixteen pages on the poet's use of such words (1977: 232–48). However, it should be pointed out that this kind of obscurity can work hand in hand with lexical ambiguity. Consider the word *peeled* in the following lines from 'The Wreck of the Deutschland' (stanza 26):

> For how to the heart's cheering
> The down-dugged ground-hugged grey
> Hovers off, the jay-blue heavens appearing
> Of pied and peeled May!

Milroy (1977: 240) records Wright's observation that *peel* is a dialect form of 'pool' which results from 'a month of clouds and showers', so that, by association, the expression *peeled May* may be read as 'showery May'. This contrasts with the standard interpretation of *peeled* as 'stripped', giving rise to the following reading: 'The drooping, grey clouds of winter are "peeled" back to reveal the blue and white skies of spring' (Phillips 1986: 340). There is, then, local ambiguity in the word *peeled*, although at a more global level, the significance of cheer emerging out of gloom remains essentially unchanged.

The second type of obscurity which results from a use of recondite vocabulary is exemplified in the following lines from Allan Tate's 'Horatian epode to the Duchess of Malfi' (quoted in Ruthven 1979: 36):

> You have no more chance than an infusorian
> Lodged in a hollow molar of an eohippus.

A check with the dictionary helps to clear up the difficulty posed by the words *infusorian* and *eohippus*. Similarly obscure are '*Degged* with dew' ('Inversnaid'), which means 'sprinkled' or 'bedewed' (see Phillips 1986: 366 and Yasuyoshi 1987: 109), and 'a *wuthering* of his [bird] palmy snow-pinions' ('Henry Purcell'), where *wuthering* describes the sound of the wind; both examples are from Hopkins.

This type of obscurity, like ambiguity, is based on denotative meaning. However, whereas obscurity due to the use of recondite words can, in principle, be easily eliminated, (lexical) ambiguity is not subject to elimination. As with the first type, an obscure word of this kind can become ambiguous if it contains more than one meaning that is relevant to the context.

In the last type of obscurity on our list, the individual words make sense but there is difficulty in understanding their relations to one another. This is exemplified by the opening stanza of 'If My Head Hurt a Hair's Foot' by Dylan Thomas, which is quoted below:

> If my head hurt a hair's foot
> Pack back the downed bone. If the unpricked ball of my breath
> Bump on a spout let the bubbles jump out.
> Sooner drop with the worm of the ropes round my throat
> Than bully ill love in the clouted scene. . .

Although the words are stringed into what appears to be grammatical constructions, the whole text amounts to apparent nonsense at first reading. The stanza was, in fact, labelled 'nonsense' by Robert Graves who then challenged anyone to make sense of it. Hodgart took up the challenge, and although there was really no resolution as to the actual meaning, both his attempt and those of subsequent critics to interpret the lines indicate that it is usually possible to find sense in what appears to be obscure. (For a record of the exchange between Graves and Hodgart, see Moynihan 1966: 72–6, who also summarizes the readings of some other critics.)

Since type (iii) obscurity involves relations between words, it really goes beyond the lexical level to that of context. In the Dylan Thomas example, the opaqueness which leaves an unending debate over what is intended by the poet or the text itself is largely compounded by obscurity at the contextual level. Phrased differently, there is a correlation between word-obscurity and context-obscurity. Based on the opposing values of clarity and obscurity, there are theoretically four kinds of relation: (a) that between a clear context and an obscure word; (b) that between a clear word and an obscure context; (c) that between an obscure word and an obscure context; and (d) that between clear words in a clear context. Only the first three involve obscurity, but the last is nevertheless listed, as it is important in helping us to make out 'islands of sense' from which we build in our attempt to understand a generally obscure text.

Relation (a) provides the most encouraging environment for facilitating the decoding of word obscurity. Much of our earlier discussion, including that for obscurity of types (i) and (ii), has largely presumed this kind of relation, as indicated by a brief recall of the *spell* example given earlier. The clear context allows attention to be focused on the obscure word, and serves as a jigsaw frame which guides the selection and fitting together of the right semantic pieces.

Relation (b) occurs in the Dylan Thomas example for type (iii) obscurity, where the words, in isolation, have defined (dictionary) meanings, but the way they are combined (involving apparently irrational relations between the words) generates a context that is obscure. Whereas in (a) context functions to clarify, the reverse is true of (b). What baffles the reader is not so much the question of 'What is the meaning of this or that word?' as that of 'What is the poet talking about?' or 'What is the poem about?' In order to make sense of the poem, the reader needs to reinterpret the words. Strategies resorted to in the process of reinterpretation include the need to understand metaphor, symbolism and other figurative use, all of which open up the possibility for a play with ambiguous meanings.

Of the three types of relation involving obscurity, (c) generates the greatest degree of unintelligibility. This follows from the underlying principle of the reciprocity between word-obscurity and context-obscurity. If clarity at word or context level helps to shed light on obscurity at context or word level, then it is only logical to expect that obscurity will be reinforced if it occurs at both word and context levels. Consider the last four lines from the sestet of 'Henry Purcell':

> . . . so some great stormfowl, whenever he has walked his while
> The thunder-purple seabeach, plumed purple-of-thunder,
> If a wuthering of his palmy snow-pinions scatter a colossal smile
> Off him, but meaning motion fans fresh our wits with wonder.

There are 'islands of sense' which we can make out from the collocations of certain words, such as the great stormfowl, which has purple-of-thunder plumage, has walked the beach that is of a thunder-purple colour, and it is intending to move ('meaning motion'). These pockets of intelligible meanings exemplify the fourth relation, (d), which is not directly involved with the issue of obscurity but is indispensable for providing us with anchors to make sense of other obscure parts of the text. In the lines from 'Henry Purcell' above, the last two are probably the most difficult to understand, a difficulty that is not lessened by the use of words like *wuthering* and *palmy*. Hopkins explained the former as 'a Northcountry word for the noise and rush of the wind' (McChesney 1968: 91); as for the latter, Milward (1969: 58) considers it ambiguous in its reference to palm-branches or palm of the hand; or it could mean 'triumphant' in the sense it is used in *Hamlet*: 'in the most high and palmy state of Rome'. Hopkins admitted that the sestet, which includes these lines, 'is not so clearly worked out as I could wish' (see Milward 1969: 56); however, a determined reader can still attempt to make sense of such obscurity. The implication is that there always exists the possiblity of discovering hidden meanings. This idea of discovery or recovery is also present in Todorov's description of obscurity as a phenomenon which results from an 'occultation of referent' (see Riffaterre 1981: 238). In other words, there are identifiable meanings which are obstructed from the reader's view for the time being, and which can, with effort on the reader's part, be uncovered. Such a notion of obscurity is important as it means that obscurity is potentially valuable for ambiguity.

In practice, obscurity occurs only when there is an inability to decipher a word's meaning at *a given point in time*. This points to the transitoriness of the stage of undecipherability for all occurrences of obscurity except the extreme kind of total unintelligibility. In fact, obscurity is dynamic in the sense that it can move along a scale from impenetrability towards some discoverable meaning, or, to an apathetic reader, an obscure word may be considered 'impenetrable' when its meaning is actually 'discoverable'. For instance, consider *combs* in the following lines from stanza 4 of 'The Wreck of the Deutschland':

I am soft sift
In an hourglass – at the wall
Fast, but mined with a motion, a drift,
And it crowds and it combs to the fall;

In the context, it seems nonsensical to see the word as referring to the act of combing hair or to the comb on the head of a cock. Rather, there is the more esoteric use of *combs* as a verb derived from the noun form meaning 'crest' or 'ridge' (Milroy 1977: 235), thus giving us an image of sand gathering into a 'ridge' in the hourglass.

The same lines above provide another example which illustrates how ambiguity can 'emerge' out of obscurity. *Drift*, according to Milroy (1977: 237), has the special sense of 'the space between furrows; a trench cut in the ground', which collocates well with the other idiosyncratic word *combs* discussed above. However, unlike the latter, the ordinary sense referring to 'a driving movement or force' for *drift* is also applicable, tying in with the preceding description of motion. The two senses, one of which arises out of an obscure use, opens up a possibility for ambiguity in the context. However, it is maintained that obscurity remains distinct from ambiguity, although the former can help to contribute to the latter.

6.5 Pun

In contrast to the phenomena discussed in the last three sections, the pun is a sister phenomenon of ambiguity; that is, the pun may be considered to be a manifestation of ambiguity. Leech (1969: 209) describes the pun as a 'foregrounded lexical ambiguity', and Attridge (1988: 141) as 'ambiguity *unashamed of itself* . . . the pun is the product of a context deliberately constructed to *enforce* an ambiguity . . .'. This relation can be gathered from the usual definition given to a pun as 'the use of a word in such a way as to suggest two or more meanings or the use of two or more words of the same sound with different meanings; a play on words' (Charnley 1975: 28). Both puns and ambiguity depend on similarity of form and disparity of meaning. In both, 'there are always two or more levels, manifest and latent, in some kind of coexistence, sequence, alternation or tension' (Redfern 1984: 22).

As puns may consist in the repetition of the same word-form, or in a single occurrence which is ambiguous between two senses, there is considerable overlapping between pun and ambiguity. Hill (1985: 450), for instance, sets up three principles which he considers to govern the 'reality of double-meaning puns', but these principles apply equally to ambiguity, so they reinforce the similarity between the two phenomena. The principles given are: (a) the presence of a double context, with each offering support for one meaning (although the pun or ambiguity can also occur in a single context which can support more than one meaning); (b) the homonymous or polysemous nature of words, which Hill calls a 'hinge'; and (c) the presence of a 'trigger' which 'calls the hearer's or reader's attention to the double meaning' (Hill 1985: 450). This 'trigger' can be set off by means of foregrounding.

That the pun and ambiguity are really sister phenomena can be further clarified by taking a look at Heller's (1974) typology of the pun. He posits four types which share the common structural characteristic of having 'a single manifesting mark [a word form; symbolized by 'M' below] signal more than one conceptual function [i.e. sense; symbolized by 'F' below]' (1974: 271). The basis of differentiating between the types depends on whether what is initially perceived correlates with the subsequent interpretation or reinterpretation. The four types are reproduced in Figure 6.3 (Heller 1974: 272–3). Each type has two structures, the initial one representing a potential state, and the second one the actual state which results from a retrospective stage of interpretation, where the ambiguity is either resolved or retained.

Heller (1974: 271–2) illustrates the first type with the following example:

The doctor fell into the well
And broke his collar bone.
He should have tended to the sick
And left the well alone.

It is evident that the second *well* has the two senses 'place for collecting water' and 'people who are healthy', and that these senses are directly mapped on to the second structure in Figure 6.3. This form of pun is identical to lexical ambiguity, and because the context and 'narrative' of the poem so clearly draws attention to *well* as a pun, this pun is, indeed, what Leech (1969: 209) describes as a

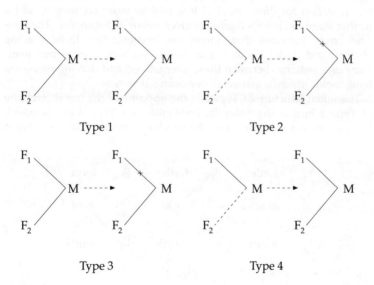

Figure 6.3

foregrounded lexical ambiguity. Heller (1974: 272) calls this a 'retentional, nondisambiguational pun'.

The second type is illustrated with a line from Joyce's *Ulysses*:

> Come forth, lazarus! And he came fifth and lost the job.

The pun is on *forth* which, in itself, signifies direction, but in the context, it is made to echo *fourth*, and reinterpreted as an indicator of sequence, not direction. This is a case of homophones, which differ in the written but not the spoken form (see the end of this section). Heller describes this pun as non-retentional (because the initial meaning is eliminated) and disambiguational (only one function, the second or reconsidered one, is adopted). In fact, Heller's account is not complete. We could say that, although there is disambiguation, a form of retrospective ambiguity is present in this Type 2 pun. Two contexts have been created here, each of which supports one sense. The play of these two contexts, one against the other, generates a play of two mutually exclusive alternatives. In encountering the word *fifth* further on in the utterance, the reader backtracks to read 'fourth' (F_2) into the word *forth* (compare garden-path ambiguities in syntax), but this 'new' sense does not eliminate the original one to the extent that only the new reading remains, as seems to be represented by Heller's figure for Type 2. The expression 'Come forth' still contains the interpretation for direction (F_1). It would be more accurate to add a further stage to Heller's figure, as given below in Figure 6.4. The two-way arrow indicates that, under one context, the 'forth' reading obtains, and under another, the 'fourth' reading is more pertinent. The mind switches between these alternatives, and, having perceived both, holds them together as coexisting disjuncts.

The initial structure of Type 3 is the opposite of the initial structure of Type 2 in that the potential ambiguities for Type 3 are manifest, but the second structure (i.e. the resultant state) for the two types

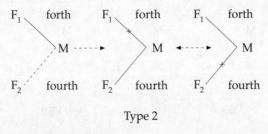

Type 2

Figure 6.4

contains disambiguation.[8] For instance, consider the example from Milton's *Paradise Lost* III: 214–15:

> Which of ye will be mortal to redeem
> Man's mortal crime, and just the unjust to save?

The word *mortal* is polysemous (F_1 and F_2 below), but the context also clearly indicates which sense is intended in each of its occurrences (the first has the sense 'subject to death' and the second, 'deadly'), so that Type 3 pun is, as Heller says, disambiguational and non-retentional. As in the case of Type 2, Heller has stopped short of a further stage of interpretation. Supposing we concentrate on the second occurrence of *mortal* found in 'Man's mortal crime', with the sense 'deadly', we could represent the stages of interpreting the pun in the manner given in Figure 6.5. The proximity between the two occurrences of *mortal* in Milton's lines encourages a link to be established between them, so that the second *mortal* carries an echo of the sense found in the first *mortal*, as represented in the third structure in the figure above. The faint cross, marked by broken lines, indicates that F_1 is not the most salient reading in the given context for the second *mortal*, but it is nevertheless relevant in a 'wider' interpretation where the mortality of man is related to his mortal crime. This analysis applies in a similar manner if 'M' in the figure above is made to stand for the first *mortal*.

From Heller's figures, it can be seen that Type 4 is similar to Type 1 in being obviously ambiguous. If we consider the initial structure of each type to be the potential state, and the second structure to be the actual state, then it can be seen that, whereas the potential ambiguities for the pun of Type 1 are overt and manifest (represented by the unbroken lines in the figure), one of the senses in the potential state for Type 4 pun becomes evident only on retrospection (represented by the change from broken to unbroken lines). Type 4

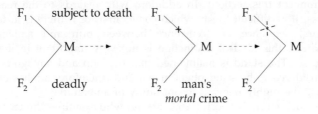

Type 3

Figure 6.5

pun can be illustrated with the following example (Heller 1983: 441): the expression 'He took a turn for the nurse', in a hospital setting, has an overt context which makes a literal reference to 'nurse', and a covert context suggested by the established cliché 'took a turn for the worse', so that this other interpretation is juxtaposed with the literal one. The proximity in sound between *nurse* and *worse* further encourages one to postulate a relation between the two words.[9]

Types 1 and 3 may be said to contain items which bear type-ambiguity. In the examples *well* and *mortal*, for instance, the presence of type-ambiguity is the reason why the context and, in the case of Type 3, repetition can cause the reader to become aware that these words are each capable of bearing two meanings. At the token level, one or both meanings may be intended. In the case of Types 2 and 4, on the other hand, only one meaning is really inherent in the lexical item concerned at type level, while the other is attributed to the word (in its token occurrence) by the context (linguistic or non-linguistic). In this way, we can talk about ambiguous meanings which are 'created' by the context.

The typology of the pun described above shows how closely pun is interwoven with lexical ambiguity. This close interrelationship makes it difficult to determine which phenomenon comes before or after the other. Muir (1950: 475) considers the pun to be a source of ambiguity: 'Sometimes the use of overt or concealed puns causes an ambiguity.' Similarly, for Quirk (1951: 81–2), 'the term *pun* can also cover plays on words for which a word has only to be capable of *suggesting* another one of different interpretation'. Consider the *nurse/worse* example above, where the ambiguity in the given expression is 'reflected' from allusion to another context. In such a case, then, puns can be said to be a source of an ambiguous double image. However, it would seem that the reverse is the case (i.e. the pun is brought about by ambiguity, or, in many cases, by polysemy or homonymy) in the numerous definitions of pun in terms of ambiguity (see the beginning of this section). In addition, with regards to the reading process, it is difficult to say which comes first, or if there is in fact a temporal sequence of occurrence between pun and ambiguity. Ultimately, this kind of distinction is not very important in literary discourse. The stand is maintained that the pun and ambiguity can be considered to be sister phenomena, and, therefore, studies of the pun will be highly relevant to our study of ambiguity.

One such study is Leech (1969: 209–14) who examines the technical aspects of punning. Leech provides a convenient list of punning methods which may be examined for the way pun and ambiguity work hand in hand. For example, repeating a word while shifting

AMBIGUITY AND COGNATE PHENOMENA

from one of its meanings to another is a popular way to pun, and has been noted in classical rhetoric as 'antanaclasis' (Vickers 1970: 129). In terms of Heller's typology, it may be said to correspond to Type 3. The *mortal* example above is an instance of punning repetition, and as the pun–ambiguity relation has been described, it will not be discussed further here. An instance of the repetitive pun in Hopkins is found in *mind* towards the end of the poem 'The Lantern Out of Doors':

Death or distance soon consumes them [men]: wind
What most I may eye after, be in at the end
I cannot, and out of sight is out of mind.

Christ minds: Christ's interest, what to avow or amend
There, eyes them, heart wants, care haunts, foot follows kind,
Their ransom, their rescue, and first, fast, last friend.

The first *mind* (a noun) occurs in a conventional expression which defines a feature characteristic of the poet (and of mankind). Its immediate reappearance as a verb in the next line specifies Christ's active care for the men ('them'). An implicit contrast between the poet's attitude and that of Christ is, therefore, set up, not only by the close proximity of the words, but also by the punning repetition. This pun on *mind* in the poem serves a thematic significance of comparing the poet's short-lived care and remembrance with the everlasting care of Christ who will always keep the men in mind.

Other forms of repetition which link divergent meanings are what may be termed 'reversibles', such as *live* and *evil*, *scared* and *sacred*, *hated death* (Culler 1988: 5), which have semantic components that are mutually exclusive. Manifestations of reversibles take the forms of anagrams, palindromes and chiasmus (see Rimmon 1982: 29). The basis of an anagram is the writing system. Thus, Samuel Butler's 'Erewhon' is an inverted 'Nowhere', Dylan Thomas's 'Llareggub' in *Under Milk Wood* also makes use of anagram to mean 'nothingness' (see Ahl 1988: 26). Anagrams are more than just riddles to amuse the reader, but can be a revealing expression of reality as, in Socrates' opinion, 'writing is not . . . the *recording* of reality in words, but the *imitation* of reality in letters and syllables' (Ahl 1988: 27). Anagrams function in the way rhyme does, for emphasis and to suggest certain semantic connections.

One offshoot of punning repetition is the chiasmus which is an inversion of the order of words (see Ullmann 1962: 138; Rimmon 1982: 29). Puttenham calls the chiasmus 'Crosse-Copling', which mirrors the criss-crossing of opposites: 'Some co-eds pursue learning, others learn pursuing' (Redfern 1984: 23–4). It involves a rearrangement in order to call attention to the different senses present in the same word: for instance, *extraordinary* in 'ambassador extraordinary' carries a different sense ('additional or subordinate') from that in 'extraordinary ambassador' ('unusual'; see Ullmann 1962: 170). Although there is disambiguation at the token-level, this form of punning through repetition is not to be dismissed, as the different senses suggested may have psychological significance, in that the disparate senses may coexist in the mind of the reader and have an effect on his subsequent interpretation.

What may be included as a further form of punning repetition is the 'syllepsis', when this is used in the sense of a zeugma. This occurs when 'two superficially alike constructions are collapsed together, so that one item is understood in disparate senses' (Leech 1969: 211).[10] Taken in this latter definition, syllepsis becomes an ellipted form of punning through repetition. Consider Pope's lines from *The Rape of the Lock*:

> Or stain her honour, or her new brocade,
> Or lose her heart, or necklace, at a ball.

Each of the two verbs has two coordinated nouns as objects, but each usage carries a different sense. Because one word is clearly made to stand for two senses, the reader sees the type-ambiguity involved, but at the level of the token, it is quite clear which meaning is intended in the particularized context. 'Stain her honour' has to do with chastity, while 'stain her brocade' describes something more prosaic, i.e. literally to dirty an object. Similarly, 'lose her heart/ necklace' is an unholy yoking together because of the disparate senses of the verb in each particularized context. Because only one word is used to describe two contrasting activities (one literal and the other metaphorical), the connections are more apparent, and a satirical effect is achieved.

Another way to pun is to play on antonyms, which involves using 'two words which are normally antonymous in non-antonymous senses' (Leech 1969: 210). Leech illustrates this with an example from *Romeo and Juliet*:

> therefore pardon me,
> And not impute this yielding to *light* love,
> Which the *dark* night hath so discovered.

Leech's comment will be quoted to show how the pun here suggests ambiguity: '*Light* is used here in the Shakespearean sense of "frivolous", and yet at the same time we are made aware of it as an antonym to *dark'* (1969: 211). As an antonym to *dark*, *light* would take the senses of 'bright' or 'shining' (and the connotation of 'intense' which is a contrast to 'frivolous'). Although the first sense of 'frivolous' is dominant, the second sense is possible. At the linguistic level, the two senses are incompatible, but at the pragmatic level of interpretation, the two senses coexist in the reader's mind. This play on antonyms as a punning method clearly involves lexical ambiguity, and exemplifies Heller's Type 1 pun.

The third method is 'asyntactic pun' where 'one of the meanings does not actually fit into the syntactic context' (Leech 1969: 211). The well-known example of Mercutio's utterance, 'Ask for me tomorrow and you shall find me a grave man', is given. As Leech observes, *grave* can only occur as an adjective grammatically, and thus with the meaning 'serious'; but the context of Mercutio dying invites us to view the word as a noun as well, i.e. with the meaning 'a man in the grave'; 'dead'. At the overt, token-level, the syntactic structure dictates the appropriate meaning, so that the possibility of actualizing the potential ambiguity is suppressed. However, the context is a strong factor here, with the result that the two alternative senses play on the mind of the reader. The obvious ambiguity at the pragmatic level suggests that this kind of pun can be considered to correspond to Heller's Type 4.

Etymology is a fruitful source that poets draw upon for pun, which is hardly surprising, considering that in both etymology and pun there is a use of related forms to connect disparate meanings (Culler 1988: 2). This kind of pun invites a comparison between an etymological but obsolete meaning and a current meaning, both of which are usually in contrast with one another. Since an etymological meaning reflects the origin of the word but is no longer current, a pun which makes use of etymology will be different from other puns based on current meanings. An instance is *martyr* in the compound *martyr-master* which is addressed to Christ ('The Wreck of the Deutschland', stanza 21). Here, the current sense of 'being put to death because of one's religious beliefs' applies. However, in the context of the poem, there is also an oblique reference to the nuns as martyrs (the Franciscan nuns were exiled because of their faith, which led to their death by shipwreck). Strictly speaking, since their death was not directly caused by oppressors, they could not be described as *martyrs* in the conventional sense; but this term applies if we interpret it in the etymological sense 'witness'. Similarly, in the poet's praise of the falcon or Christ in 'The Windhover', the word *dangerous* draws upon the current and non-current senses of 'perilous' and 'dominant' (from Latin *dominium*) respectively:

... AND the fire that breaks from thee then, a billion
Times told lovelier, more dangerous, O my chevalier!

Another example is the following from Hopkins's 'Andromeda'
which, at one level, narrates the story of how Andromeda is saved
from being sacrificed to the dragon or beast:

Her flower, her *piece* of being, doomed dragon food.

Milward (1969: 71) tells us that *piece* carries an obsolete, Shakespearean
reference to a rare woman. Conventionally, the word is also used for a
bit of matter or food; hence, there is a pun here which plays on the
idea of a rare woman who is doomed as food for the dragon. This
kind of pun is, in effect, no different from any polysemic or
homonymic pun; that is, its relation to ambiguity depends on how it
is used (whether in punning repetition or as a syllepsis, for instance).

Finally, there is a kind of pun that is based on words with identical
sounds (homophones)[11] or on words that sound similar (paronomasia).
This type of pun which depends on the phonological identity or
similarity is considered to be so common and important that it
represents the epitome of the pun for some investigators into the
phenomenon. For instance, Geoffrey Hartman defines the pun as 'two
meanings competing for the same phonemic space or as one sound
bringing forth semantic twins' (quoted in Fried 1988: 85), and
Koestler describes the pun as 'the bisociation of a single phonetic
form with two meanings – two strings of thought tied together by an
acoustic knot' (quoted in Ackerley 1978: 169). When two words sound
alike, there is a tendency to postulate a relationship between them.
This is in accordance with Jakobson's (1960: 368) claim that
'equivalence in sound, projected into the sequence as its constitutive
principle, inevitably involves semantic equivalence', and that 'two
similar phonemic sequences near to each other are prone to assume a
paronomastic function' (Jakobson 1960: 371). Consider the following
example (Fried 1988: 96):

And naked to the hangman's noose
  The morning clocks will ring
A neck God made for other use
  Than strangling in a string.

('A Shropshire Lad xı', A. E. Housman)

There is a pun on *ring* which is a homophone with *wring*, the latter
being strongly suggested by the contextual environment of 'hangman's
noose' and 'neck'. At one level of reading, the two senses alternate
with each other in true ambiguity fashion, with *ring* in the company

of clocks on the one hand, and *wring* associated with 'neck' on the other. However, at a higher level, these two senses integrate to amplify the theme of the 'deathly force of perfect timing' (Fried 1988: 96). Similarly, the near-homophones *wrack* and *wreck* in 'is the shipwrack then a harvest' (Hopkins, 'The Wreck of the Deutschland', stanza 31) offer a double image. Apart from the more obvious meaning of 'ruin' as in the wreck of the ship that the narrative of the poem deals with, the 'wrack' of seaweed is a harvest (MacKenzie 1981: 53), so that the idea of destruction coexists with the idea of salvation. Thus, in these examples, the pun is intimately related to ambiguity and the two are significant contributing factors to an interpretation.

6.6   Conclusion

From the comparisons made of the various phenomena which have often been confused with ambiguity, we have distinguished indeterminacy, vagueness and obscurity as being different and distinct from ambiguity, multiple meaning as being a wider phenomenon that embraces ambiguity, and the pun as a sister phenomenon of the latter.

Notes

1. This view is held not only by literary critics, but by philosophers as well, such as Clark and Welsh (1962, Chapter 3, section 3) who distinguish multiple meaning and ambiguity according to whether they have value: the former has, and is found in poetry (in forms such as puns), whilst the latter is a defect or error which arises from 'failures in expression' (1962: 153) when the meaning comprehended is not the same as the intended meaning.
2. Empson (1961: 11) states this explicitly: 'I do not deny that the term had better be used as clearly as possible, and that there is a use for a separate term "double meaning", for example, when a pun is not felt to be ambiguous in effect.'
3. As we saw in Chapter 3, section 3.2.1, mutual exclusion is not a necessary condition for ambiguity to occur; it is sufficient that there is a difference between senses that are distinct and disparate. However, this does not

detract from the point being made here, that ambiguity is a subset of the broader category of multiple meaning.

4. Cited in Bahti (1986: 209).

5. In what is known as the 'Rorschach test', psychologists offer standard inkblots to their subjects to diagnose their response, and their findings reveal the importance of projection in the act of interpretation. What image is perceived depends on what the subject projects into the indeterminate shape of the blot. For a brief description of this test, see Gombrich (1977: 89, 155).

6. Quoted in Coates (1983: 13).

7. Hopkins directed this comment at 'The Wreck of the Deutschland', but it is applicable to his poetry in general.

8. Heller (1974) does not give any direct illustration of the Type 3 pun.

9. Note that the pun for *forth/fourth* is governed by mainly linguistic considerations (phonological identity, collocational juxtaposition, and so on), but the pun for *nurse/worse* is more dependent on the contextual factor (the phonological similarity is crucial).

10. In classical rhetoric, the term 'syllepsis' refers to the use of one word to suggest two senses (Vickers 1970: 148), thus making it difficult to differentiate from lexical ambiguity. For instance, in the line from Shakespeare's Sonnet 138, 'Therefore I *lie* with her, and she with me . . .', *lie* is considered a syllepsis, but it is also a homonymic ambiguity. Less clearly homonymous, but still evidently a syllepsis, is the example of *concerned* in 'The Eurydice – it *concerned* thee, O Lord' (Hopkins's 'The Loss of the Eurydice'), where the word is a pun between the sense of 'involved' with the connotation of 'being responsible', and the sense of 'worried' because of care. If syllepsis is used in the way intended by classical rhetoric, then it may be considered to correspond to Heller's Type 1 pun.

11. Note that 'homophone' is sometimes limited in its use to words which are spelled differently (e.g. *forth/fourth*, given earlier). At other times it refers to words which sound alike whether or not they have different spellings. In either case, what is crucial is the phonological identity or similarity between different words.

CHAPTER SEVEN

Sources of lexical ambiguity

Chapter 2, section 2.1.2 discussed the two important sources for potential lexical ambiguity: polysemy and homonymy. This chapter will consider further other means by which ambiguity is derived, such as tropes (sections 7.1 and 7.2) and lexical innovation (section 7.3), both of which often play on the polysemous and homonymous nature of language. In addition, section 7.4 discusses referential uncertainty as another source of lexical ambiguity.

7.1 Metaphor

Tropes such as metaphor, metonymy, irony, symbol, allegory and paradox are all based on the play of two or more layers of meaning, usually literal versus figurative. This characteristic is the basis for their potential as sources of ambiguity. Moreover, as poetry is infused with metaphor and the other figures mentioned, it is profitable to try to establish a relation between them and ambiguity for two purposes: the first, as previously stated, is the rich source of data provided by such figures for ambiguity in poetry; and the second is the more complete picture gained of ambiguity as a poetic device when examined in relation to the other important poetic devices given above.

Since metaphor is generally acknowledged to be the most pervasive in poetry (and, according to Lakoff and Johnson 1980, in ordinary and standard language as well), it is appropriate to begin with this trope. The etymological sense of 'metaphor' is derived from the Greek word 'metapherein' which means 'to carry over' or 'to transfer'.[1] The traditional definition of metaphor is based on the notion of transference which consists in presenting one idea or object by using the name or linguistic sign of an altogether different idea or object. Compare Aristotle's definition: 'Metaphor consists in applying to a thing a word that belongs to something else; the transference being either from genus to species or from species to genus or from species to species or on grounds of analogy' (quoted in Nowottny 1962: 49). From this basic process of transference, discourses on metaphor attempt to explicate the phenomenon in terms of relations such as resemblance, implied comparison, analogy, substitution, interaction and others. In all these explications, the fundamental point that is returned to again and again is that the metaphor involves the working together of two mutually exclusive meanings. This is also the point from which we may begin to look at metaphor as a source of ambiguity.

Characteristic of metaphor is the clash or opposition between the literal meanings of the term designating what Richards (1936: 96) calls the 'subject' or 'tenor' and the 'vehicle'. For instance, in metaphors such as *love is a rose*, it is explicit that the literal senses of the two entities compared (*love* as tenor and *rose* as vehicle) are incongruous. The literal interpretation of the tenor–vehicle pair may be blocked semantically through logical absurdity, or pragmatically through factual impossibility or factual implausibility.[2] In order to resolve this clash so as to make sense of metaphor, there occurs a shift from the literal to the figurative meaning. 'Literal' here may be read as referring to denotation, or the criterial properties of a word, while 'figurative' is a little more complex. It is best understood as the meaning which comes about when a term which literally denotes some entity is transferred to another entity which is not usually regarded to be related to the first entity in any direct way. It is usually, but not necessarily, restricted to connotation. Although the figurative meaning is fundamental to understanding metaphors, the literal denotative meaning of a word used metaphorically has its part to play as well. There is no doubt that to call someone a *cesspool* is to use a metaphor that depends on the denotation of 'filthiness' or 'waste' which characterizes the word. Connotation is, on the other hand, dominant in Hopkins's *black hours* where it is not the hue of the colour that is important, but its connotation of 'misery' or 'hopelessness'.[3] It is clear that the designating properties of a person and a cesspool, and of hours and blackness, are incompatible.

At the lexical level, the interrelatedness of ambiguity and metaphor is borne by what Black terms the 'focus', or the word that bears the shift in meaning from literal to figurative. In 'The chairman plowed through the discussion', the word *plowed* is the focus of the metaphor, while the rest of the sentence, which is used literally, provides the 'frame' within which the focus is interpreted (Black 1962: 27–8). Metaphor is, of course, not only a 'one-word trope' (Ricoeur 1977: 101–2), but viewing it at the word level (see Ricoeur's argument that 'The theory of the statement-metaphor refers back to the word-metaphor'; 1977: 131) has the advantage of naturally suggesting its link with the essential characteristics of lexical semantics, that is, polysemy and homonymy.[4]

The coexistence of the literal and figurative meanings stems from the polysemic character of language. From our previous examination of polysemy, we noted that it is semantic difference rather than semantic similarity that is relevant to ambiguity. The same principle holds for metaphor as a form of ambiguity. The polysemy factor comes into play in the shift from the literal to the figurative meaning. Often, the figurative meaning is regarded as an extension of the literal meaning, which implies that there is no mutual exclusiveness between the original and the extended meaning. As figurative meaning is usually based on connotation, it is to be expected that there will be some kind of semantic similarity with the literal meaning, since connotation is, in a sense, derived from the denotation of the term concerned. However, as we resort to the figurative meaning in order to understand a metaphor, it is logical to expect some underlying semantic difference within the two meanings in the focus, so that, whereas the literal meaning is inapplicable, its figurative counterpart will be relevant. To return to Hopkins's *black hours*, *black* ('colour') in a literal sense has to modify a noun with the semantic feature +CONCRETE (accompanied by physical and spatio-temporal qualities). *Hours* has a temporal quality and is therefore essentially an abstract entity, designated with the feature −CONCRETE. The combination *black hours* shows a violation of selection restrictions which results in the literal 'colour' meaning being blocked;[5] to make sense of the expression, we seek a non-colour interpretation of *black*. A contextually appropriate figurative meaning such as 'misery' is then selected, probably because the connotation of 'misery' is pragmatically (or conventionally) associated with the colour 'black', but, semantically, these two meanings are poles apart.

It can be safely said that polysemy makes possible the existence of metaphor, since the latter depends on the characteristic of multiple senses of one word, whether the semantic plurality is at the same level (literal vs literal, or figurative vs figurative), or at different levels (literal vs figurative). But the relationship between polysemy and metaphor is two-way, in that just as polysemy is a source that metaphor draws upon, metaphor also contributes to polysemy and, consequently, to ambiguity. This contribution results, to a large extent, from the propensity of the metaphor to create new meanings. Connotation, which is the basis of figurative meaning, differs in a very important aspect from denotative meaning, and that is, in its openness to semantic change or innovation. It follows that connotation is seen to reside in the marginal meaning the peripheral circle of which is expandable and fluid. (Beardsley 1962: 297, for instance, explicates the metaphor in terms of the central meaning of the term, which is equated to denotation, and the marginal meaning, which is equated to connotation.) In comparison, any alteration or addition to the denotation as central meaning occurs much more slowly as the factor of 'institutionalizing' the meaning has to be taken into account. Black (1962: 33) calls the process of injecting new senses into old words 'catachresis', and observes that 'if a catachresis serves a genuine need, the new sense introduced will quickly become part of the *literal* sense'. This is evident in the assimilation of well-established metaphors into the core meaning of a word. For instance, *crane* originally referred to a long-necked bird and was figuratively extended to refer to a device for lifting heavy objects. For a present-day speaker, the link between the original and derived senses is not so clear, and the figurative meaning has a separate entry in the dictionary. A similar development is seen in *tank*, with the original meaning of a metal box-like container for water or fuel and its extended meaning of an engine of war.[6] Such metaphors are 'fossilized' and so may be considered to have a semantic status equivalent to any homonymous or polysemous item which has acquired meanings through means other than metaphorical extension.

The place of homonymy in metaphor is best seen in terms of the connection between the pun and metaphor, both being forms of ambiguity. In both, there is a yoking together of incompatibilities, resulting in a simultaneous perception of two disparate meanings. This factor forms the basis of their relation, and of Brown's (1956: 18) description of the pun as 'the first step toward the achievement of symbolic metaphor'. The pun seems to achieve this metaphorical status when the disparate meanings are discovered also to yield similarity: 'When the pun discovers that two things, two different concepts, or two widely separate experiences bearing the same name also share deeper affinities, it is a metaphor' (Welsh 1978: 245; quoted in Redfern 1984: 97). This is illustrated below:

> . . . like each tucked string tells, each hung bell's
> Bow swung finds *tongue* to fling out broad its name;
> Each mortal thing does one thing and the same:
>   Deals out that being indoors each one dwells;
>   Selves – goes itself; myself it speaks and spells,
> Crying What I do is me: for that I came.
>
> (Hopkins, 'As kingfishers catch fire . . .')

The word *tongue* integrates the two forms of wordplay, pun and metaphor. The literal meaning refers to a part of the anatomy (cf. the human tongue). This is conventionally given the metonymic reading of 'speaking', 'utterance', a reading that is clearly intended in the poem, as suggested by its linguistic environment of 'tells' and 'speaks', and 'finds tongue' which bears an analogy to 'give tongue' (i.e. 'utterance' or 'voice'). In the context, there is a metaphorical reference to the clapper of a bell as well. By punning on the metonymic and metaphorical interpretations, Hopkins spells out the distinctiveness of the bell in its sounding out of its 'self' ('Deals out that being indoors each one dwells'), and thus exemplifies the inscape of the thing.

In the poetic context, fresh and novel metaphors are interesting and rewarding, whether as an expression or as a source of ambiguity. The extension of meaning in ordinary or trite metaphors usually draws upon a stock of attributes most commonly associated with the focus. In a poem, the poet can highlight, suppress, or construct a system of implications through which he guides the reader's interpretation of a given metaphor. Even so, there is no certainty that two readers will reach the same interpretation. Fraser (1979) conducted a test on the interpretation of novel metaphors, and his results show that there is little consistency in the way different speakers interpret the same metaphors. This is because the pointers or clues do not banish a certain amount of openness and flexibility in metaphorical interpretation, fortunately, as this often serves as the stimulant to lively discussions which help to generate further insights into the poem. As the metaphor is not an explicit statement of the intended meaning, there is a good likelihood of discovering ambiguity in such metaphorical interpretations. More specifically, we can name three ways in which this can happen:[7]

(a) when a non-metaphorical reading is tenable as well as the metaphorical one;[8]
(b) when there are two or more different metaphorical readings; and
(c) when there is a combination of (a) and (b).

The basis for (a)–(c) as ways in which ambiguity can arise depends on the literal–figurative dichotomy and, without question, analysis must be carried out within a semantic–pragmatic framework.

(a)   A comparison of the two terms in a metaphor will reveal the incongruence of their designating properties; this incongruence creates a double vision which is not unlike that of an ambiguous word. The term 'vision' is used in a rather loose way here, as the visual effect of an abstract item is hardly clear. In the metaphor *black hours*, for instance, we may be able to see the 'blackness', but it is surely impossible to see 'hours'. Earlier, it has been argued that the literal sense of the term to be transposed on to the subject is blocked (or, following Ricoeur 1979: 152, suspended) as its meaning is nonsense in a metaphorical context; however, this does not mean that it is obliterated. On the contrary, it is very much present, especially in novel metaphors, which accounts for the impact metaphors have on our perception (or vision).[9] As Ricoeur (1977: 116) points out, it is the cumulative capability of the word which is the foundation of semantic innovation in language, including creativity by means of the metaphor. This is clearly expressed by W. M. Urban in *Language and Reality* (1939: 112; quoted in Ullmann 1962: 163):

> The fact that a sign can intend one thing without ceasing to intend another, that, indeed, the very condition of its being an *expressive* sign for the second is that it is also a sign for the first, is precisely what makes language an instrument of knowing. This 'accumulated intension' of words is the fruitful source of ambiguity, but it is also the source of that analogous predication, through which alone the symbolic power of language comes into being.

Consider also Davidson's (1979: 33) observation: 'Imagine the literal meaning as latent, something that we are aware of, that can work on us without working in the context, while the figurative meaning carries the direct load.' Thus, the metaphor may be said to have two different kinds of meaning at once, the literal and the figurative, and so poses as a possible form of ambiguity.[10]

Sometimes, moreover, there is uncertainty as to whether the literal reading is in fact blocked or whether it counts as one of the readings. Ambiguity can arise from cases which offer both a literal as well as a figurative reading in a given context. Proverbs are especially susceptible to ambiguity of this sort: as Leech (1969: 161) notes, ' "A rolling stone gathers no moss" and "Empty vessels make the most sound" are both true, if trite, as literal propositions; as proverbs, however, we understand them to refer figuratively to human character.' A little different is an example found in Hopkins's 'The Loss of the Eurydice', which describes the wreck of three hundred seamen off the coast of England:

> No Atlantic squall overwrought her
> Or rearing billow of the Biscay water:
> Home was hard at hand
> And the *blow* bore from land.

Within the context of the stanza quoted, *blow* makes a literal reference to the wind that blows from the coast, but the word has another meaning of 'a hit'. The ambiguity arises from a metaphorical version of the second sense, since in the wider context of the poem which is concerned with the lost spiritual state of England, there is also a reference to the spiritual blow occasioned by the division within the Church in England.

The same poem offers several other examples of ambiguity between literal and non-literal interpretations:

> Marcus Hare, high her captain,
> Kept to her – *care-drowned* and wrapped in
> Cheer's death, would follow
> His charge through the champ-white water-in-a-wallow,

The compound *care-drowned* encourages more than one reading; it can take the literal sense of 'drowned because of care for the ship', which is valid because of Marcus Hare's position as the ship's captain, or it can be interpreted figuratively as 'drowned in cares' (i.e. despair), which parallels the structure of 'wrapped in Cheer's death', or it can be further interpreted as 'having drowned his cares' by analogy to the common idiom 'drown one's sorrows'. Similarly, both literal and metaphorical interpretations are found in the phrase 'the breathing temple and *fleet* / Life', where *fleet* is a pun referring to the ship and its crew as well as to the 'shortness of passing life' (most of the seamen being 'boldboys soon to be men'). This doubleness of reference is an instance of how Hopkins goes beyond rendering a mere account of the shipwreck, and serves to suggest the poignancy of the waste of young, innocent lives.

The traditional method of analysing metaphors in terms of tenor and vehicle shows another way in which ambiguity can arise out of the tenability of the literal as well as figurative interpretations. An illustration is the example discussed in Chapter 2, section 2.1.1, *a human elephant*. Depending on which element is perceived to be the tenor and which the vehicle, we get the two different readings of 'a human being like an elephant' and 'an elephant like a human being'. To a great extent, the decision on which is the tenor or vehicle is determined by the context, but this does not rule out the possibility of a reversal. In the sonnet beginning with 'I wake and feel . . .', the persona is depersonified into a set of biological conditions:

> I am gall, I am heartburn. God's most deep decree
> Bitter would have me taste: my taste was me;

The persona is not only filled with bitterness or searing pain; he has become 'gall' and 'heartburn', so that *my taste was me* is the taste of bitterness. However, because the act of tasting presupposes a person or animate being as subject, the depersonification is reversed. Thus, on the one hand, *my taste* is metaphorically equivalent to 'gall', 'heartburn' or 'bitterness'; on the other, it literally refers to the taste of a person. Similarly, *me* is literally the persona, but metaphorically it is gall, etc. But the reversal is incomplete as the subject is also the object. This creates a complexity where the 'subject-self' is identical with, and yet separate from, the 'object-self'. The literal and the metaphorical shift in and out of each other, or, in the words of Jakobson, 'The double-sensed message finds correspondence in a split addresser, in a split addressee, and what is more, in a split reference' (1960: 371).

(b) In addition to ambiguity of a literal–figurative nature, there is also that which occurs between two or more figurative interpretations. Metaphorical meaning which is born out of a semantic clash at the literal level emerges as a new meaning. It is the propensity of metaphor to generate new meaning that makes it so productive as a source of ambiguity.

One means of discovering the metaphorical meaning is to look for the ground of comparison between the tenor and the vehicle. The ground is covert in a metaphor, which encourages the possibility of different figurative readings for the metaphor. This, in turn, opens out to possible ambiguity. As noted by Leech (1969: 157): 'Metaphor . . . is inexplicit with regard to both the ground of comparison, and the things compared. This is not only a matter of indefiniteness . . . but of ambiguity.' Take, for instance, the following lines in the first stanza of

Hopkins's 'St Alphonsus Rodriguez' which describes honour gained at war:

> And those strokes once that gashed flesh or galled shield
> Should . . . on the fighter, *forge* his glorious day.

The focus is *forge*, which has ambiguity at the metaphorical level arising from ambiguity at the literal level: on the one hand, the ground of comparison is the blacksmith's forge where metal is beaten into shape, and on the other, there is a comparison to fraudulent imitation (of signature, etc.) which undercuts the former interpretation. This generates an ambiguity of whether the glory attained at war is genuine or is a sham.

A line from Tennyson serves as another illustration of ambiguity arising from different metaphorical interpretations:

> The *wrinkled* sea beneath him crawls.[11]

The metaphorical expression is not limited to just one word here, but we shall focus on *wrinkled*. This can be interpreted in terms of appearance: 'the sea looks wrinkled because of the waves'; or it can be seen in terms of age: 'the sea is wrinkled with age' (i.e., 'the sea is ancient'). These two interpretations remain separate although both are tenable, and may be superimposed one upon the other as a case of 'extralocution' (see Chapter 2, section 2.1.1), which adds to the poetic complexity of the line.

(c) A third way for metaphor to be a source of ambiguity occurs when there is a play of literal versus figurative meanings, as well as a play between different figurative interpretations, i.e. a combination of (a) and (b) discussed above. Consider the example from Hopkins's 'Henry Purcell' below:

> Let him oh! with his *air* of angels then lift me, lay me!

The word *air* can be literally glossed as 'atmosphere' or 'sky', so that *air of angels* could read 'sky filled with angels'. This may be a possible reading in the light of the bird image that follows, especially since there is cohesion in the collocation between *air*, *lift*, *wings* and, perhaps, *angels* (who are conventionally depicted with wings). More obvious is the figurative reading referring to 'music', hence, 'angelic melody' or 'heavenly music'; less obvious is another metaphorical interpretation referring to 'a person's distinctive bearing', which coheres with the poet's description of Henry Purcell as 'arch-especial a spirit' in stanza 1 – after all, it is not Purcell's music *per se* which impresses the poet, but the 'forged feature', 'the rehearsal / Of own, of abrupt self'. Each reading seems to get some form of contextual support that makes it viable, and one interacts with another to give visual immediacy and significant depth to the poem.

7.2   Other figures

The play of literal and figurative meanings is also the basis for ambiguity arising from other figures such as metonymy, symbolism, and so on. It is, in fact, possible for ambiguity to exist between different types of figures. An example discussed earlier, *black hours*, for instance, has been shown to be a metaphor. However, if we give another interpretation of 'hours of darkness' (i.e. night), then the metaphor can also be a metonym.

7.2.1   *Metonymy*

Wales (1989: 297) describes *metonymy* as 'a rhetorical figure or trope by which the name of a referent is replaced by the name of an attribute, or of an entity related in some semantic way (e.g. cause and effect; instrument; source)'. Thus, Hopkins's use of *redcoats* for 'soldiers' in 'The Soldier' is an instance of metonymy. More interesting is the use of *scarlet* in the same poem:

> So feigns it [the heart] finds as sterling all as all is smart,
> And *scarlet* wear the spirit of war there express.

The word *scarlet* refers back to the metonym *redcoats*, and may be seen as a 'twice-removed' metonym, since the colour 'red' is an attribute of *redcoats* which is an attribute (by way of uniform) for 'soldiers'. At the same time, *scarlet* may refer to something different, i.e. 'blood', which is commonly associated with war. Within the context given, then, there are different metonymic interpretations for *scarlet*. This play on the ambiguous interpretation of *scarlet* hints at the poet's sceptical attitude towards the notion of honour derived from the battlefield.

7.2.2 *Symbolism*

Symbolism also depends on the interaction between the literal and figurative meanings. It is described by Leech (1969: 162) as an 'optional extension, as it were, of the meaning from literal to figurative', and by Nowottny (1962: 175) in the following manner:

> With metaphor, the poet talks about object X as though it were a Y; he uses Y-terminology to refer to X. With symbolism, he presents an object, X, and without his necessarily mentioning a further object, his way of presenting X makes us think that it is not only X, but also is, or stands for, something more than itself – some Y or other, or a number of 'Y's; X acts as a symbol for Y, or for 'Y's.

Two simple examples taken, again, from 'I Wake and Feel . . .' serve to illustrate the coexistence of the literal and the symbolic meaning:

> I wake and feel the fell of dark, not day.
> What hours, O what black hours we have spent
> This *night*! what sights you, heart, saw; ways you went!
> And more must, in yet longer *light's* delay.

Night can refer to the 'material night which ends with day' or it can take on a symbolic reading which refers to the 'dark night of the soul'; similarly, *light* can refer literally to the 'daylight' or symbolically to the 'light of Christ's second coming'. Within the context of a poem which centres on the individual's spiritual experience, the symbolic interpretations are derived from biblical associations. For instance, Christ is equated with *light*, and the poet, a Jesuit, awaits his Second Coming to dispel the *night* (Milward 1969: 119–20).

Whereas the above examples show how ambiguity can arise through the coexistence of the literal and symbolic, the following example illustrates a type of ambiguity that comes about because of two possible symbolic readings. In Hopkins's poem 'The Caged Skylark', there is a literal reference to the bird, but in its comparison with man throughout the poem, the caged skylark comes to represent something more. Consider the first stanza:

> As a dare-gale skylark scanted in a dull cage
> Man's mounting spirit in his bone-house, mean house, dwells –
> That bird beyond the remembering his free fells;
> This in drudgery, day-labouring-out life's age.

The bird symbolizes the imprisoned spirit which has forgotten its original freedom, just as man has forgotten his mounting spirit. Within the textual context, there is a play between a concrete entity 'bird' and an abstract entity which bears the symbolic meaning. In addition, the symbolic meaning derived from the text can be compared to the meaning assigned to symbols by poetic convention or culture. According to Eitner (1978: 16, cited in Yasuyoshi 1987: 150–2), a *caged skylark* is a familiar symbol used in the second half of the eighteenth century to represent a state of sheltered innocence, security and natural piety – attributes which are favourable. There is support for this positive view in the third stanza:

> Why, hear him, hear him babble and drop down to his nest,
> But his own nest, wild nest, no prison.

There is a contrast of the ideas of 'imprisonment' and 'shelter'. These need not be contradictory, but they are sufficiently different to cause the *caged skylark* as a symbol to be ambiguous.

7.2.3 Allegory

A trope that is a close relation of the symbol is *allegory*, which is viewed by some scholars in terms of the former: Leech (1969: 163) describes it as a 'multiple symbol' the interpretation of which is derived from a combination of the individual interpretations of different symbols, and Wales (1989: 17) sees it as 'a systematic, structural kind of symbolism'. As such, like symbolism, allegory will also rest on the play of literal and figurative meanings to generate ambiguity.

A traditional definition of allegory is embodied in Preminger (1965: 12): 'As a technique of literature, allegory is a technique of fiction-writing, for there must be some kind of narrative basis for allegory. We have allegory when the events of a narrative obviously and continuously refer to another simultaneous structure of events or ideas, whether historical events, moral or philosophical ideas, or natural phenomena.' The precondition of the narrative as a basis for allegory should not obscure the usefulness of considering the phenomenon at a lexical level. As Quilligan (1979: 33) observes: 'The plots of all allegorical narratives . . . unfold as investigations into the literal truth inherent in individual words.' The dual structure of an allegorical narrative can then be studied in terms of the tensions generated 'between meanings of polysemous words, that is from the integration of the literal and the non-literal meanings of and in a key-word' (Ronen 1988: 116).[12]

An example of an allegorical narrative is Hopkins's 'Andromeda'. At one level, this is a mythological story about Perseus's rescue of Andromeda from the beast. At another level, an analogy can be made

to Christ (as Perseus) saving the Church (Andromeda) from the devil
or sin (the sea-monster).[13] Within the allegory's dual structure of
signification, some words take on symbolic references: in the first
line,

Now Time's Andromeda on this *rock* rude,

rock is literally the physical entity 'big stone', but the allegory
encourages reference as well to 'Peter' the rock on which Christ built
his church (Matthew 16:18). (Conversely, one could say that the
double meaning of *rock* helps to suggest an allegorical reading.) A
closer look at the first stanza will reveal other words which are
ambiguous:

Now Time's Andromeda on this rock rude,
With not her either beauty's equal or
Her injury's, looks off by both horns of shore,
Her flower, her piece of being, doomed dragon food.

Time past she has been attempted and pursued
By many blows and banes; but now hears roar
A wilder beast from West than all were, more
Rife in her wrongs, more lawless, and more lewd.

In the context of the allegorical reading of the poem, *horns* can refer to
'promontories' and to 'the devil's horns'; *piece* has its homophonous
counterpart in *peace* – hence the possible readings that Andromeda is
dehumanized into a 'piece of being', and the peace for the Church is
doomed; *dragon* refers to the beast to whom Andromeda is sacrificed,
but it is also a traditional symbol for Satan; the pronoun *she* takes a
double reference to Andromeda on the one hand, and to the Bride of
Christ, the Roman Catholic Church, on the other; *attempted* carries the
sense 'attacked' applied to the mythological story and the sense
'tempted' applied to the Church which is so often tried and tested;
beast shares with *dragon* the literal and allegorical references; and
West is the direction from which the beast comes, but also the
Western countries where the Church was threatened by develop-
ments and values which were 'against faith and morals' (Gardner
1969: 186 interprets the 'wrongs' brought by the 'wilder beast from
West' as rationalism, Darwinism, the new paganism of Whitman, and
similar forces). The double readings for the words discussed result
from the allegorical structure of the narrative, and involve, in the
words of Fletcher (1964: 18), the 'two [or more] attitudes of mind'
required to apprehend allegory.[14]

One means of expressing allegory is personification, by which is
meant not the attribution of human qualitites to an object, such as the

dancing of daffodils, but the naming of an actor or character with a concept, such as *Killjoy* (Barney 1979: 20). In other words, the verbal personification juxtaposes the concrete with the abstract. Consider the first half of stanza 15 of 'The Wreck of the Deutschland':

> Hope had grown grey hairs,
> Hope had mourning on,
> Trenched with tears, carved with cares,
> Hope was twelve hours gone;

The abstract idea of *hope* is personified into an allegorical figure, so that by the fourth line there is present the image of *Hope* as an agent who has gone away, as well as the more literal, intellectual conception of 'hope' that has long been in abeyance for the victims of the shipwreck. There is a coexistence of personification with its reversal back to the literal sense.

7.2.4 Paradox

Like the other figures discussed so far, paradox makes use of the play of literal and figurative meanings. Paradox is a statement which contains an apparent self-contradiction so that, semantically, it seems absurd, but pragmatically, it can be sensibly interpreted.[15] For instance, consider the following:

> Not, I'll not, carrion comfort, Despair, not feast on thee;

The example above contains a double paradox found in the noun phrase *carrion comfort* and in the appositional pair *comfort, Despair*. There is a surface incongruity which may be generally captured as equating a 'negative' value (e.g. the unfavourable associations in *carrion* and in *Despair*) with a 'positive' value (*comfort* is usually regarded as desirable). More specifically, the image of 'rotting flesh' in *carrion* is at odds with the conceptual notion of 'ease', 'solace' or 'relief from grief' in *comfort*; and *comfort* and *Despair* are antithetical in that implicit in the latter is the feature −COMFORT. There is an initial shock at such unexpected juxtapositions. However, paradoxes are meant to be resolved, and this is carried out by going beyond the literal plane to the figurative one in order to make sense of the apparent absurdity, often by adopting a strategy of 'erasure and replacement' (Ching 1975).[16] In the process, the reader may gain a perspective that is different from, perhaps contrary to or incompatible with, the conventional notion. Thus, *comfort* gets reinterpreted as something undesirable, but its established sense is not quite abandoned or erased, so that there is an ambiguous play between the 'new' and the 'old' meanings in the mind of the reader.

Another instance of paradox is seen in 'Binsey Poplars', a poem about the felling of poplar trees:

> Where we, even where we mean
> *To mend her we end her,*
> When we hew or delve:

The result is the opposite of the intention, and the rhyme between the key words *mend* and *end* brings out the irony in the paradox, pointing out the destructiveness of man's interference with nature, whatever his good intentions. In the context, then, the sense of destruction overshadows the usual dictionary sense of 'become better' or 'heal' in the word *mend*.

Many paradoxes are located in the juxtaposition of two lexical items which are semantically incompatible, taking the form of an oxymoron. This is seen in the combination of *reaving Peace* in the poem 'Peace'. Hopkins explained that *reave* is to be read as 'rob, plunder, carry off',[17] which creates a discord in our conception of the quality of harmony which underlies 'peace' and the violence attributed to it in the expression. Sense can be unravelled from this paradox when reading it in the context of the whole poem where peace is concretized as a 'wild wooddove' that seldom stays with the persona (who is pictured as a tree):

> When will you ever, Peace, wild wooddove, shy wings shut,
> Your round me roaming end, and under be my boughs?

In the light of the above image, the paradox of *reaving Peace* is resolved only by considering the noun as ambiguous between the proper name (reinforced by the capitalization) for a figure, and the common name for a concept. Thus, it is possible to interpret the paradox as *Peace* (figurative) which robs the poet of his *peace* (literal). Paradox may be said to encourage a perception of *Peace* as ambiguous in *reaving Peace*.

7.2.5 *Irony*

Irony is a double-layered phenomenon which has been traditionally seen as a contrast between an apparent (usually also literal) meaning and an assumed (usually also figurative) meaning. The literal meaning in an overt linguistic construction conceals an intended

opposite meaning which often expresses some form of disapproba-
tion. The idea that some kind of moral or social judgement is
associated with irony is reflected in de Wolff's (1985: 230) observation
that 'The traditional accounts of irony indicate, albeit in a rough and
very implicit way, the fact that ironical language involves a relational
comparison between systems of values . . . . The important thing is
that the outcome of this comparison does not turn out to the
advantage of the object in question . . .' The surface meaning is
rejected because of its incongruity with an implied proposition.[18]
Muecke (1969: 49) sums up the definition of irony as consisting of 'the
duality, the opposition of the terms of the duality, and the real or
pretended "innocence" '.

An ironic reading is often arrived at by means of conventional or
cultural knowledge which throws into relief the incongruity of ideas,
propositions and events found in the text. For instance, 'His designs
were strictly honourable, as the saying is; that is, to rob a lady of her
fortune by way of marriage' (cited in Leech 1969: 172). Going by the
ethical code of most societies, marrying someone for no other reason
than financial gain is anything but honourable. The author further
indicates that an opposite meaning is intended by using the highly
pejorative verb *rob* which directly contradicts the honorific implication of *honourable*. Since irony is dependent on contextual clues from
the text as well as from real-world knowledge, it is a phenomenon
that is not inherent in words or linguistic expressions: thus, the word
honourable (or any word) is not ironic out of context. But, as in the
case for metaphor, we can posit a 'focus' for irony, which may centre
on a word. In an ironic reading, this word takes on a negative value
which replaces, but does not eradicate, the literal sense.

Because the surface meaning is not eradicated, there is a possibility
for what Muecke (1969: 29), in citing Alan Rodway, describes as a
'double exposure . . . on one plate', involving 'two co-existing but
irreconcilable, irrelatable "realities" ', to occur. The last lines of
Hopkins's 'That Nature is a Heraclitean Fire and of the Comfort of the
Resurrection' play with a reversal between the literal and non-literal,
or ironic and non-ironic readings:

> In a flash, at a trumpet crash,
> I am all at once what Christ is, since he was what I am, and
> This Jack, joke, poor potsherd, patch, matchwood, *immortal diamond*,
> Is immortal diamond.

The focus is underlined in the above text. Following a series of
unflattering nouns, the sudden occurrence of *immortal diamond* seems

out of place. The discrepancy suggests an ironic interpretation of this metaphor. However, this irony is reversed in the second occurrence of the same metaphor, affirming the incorruptible worth in man when he is 'all at once what Christ is'. The 'double exposure' in these lines is complicated as the subject is not just man (represented by the persona), or man reconciled to God, but also Christ Incarnate. As such, the first *immortal diamond* may also be non-ironic in its reference to Christ who, though human, never ceased to be a 'diamond'.

From the above, it seems that there are two ways in which irony can act as a source of lexical ambiguity: one is to assign an antonymous meaning (symbolized by a 'minus' sign) to the literal sense of the focus, and the other is to generate uncertainty between an ironic and a non-ironic reading. But in many instances the presence of lexical ambiguity arises not because an 'extra' meaning has been created, but because the focus word is inherently polysemous. Irony calls attention to this polysemy which is actualized as ambiguity, as shown in an example discussed earlier:

Honour is flashed off exploit, so we say;
And those strokes once that gashed flesh or galled shield
Should tongue that time now, trumpet now that field,
And, on the fighter, *forge* his glorious day.

                          (Hopkins, 'St Alphonsus Rodriguez)

The phrase 'so we say' is a telling indicator of an ironic implication in the description of a soldier's honour that is 'flashed off exploit'. The word *forge*, as we have seen earlier, can mean 'beating something into shape' or it can take a less favourable meaning of counterfeit. The first sense is unquestionably the obvious one in the context, but the ironic implication in this stanza calls into play the second sense as well. Irony here functions less as a source than as a means for the realization of lexical ambiguity. In fact, one can adopt a reverse perspective of seeing irony, not as a source, but as an effect of lexical ambiguity.

7.3   Lexical innovation

No language can possess all the necessary, established words to express all the complexities of human experience and shades of emotion, or the new ideas, concepts and discoveries in our dynamic world. However, language is itself dynamic, and is capable of generating new words from existing elements in order to provide us with the means to capture succintly what has to be, otherwise, described in phrases, sentences or paragraphs. This happens in all kinds of registers such as scientific language, journalism, advertising, academic writings, ordinary conversations and poetry. Lexical innovation is obviously present in Hopkins's poetry. Milroy (1977: 113) tells us that 'It is the extent to which he uses such devices [alliteration, compounding, word-blending and syntactic premodification] and the ways in which he applies them that are uniquely his; and the intensity and richness of his mature poetic diction result from them.'

The manufacturing of new words, or lexical innovation, involves not only the novel forms of words, but also the novel use of familiar lexical items in unfamiliar and unconventional ways. The former is exemplified by examples such as *seathumbed* (Dylan Thomas, 'Author's Prologue'), *foresuffered* (T. S. Eliot, *The Waste Land*), and *brillig* (Lewis Carroll, *Through the Looking Glass*). The latter is illustrated by an example from Hopkins's 'The Wreck of the Deutschland', where the noun *Easter* is used as a verb in 'Let him easter in us'. Obviously, 'new lexical units' or 'new words' constitute the most clear-cut category of lexical innovation, but it is sometimes difficult to draw the boundary between 'new' words and 'old', or, more appropriately, familiar words, since the degree of novelty is relative to the reader's competence in language and to his experience in reading poetry. Generally, the dictionary can be used as a guide. But there is another sense of 'new' which is different from the preceding description, and that is the sense of novelty associated with the context in which a word (new or familiar) is used. What is implied in this is that our discussion of lexical innovation should not be restricted to formal or semantic matters, but should consider the aspect of pragmatics as well. A semantic–pragmatic framework, which has been consistently used throughout this thesis, will also be applicable to a study of neologism as a source of lexical ambiguity.

Neologisms are potentially ambiguous because they have no established or conventional interpretations attached to them, so they carry some uncertainty as to what they mean. Apart from 'newness', other features which contribute to their potential for ambiguity are their compactness or economy, their deviation from the linguistic norm (this is related to the characteristic of novelty), and their tendency to formulate new concepts (for the last point, in particular, see Leech 1969: 44). All these characteristics make neologism especially suitable and valuable to a genre such as poetry which is creative, compact and often insightful in highlighting or exposing aspects of life and the universe.

The main method that the poet uses to create new words is word-formation.[19] Word-formation is a process which makes use of existing elements such as roots and affixes to form new words. There are rules which help to predict some likely meanings, such as are found in the suffixation of *-er* which converts the base it is attached to into a noun, carrying an agentive sense, or into an adjective, carrying a comparative sense. But in some cases, the rules of word-formation do not unfailingly give a ready guide to the correct interpretation. As Wales (1989: 317) observes about poetic coinages, 'their MOTIVATION for creation comes from the CONTEXT of the text'. Similarly, interpretation of neologisms must also be context-based. Consider the example *ring-wise* (this is illustrated by Meys 1975: 93). The word by itself will be seen as similar in its structure (noun + semi-suffix)[20] to *clockwise, festoon-wise, lengthwise*. However, from the context 'Billy Walker beat the ring-wise Doncaster heavyweight Peter Bates', the element *wise* has the meaning of 'experienced', 'being wise', and not the suffixal meaning of 'in the form, manner, or the like of – ' (Marchand 1969: 358). Thus, word-formation rules here contain an ambiguity between *-wise* as a suffix and *wise* as an adjective. As in other cases of ambiguity, (ir)resolution is effected only within context. In what follows, we shall consider two prominent methods of word-formation, i.e. compounding and derivation.

7.3.1 *Compounding*

A major, productive process of word-formation is compounding, whether in general language usage or in poetry. A compound can be generally described as a lexical unit formed from a combination of two or more separate words. This is, of course, a simplistic explanation of a complex concept. In fact, the compound as a concept is so difficult to pin down that Levi (1978: 14) calls it a 'fictitious beast'. Linguists have tried to determine what constitutes a compound by applying various criteria, such as frontal stress, semantic specialization, permanent association between the elements, and isolation as a word-unit; none of these is satisfactory on its own.

There are essentially two ways to characterize the compound semantically. The first is to attribute to the compound semantic specialization where 'the meaning of the whole cannot be logically deduced from the meaning of the elements separately' (Jespersen 1942: 137). This is especially characteristic of idiomatic and institutionalized compounds such as *greenhouse* (house made of glass for the growing of delicate plants), *moon-struck* (deranged in mind) and *gatecrash* (join a party uninvited). Such compounds cannot be directly paraphrased (i.e. by using the component words), and, if used conventionally, are unlikely to be ambiguous at the semantic level. However, at the pragmatic level, such lexicalized compounds can be made to take on new meanings through a creative use of context. An interesting example pointed out by Bauer (1979: 46) is the peculiar use of the compound *fireman* in Ray Bradbury's novel *Fahrenheit 451*. Conventionally, this compound denotes a trained professional who fights fires by putting them out. In the novel, society destroys all books by burning them, and professionals (i.e. 'firemen') are engaged to do this. Hence, *fireman* here has an opposite meaning to the standard one: in the latter instance, the underlying verb is 'put out' (fire), and in the former, it is 'light' (fire). In arriving at the deleted verb in the compound, the crucial determining factor is the pragmatic knowledge of what a fireman is expected to do within the context of the society, actual or fictitious. What is set up in the mind of the reader now is a potential situation for ambiguity, with a play of the conventional meaning against the created meaning. Whether this potential is actualized depends on whether the story, at any point, deliberately obscures the context in a way that causes uncertainty and undecidability in the reader between the meanings. In terms of effect, there is no doubt that the new meaning of the compound *fireman* is surprising because it is contradictory to the conventional meaning, and the contrast forces us to see the compound with new eyes.

In general, it is doubtful that newly created compounds will be as 'opaque' as the more idiomatic compounds such as *moon-struck*, as the poet will need to provide clues for the reader to understand the compound created. It is more likely for poetic compounds that are instances of neologism to take on the second form of semantic characterization, which enables compounds to be readily understood through a direct paraphrase from the surface constituents. Some examples from Hopkins are: a *'dare-gale* skylark' (skylark which dares the gale), *manmarks* (marks made by man), and *'wind-beat* whitebeam' (whitebeam, a kind of tree, that is beaten by wind). To interpret such compounds, the reader looks for the relationship between the two familiar component units. Sometimes, this semantic relationship becomes quite clear through consideration of the constituent elements, but sometimes, it is not apparent from the surface elements alone. As a result of the unstated relationship in a compound, ambiguity may arise. In principle, a compound like *horse-cart*, as Gleitman and Gleitman observe (1970: 90), can mean:

(a)   cart that is shaped like a horse (cf *box-car*)
(b)   cart that is drawn by a horse (cf *dog-sled*)
(c)   cart that a horse rides in (cf *passenger-car*)
(d)   cart for a horse (cf *hay-wagon*)
(e)   cart that is as big as a horse (cf *horse-radish*)

As *horse-cart* is an institutionalized lexical unit, its 'frozen' meaning screens off other possible meanings except one, i.e, sense (b). Less well-established compounds may retain more than one underlying relation between the components of the compound, as in *martyr-master* (stanza 21) and *heaven-haven* (stanza 35) which may be coordinates with an underlying 'and' as the connecting link, or copulas signalled by an underlying 'is'.[21] Even more distinctively different is the interpretation of 'master of all martyrs' for the former compound, and 'a haven for heaven' for the latter. The compound, *dapple-dawn-drawn* (falcon) in 'The Windhover', also exhibits ambiguity between the readings 'the falcon is drawn forth (i.e. attracted) by the dappled dawn', and 'the falcon is drawn against (i.e. etched against) the dappled dawn'.

The ambiguity in the last compound discussed is attributable, in part, to the various possible relations underlying the compound, and in part to the polysemy of *drawn*. The difficulty of unravelling the meaning of the compound is increased if one or both of the component words is/are polysemous or homonymous, so that, in some cases, there is no certainty about the intended meaning: one reader may arrive at an entirely different reading from another reader. We can see this happen with *trambeams* as it occurs below:

> Some candle clear burns somewhere I come by.
> I muse at how its being puts blissful back
> With yellowy moisture mild night's blear-all black,
> Or to–fro tender trambeams truckle at the eye.
> By that window what task what fingers ply,
>
> (Hopkins, 'The Candle Indoors')

Tram and *beam* as individual constituents have more than one meaning. With the help of the *OED*, we can gloss some of the meanings of *tram* as:

(a)   woof or weft; silk-thread;
(b)   a cunning contrivance or device; a machination;
(c)   tackle or gear of ship;
(d)   balk, beam;
(e)   a track of wood, stone or iron;

and some meanings of *beam* are:

   (i)   the rood-tree or cross;
   (ii) a large piece of squared timber as part of the structure of a house or ship;
   (iii) wooden roller or cylinder in a loom;
   (iv) a bundle of parallel rays, such as light;
   (v) a radiant smile.

Theoretically, *trambeam* has twenty-five (5×5) possible meanings, or is twenty-five-ways potentially ambiguous.[22] Some of these meanings would be ruled out by the context in which the compound occurs (e.g. sense (c)), or by impossible combinations (e.g. (e) + (v)). But there remain enough multiple senses for the compound to be ambiguous, as can be gathered from the different interpretations given by different critics:

> Tram is basically a beam, bar or shaft. Ogilvie comments that a tramway, a plate railway, is prepared 'by forming the wheel tracks of smooth *beams* of wood . . . plates of iron'; these would seem to be *trambeams*. Schoder comments that 'silk threads used in weft' are called *trams*, hence the idea here is probably of wavy silk-like beams, but H[opkins] may mean *straight*, not wavy, beams of light.

(Milroy 1977: 246)

To capture the need for pragmatics in interpreting compounds, Bauer (1979: 46) puts forward the following proposal: 'There is a connection between lexeme A and lexeme B in a compound of the form AB such as can be predicted by the speaker/hearer partially on the basis of her knowledge of the semantic make-up of the lexemes involved and partially on the basis of other pragmatic factors.' To Bauer's proposal, we should make explicit the role of the reader: it is usually left to the reader to work out the exact relation between the two elements of a compound, and sometimes the answer is uncertain.[23] An exemplification of this is found in Short and Van Peer (1989: 28), where two readers interpreted the compound *rollrock* in Hopkins's 'Inversnaid' variously as 'rocks [which] can be rolled', 'rolling down from the rocks', and 'rolling down and rocking':

> This darksome burn, horseback brown,
> His *rollrock* highroad roaring down,

As the authors noted (1989: 50), the context is not very helpful in resolving the ambiguities in the interpretation of the compound.

A more day-to-day illustration of the need for pragmatics in the interpretation of compounds is *rat-poison*, which is 'poison for rats' because, pragmatically, rats are undesirable. But *snake-poison* cannot be unambiguously interpreted as 'poison for snakes', although this is a possibility, for pragmatically, not all snakes are undesirable and some snakes produce a certain venom which can be extracted, so that the compound can also be interpreted as 'poison from snakes' (in fact, this is the lexicalized reading). Other simple pairs such as *man trap* and *baby trap*, *flourmill* and *windmill*, also show the potential ambiguity. Even a collocation, sometimes considered to be a compound, such as *London train*, is ambiguous in direction between train going to or coming from London (see Bauer 1983: 47).

7.3.2 Derivation

Derivation is another major process of word-formation. It may be divided into derivation by affixation and derivation by zero-morpheme attachment (known as 'zero-derivation'). The former involves adding an affix to a base form to produce new lexemes (Lyons 1977: 522);[24] for example, the adjectivized noun in *'belled* fire' ('The Wreck of the Deutschland') is derived from noun + *-ed*. The latter is an alternative label for conversion, or the change in word-class for a base form without any change of form; for example, the past form of a verb is used as a noun in 'a lonely *began*' ('To Seem the Stranger Lies My Lot').

Like compounds, words formed through derivation have the property of economy. For instance, instead of saying 'fitted to be, behaving like, a companion', compactness is gained by affixation in the word *companionable*. In a manner similar to the possible presence of polysemy in the lexical constituents of compounds, some affixes have more than one interpretation, as can be seen, for instance, in two other combinations with *-able*: *acceptable* ('can be accepted') *knowledgeable* ('having knowledge'). In connection with the *-able* suffix, Marchand (1969: 230) notes that it can carry an underlying active or passive sense, 'fit for doing' or 'fit for being done', as instanced by the following: *agreeable* (active) and *blameable* (passive); but two examples which can be interpreted either way are *changeable* and *passable* (see Marchand 1969: 230 for these and many more examples). Another suffix which offers possible ambiguity is the nominalizing *-tion* or *-ation*, which can carry an active or passive sense, e.g. *exploitation*, or the meanings of 'action' or 'state', e.g. *explanation*.

As in the case of compounds, compactness leaves something unsaid or some meaning implicit, which creates a favourable environment that encourages potential ambiguity. For instance, *un-* is not only a negative prefix, but it can also function as a reversative or privative. In coinages such as *unchilding* and *unfathering* (created in the order of *un-* + *child/father*; *unchild/unfather* + *-ing*), there are two possible interpretations: 'to cause not to be a child/father' and 'to deprive of children and fathers' (Milroy 1977: 160–1). Although the second reading is preferable to the first in the context 'the widow-making unchilding unfathering deeps' ('The Wreck of the Deutschland', stanza 13), the first remains a possibility. Further, consider *unchrist* in Hopkins's 'The Loss of the Eurydice' (lines 95–6):

> These daredeaths, ay this crew, in
> Unchrist, all rolled in ruin –

Un- is often prefixed to adjectives (as in *unpopular*), participles (e.g. *untested*), verbs (e.g. *untwist*) and sometimes nouns (e.g. *unhorse*). *Unchrist*, however, is strikingly innovative because the prefix is added to not only a personal noun, but also a proper noun. Prefixed to a noun, *un-* takes on a reversative or privative function (Quirk, et al. 1972: 983), as instanced by *unchild* and *unfather* above. However, in the lines quoted, *unchrist* can also be seen to take the meaning of 'lack of-, absence of-' (Marchand 1969: 204); i.e. it describes the state of the crew of being without Christ. In this example, then, the prefix *un-* has two underlying binary states of +PASSIVE (contained in the second reading) and +ACTIVE (contained in the reversative reading), which play against each other. Moreover, in the latter, there is an implication that something must, in the first place, be present before it can be reversed; such an implication is absent in the former reading.

Uncertainty over the form of a word created through derivation may be another cause of potential ambiguity. For instance, *disseveral* in 'Manshape, that shone / Sheer off, disseveral, a star' ('That Nature is a Heraclitean Fire and of the Comfort of the Resurrection') may be interpreted as *dis-* + *several*, giving the meaning of 'not several', or it may be seen as an adjectivized form of *dissever*, giving the reading 'cut off' (cf. pun on the collocate *sheer off*).[25]

7.4 Referential uncertainty

Under the sub-section 'Denotation and reference' in Chapter 2, we indicated the importance of considering reference in our study of ambiguity. The reference of a word is based on the relation between the lexical unit and the referent, and, thus, reference is determined partly by the inherent meaning of the word (derived from the denotative sense or senses of the lexical unit), and partly by the context which enables us to identify the referent. This interaction between sense and context is seen, for example, in:

Margaret, are you grieving
Over Goldengrove unleaving?

(Hopkins, 'Spring and Fall')

You refers to the person addressed, but it is the context (provided by the textual environment in this case) which particularizes such a person by the name of Margaret.

You belongs to a type of words called deictic which constitutes an important group of referring expressions. Deictic, and the noun deixis, come from the Greek word meaning 'pointing' or 'showing', and the essential property of deixis is that 'it determines the structure and interpretation of utterances in relation to the time and place of their occurrence, the identity of the speaker and addressee, and objects and events in the actual situation of utterance' (Lyons 1981: 170). Deictic elements include personal pronouns (*I, you*), demonstratives (*this, that*), and temporal and locative adverbs (*now, then, tomorrow, here, there*).

Even though, as Lyons (1981: 170) observes, 'deixis is all-pervasive in the grammar and vocabulary of natural language', deictic elements are often unambiguously assigned specific referents by the context in which they occur. But these referents are not fixed, in the sense that they vary according to the different contexts they occur in: i.e., the same expression may refer to different entities on different occasions, and different expressions may refer to the same entity (e.g. *he, John, Mary's husband*, etc., could refer to the same person, in which case these expressions are said to be co-referential). Sometimes, within a situation of occurrence, there may be difficulty in deciding on the referent intended. As for the preceding cases, such referential uncertainty is closely bound to the context. An example which will show how ambiguity can be generated out of referential uncertainty is Hopkins's 'Spring and Fall':

Margaret, are you grieving
Over Goldengrove unleaving?
Leaves like the things of man, you
With your fresh thoughts care for, can you?
Ah! as the heart grows older
It will come to such sights colder
By and by, nor spare a sigh
Though worlds of wanwood leafmeal lie;
And yet you will weep and know why.

Now no matter, child, the name:
Sorrow's springs are the same.
Nor mouth had, no nor mind, expressed
What heart heard of, ghost guessed:
It is the blight man was born for,
It is Margaret you mourn for.

At the beginning of this section, we quoted the first two lines of the poem above to show that context determines the referent of the pronoun *you* as Margaret. Throughout this poem, the poet continues to use this second person pronoun and its various forms, and the addressee remains constant, that is, Margaret the child. But there are two points in the poem when this deictic becomes ambiguous: one towards the middle of the poem and the other at the end. The dedication in the title of the poem ('to a young child') and the direct mention of 'child' in line 10, indicate that Margaret is a child. The first four lines of the poem are a description of a child's response to the symbolic deaths in nature. But following these lines, the poet also describes a passage of time which can refer, in particular, to Margaret having grown older, or it can have a more general reference to anyone whose 'heart grows older' (the uncertainty is caused by the ambiguous reference of the definite expression 'the heart'). Whereas the first four lines introduce an image of a child-Margaret, the next four lines create an image of an older Margaret, so that by the time we reach line 9, there is uncertainty whether *you* refers to the child-Margaret or the older Margaret.[26] Line 9, 'And yet you will weep and know why', can then be interpreted as: (a) Margaret, when she is older and no longer able to be upset by the sight of falling and fallen leaves, will still weep and will then know why she does so; or (b) Margaret the child whom the poet is speaking to, insists upon weeping and knowing the cause.[27] In the last line of the poem, the referent for *you* seems to have changed again: here, the construction makes it awkward for *you* to refer to Margaret herself, so that a possible interpretation is to see *you* as referring to the reader, or more specifically, the implied reader. However, in the context of the interpretation for line 10 above, it is not impossible to view *you* as referring to the older Margaret mourning for the child-Margaret. What happens in the attempt to assign the referent for *you* at the end of the poem is that we have used different discoursal levels to arrive at the different referents. Within the narrative level, the whole poem is an utterance made by an implicit speaker 'I' who is not mentioned, and addressed to Margaret. At a 'higher' level, this speech situation in the poem is an utterance made by the implied author to the implied reader (see Chapter 4, section 4.3.1 which discussed the different levels of discourse in terms of the actual and fictional worlds).

Referential ambiguity can also be brought about when the context is indeterminate. For instance, the generic form of the following literary text by Keats has not been established:

This living hand, now warm and capable
Of earnest grasping, would, if it were cold
And in the icy silence of the tomb,
So haunt thy days and chill thy dreaming nights
That thou would wish thine own heart dry of blood,
So in my veins red life might stream again,
And thou be conscience-calm'd. See here it is –
I hold it towards you.

There is uncertainty whether the above text should be considered a piece of dramatic speech (it was found on a manuscript page of Keats's unfinished drama 'The Cap and Bells') or a poem addressed to a reader.[28] If it is considered a dramatic text, then the 'I' and 'you' (and the 'hand') would be visible before one another as addresser and addressee in a face-to-face spoken situation, so that the 'it' in the last line refers to the 'living hand'. Going by Bahti's (1986: 220) analysis, the response to the last line is not as clear-cut if the text is considered as a poem:

The poem insists – it is clear that I consider the text a poem, and one of Keats's best – that 'hand' be read initially as 'living', 'warm and capable / Of earnest grasping', against which sense the lines then pose an opposite instance that the reader is invited to imagine: the cold, dead hand, 'in the icy silence of the tomb'. But then it closes with 'See here it is – / I hold it towards you.' Is 'it' the living hand, or the dead one?

From our discussion so far, we see that uncertainty in determining the referent intended may result in ambiguity, and that the whole process is a pragmatic one which involves an intimate consideration of context and interpretation.

7.5 Conclusion

The discussion of sources of lexical ambiguity shows some ways in which ambiguity is derived; in addition, it also shows that, whatever the source, actual ambiguity is brought about in relation to context and reader. Thus, this helps to further exemplify, and hence, clarify, the concept.

Notes

1. See Hawkes 1972: 1 and any dictionary. There is an abundance of material on metaphor, mainly theories to explain what a metaphor is, and how we interpret it. These are very complex issues, and to discuss them adequately at all would take up too much space. As ambiguity is our concern, only aspects of metaphor which are relevant to our examination of the relation between ambiguity and metaphor will be brought in.
2. See Soueif (1977: 21–3) on these forms of deviance which signal metaphor.
3. Apart from the property of colour, *black* is given other meanings in dictionaries, such as 'completely dark', 'without hope of alleviation', 'very dirty or soiled', 'angry or resentful'. Many of these meanings have metaphorical origins, but through frequent usage and fossilization of the metaphors (e.g. 'black looks', 'black night'), the meanings have become so established that it is not always clear whether they should be considered part of the core meaning of *black*. If they are, then they would constitute denotations, but if they are not, they are possibly connotations. The line between denotation and connotation is, thus, sometimes fuzzy. In discussing *black* in *black hours*, I have chosen to see it as connotative, as it is the emotive quality that is of significance in the particular usage, which is quoted below:

    > I wake and feel the fell of dark not day.
    > What hours, O what *black hours* we have spent
    > This night!

    This also constitutes an example of a punning metaphor, since *black hours* can, by metonymy, also mean 'hours of blackness, i.e. darkness' (see section 6.2).
4. It would seem that homonymy is not as relevant in the context of metaphor, since figurative meaning, being derived from its literal counterpart, carries some form of semantic relatedness. Moreover, since polysemy is 'omnipresent in language' (Ullmann 1962: 175), it is inevitable that metaphor has connections with it. Homonymy is less common, but has, nevertheless, a relevance, especially when the metaphor is also a pun. On the resemblance between metaphor and pun, see Leech (1969: 214).
5. See Leech (1981: 138–42) for an account of selection restrictions and how utterances which violate these restrictions are interpreted.
6. These examples are given in Allan (1986: 206).
7. See Soueif (1977: 47–59) for some interesting examples for (a) and (b) in particular.

8. Ambiguity arising from such an instance is echoed, in a manner, in what Culler (1980: 65) describes as 'the potential reversibility of every figure. Any figure can be read referentially or rhetorically.'

9. 'Perception' here must be differentiated from 'understanding' or 'interpretation', the former having more to do with a sort of immediate impact on the mind's eye, or a form of recognition, while the latter two are more closely tied to 'making sense' of something.

10. A further point of interest is that the two phenomena share the feature of the correspondence of semantic distance to effectiveness: the more unlike the literal meanings of the two terms in a metaphor, the more striking is the metaphor, and similarly, the more unrelated the two meanings of an ambiguous item, the more forceful the ambiguity. Although this does not reveal the interrelatedness between the two phenomena, the parallelism is one more reason to consider their relation.

11. This example is quoted in Brown (1956: 20).

12. The dual nature of allegory is captured in Barney's (1979: 16) description: 'The word "allegory", "other-speech", *alieniloquium*, suggests that allegories present one thing by a customary route, and another thing more deviously.'

13. See Gardner (1969: 185–6).

14. Further, Fletcher (1964: 7) notes that

> The whole point of allegory is that it does not *need* to be read exegetically; it often has a literal level that makes good enough sense all by itself. But somehow this literal surface suggests a peculiar doubleness of intention, and while it can, as it were, get along without interpretation, it becomes much richer and more interesting if given interpretation.

Similarly, many of the words examined for the first stanza of 'Andromeda' are not inherently ambiguous, but when an allegorical reading assigns extra meaning to them, the text gains in depth.

15. See Leech (1969: 132), Wales (1989: 333), and any dictionary on literary terms.

16. This occurs when 'the semantic markers of one constituent are deleted and replaced by the semantic markers of the other constituent in the oxymoron [or paradox]' (Ching 1975: 49). For a typology of other interpretive strategies, see El Batanouny (1990, Chapter 6).

17. See the notes to *The Poems of Gerard Manley Hopkins* (Gardner and MacKenzie 1970).

18. The irony could be obvious, such as occurs in what Muecke (1969: 23) calls 'Simple Irony, in which an apparently or ostensibly true statement, serious question, valid assumption, or legitimate expectation is corrected, invalidated, or frustrated by the ironist's real meaning, by the true state of affairs, or by what actually happens'. Implicit in this description is the importance of awareness derived from contextual knowledge.

19. This is, of course, practised not only by poets; others who make much use of word-formation are copywriters, journalists and scientists.

20. A semi-suffix is defined by Marchand (1969: 356–7) as an element that stands midway between a full word and a suffix. Gruber (1976: 345) terms it an 'incomplete lexical entry'. Examples of semi-suffixes are: -*worthy*, -*hood*, and -*wise*, which are homophones of the independent words *worthy*, *hood* and *wise*. There is, therefore, a potential ambiguity in the use of these elements to form new words.

21. These compounds are from stanzas 21 and 35, 'The Wreck of the Deutschland', respectively. See also Milroy (1977: 181–2).

22. See Bauer (1983: 46), whose method I have followed here in order to illustrate the potential ambiguity of new compounds.

23. Sornig (1981: 13) is emphatic about the role of the reader, to the point of dismissing the importance of the originator of the neologisms, which, to me, is carrying it too far:

> it is not really the speaker who is the creator of these new quasi-meaningful sound-patterns or 'words', it is the listener, who in his decoding dilemma, when faced with a strange word, becomes active and creative. It is the listener who tries to disambiguate the absurd and meaningless sounds by relating them to something more familiar by means of a creative exploitation of misunderstanding.

24. For an account of the differences between affixes that are derivative (and thus contribute to word-formation) and those that are inflectional (and thus belong to grammar), see Bauer (1983: 22–9, 39–41) and Adams (1973: 11–13).

25. See Milroy (1977: 161).

26. It can be noted here that, unlike traditional treatment of reference as necessarily designating a real-world object, reference or referent for us need not be bound by this constraint. Rather, like Schoorl (1980: 158), I will consider a referent to be 'the hearer's private mental dossier on that object'.

27. For these two interpretations, (a) and (b), see Russell (1971: 54–5).

28. See Lipking (1981: 181).

CHAPTER EIGHT

Conclusion

The preceding chapters have been primarily concerned with explicating the concept of ambiguity. In the process, some attempt has also been made to interpret the occurrences of ambiguity in relation to the significance of the poem concerned. This relation between specific occurrences and overall significance occur at the micro- and macro-levels respectively, and similarly, ambiguity can occur at these levels which we will name micro-ambiguity and macro-ambiguity. Closely tied to this micro–macro relation is the significance of lexical ambiguity in contributing to poetic value. It is pertinent to say something about these two aspects in this concluding chapter for a more complete picture of the place of lexical ambiguity in poetry. The chapter ends with a recapitulation of what the book has tried to achieve, its limitations and some future directions.

8.1 Micro-ambiguity and macro-ambiguity

Here, 'micro-' and 'macro-' are taken to be interchangeable, respectively, with the descriptors 'local' and 'global'. Thus, at the global level, Hopkins's poetry is said to be infused with 'the tension and fusion of seemingly opposite principles: the Ignatian ideal of self-abnegation, selfless heroic endeavour, is matched by an intense self-consciousness and a dwelling on selfhood as the "final perfection" ' (Gardner and MacKenzie 1970: xxii). For Fulweiler (1972: 91–2), Hopkins's poetry is characterized by the polar extremes of the conflict in beliefs between a God who is transcendent and a God who is immanent. These illustrate the 'higher', thematic levels of meaning that represent what we call 'macro-ambiguity' in the text as a whole.

163

Our position with regard to the relation between micro- and macro-ambiguity is reflected in Armstrong's (1983: 350) observation that 'The distinction between "global" and "local" levels of discourse is important . . . because the global can help clarify local issues while local considerations can explain the practical significance of global alternatives.' Again, to return to Hopkins for illustration, we can look at one of his poems, 'The Windhover', for the significance of lexical ambiguity in influencing thematic interpretation.

This poem is peppered with instances of lexical ambiguity from the first line to the last, but not every one of them necessarily contributes to macro-ambiguity. Moreover, for the present purpose, it is sufficient to select some instances to explicate the relation between micro- and macro-ambiguity. The poem is reproduced from MacKenzie (1990: 144) below:

THE WINDHOVER:
To Christ our Lord

I caught this morning morning's minion, kingdom
    of daylight's dauphin, dapple-dawn-drawn Falcon, in his riding
    Of the rolling level underneath him steady air, and striding
High there, how he rung upon the rein of a wimpling wing
In his ecstasy! then off, off forth on swing,
    As a skate's heel sweeps smooth on a bow-bend: the hurl and gliding
    Rebuffed the big wind. My heart in hiding
Stirred for a bird, – the achieve of, the mastery of the thing!
Brute beauty and valour and act, oh, air, pride, plume, here
    Buckle! AND the fire that breaks from thee then, a billion
Times told lovelier, more dangerous, O my chevalier!

    No wonder of it: sheer plod makes plough down sillion
Shine, and blue-bleak embers, ah my dear,
    Fall, gall themselves, and gash gold-vermilion.

There is ambiguity at the start of the poem, in its subtitle 'To Christ our Lord', which can be seen either as a dedication or as an address to Christ. This phrase was added six years after the original composition, a fact which has led to the view that it is a dedication rather than an address (Donoghue 1969: 92). Many critics have found further support for the first reading in Hopkins's declaration that the poem was 'the best thing I ever wrote', and the best was to be dedicated to his God.[1] In contrast, there are others who argue for the reading of address and not dedication. In the whole poem, the only explicit mention of Christ is in the subtitle, which gives it an important role as a key to the ambiguity of the poem's concern between a phenomenal world and a spiritual one: i.e., the poem can be read, on the one hand, as a description of things as they are, and on the other hand, at a different level of meaning which explores the poet's relation with God.[2] Furthermore, whether the subtitle is seen as a dedication or an address will have a bearing on the way other specific verbal expressions are read, such as on the referential uncertainty of *thee, O my chevalier* and *my dear* in the sestet, all of which interact to affect the overall thematic interpretation which, in turn, affects the way other verbal expressions within the text are read. It would be a misconception to think that interpretation is unidirectional from micro- to macro-analysis; rather, the reading process is more like what Iser describes as 'filling in the gaps' as the reader interacts with the text (see Chapter 5, section 5.2.2), caught up with anticipation and retrospection, and drawing upon existing as well as newly acquired knowledge all the while: all these aspects of reading set up a frequent to–fro movement between interpreting at local and global levels.

The poem does not have to be about Christ in order to be dedicated to Christ; as Hartman (1969: 70) puts it, 'dedication to God is also possible by means of natural perceptions which are, as it were, the first fruits of the senses'. In such a case, it is unlikely that the reference of *thee, my chevalier* and *my dear* is to Christ. On the other hand, the reference would be to Christ in an address reading, since the falcon then becomes a symbolic analogue of Christ. There is a third possibility – a reference to the poet himself:

> My heart in hiding
> Stirred for a bird,- the achieve of, the mastery of the thing!

The introduction of *my heart* just before the sestet is descriptive of the poet's feeling, and further confuses the reference for *thee, my chevalier* and *my dear* (see the argument later). There are, thus, three possibilities for the addressee: the windhover, the poet and Christ.

The ambiguity at this micro-level reflects on the ambiguity at a more global level still, which is contained in the following interpretations: (a) the poem is a manifestation of the inscape of the windhover; (b) the poet must turn from brute beauty to spiritual beauty; and (c) the bird is a symbolic analogue of Christ. Adherents to (a) hold that Hopkins's poem is primarily an expression of sense experience, and the windhover is seen first in its individual and brute beauty (see Hartman 1969: 69–70). The bird exhibits its selfhood, realizes its innate beauty fully and perfectly, and because of that, proclaims God's glory, power and majesty. One critic, Grady (1969: 29), insists on a monist reading of the poem where 'the falcon, the chevalier, the dear, is only a bird rebuffing a big wind'. Many critics, however, not only acknowledge that other readings are possible but also accept that these different readings may coexist in the poem. As Milward (1969: 26) says, 'Amid all these possibilities, it is not perhaps necessary to make an exclusive choice, considering Hopkins's deliberate use of ambiguity in his poems.' What the presence of ambiguity highlights is the concept of 'open interpretation' for a poem, interpretation being, ultimately, a choice in the mind of the reader.

The two interpretations (b) and (c) are brought out by considering other ambiguous lexical items such as *buckle* and *here*. These occur in the sestet which is distinctly different from the octave. Whereas the octave is clearly an enactment of the falcon's flight, the sestet is a moral reflection. The last part of the sestet also contains imagery that has no apparent connection with the earlier description of the windhover. This poetic structure with its apparent change in concerns and its sudden shift in imagery, coupled with the verbal ambiguities it frames, creates the tension which arouses an 'unsettled' feeling in the reader, and which has sparked off differing views on the poem.

Most commentators have taken *buckle* as the pivotal word in the poem. Gardner describes it as 'the key to the spiritual resolution in the sestet' (in Gardner and MacKenzie 1970: xxxii). It is hardly surprising that so much attention and even controversy surrounds this word in studies of the poem, as the word is foregrounded by its position at the beginning of the line, by the exclamation mark and the capitalized conjunction which follow immediately, by its function as a verb following a series of nouns, and above all, its demand for an ambiguous reading. It has three possible meanings: 'fasten together' (as in 'buckling a belt'), 'prepare for action' (as in 'buckle to a task or to battle'), and 'crumple up' (as in 'buckle under'). The first meaning is incorporated in the interpretation of the fusion of the various attributes of the windhover which are listed at the beginning of the sestet. Following the principle of cohesion, *here* which precedes *buckle* will most likely refer to a position the bird is at, and *thee*, *my chevalier* and *my dear* refer to the bird as well. The second is found in the poet telling himself (his heart) to act against the worldly love that has been aroused by the bird so that he can be 'a billion / Times told lovelier, more dangerous' as Christ's chevalier.[3] This reading is taken in conjunction with seeing the addressee in *thee*, *my chevalier* and *my dear* as the poet himself. *Here* will then point back to *my heart*. The third meaning is present in the interpretation that the falcon's beauty buckles under in contrast to the glory of Christ's sacrifice. In the comparison of the brute beauty and spiritual beauty, the addressee in *thee* and so on is Christ, and *here* takes on the sense of 'in the immediate instance'. In addition, Deutsch (1969: 62) points out that in Scottish and northern English dialect (and Hopkins had an interest in dialectal usage), *buckle* means 'to marry'. These represent some possible readings which are all tenable. In an interplay between different parts of the text, lexical ambiguity can be used to reflect or create ambiguity at a thematic level, contributing to the polyvalent nature of poetry.[4]

This brief examination of Hopkins's 'The Windhover' shows that ambiguity illuminates a whole range of meanings and implications within a poem. Pick's (1969: 7) comment on this poem can be applied to most of Hopkins's other poetry, if not to poetry in general:

> Many lovers of Hopkins would agree that in such a poem as 'The Windhover' they find words used in such a manner that more than one of their meanings is applicable and that as a result the poem has a shimmering iridescence which is lost by insistence on more simplistic approaches.

8.2   The poetic value of lexical ambiguity

Generally, the function and significance of (lexical) ambiguity may be viewed in the context of poetry as a mode of self-expression and of knowing reality. These two modes are interrelated, since an awareness of verbal ambiguity can sharpen our perception of the complexity of the world to which the ambiguous signs refer. Furthermore, as Nowottny (1962: 162) points out, the language of art characteristically imbues the object described or referred to with some system of values or significance:

> it has, indeed, been said that art is 'the meeting-point of phenomenon and significance'. If this is so it would seem that there is a real connection between art and ambiguity, in that the ambiguity inherent in the medium itself serves as a bridgehead between 'things as they are' and the significance that may be imputed to them. The ambiguity of the medium enables the poet to meet that double demand we make of the language of poetry, that it should deal both with the phenomenal world and with the world of values.

The self-expressive or, more precisely, self-referential function of poetry is the basis of the influential concept of 'foregrounding' in stylistics (see Chapter 4, section 4.3.2). This concept refers to the highlighting of a feature against the background of a norm (linguistic, social, poetic or textual), so that attention is drawn to the medium of language itself. Foregrounding is closely linked to the aesthetic goal of poetry: in Mukařovský's words, 'Aesthetic effect is the goal of poetic expression. However, the aesthetic function . . . concentrates attention on the linguistic sign itself' (1976: 9), and 'The function of poetic language consists in the maximum of foregrounding of the utterance' (1970: 43). The aesthetic effects of poetry which arise from the medium of the poetic language itself may take the form of manipulation of linguistic elements – arrangement of words and sentences, patterning of sound, play on words, and so on. Lexical ambiguity counts as one form of word-play, and, in so far as it causes the reader to pause and puzzle over it, it becomes foregrounded. When this happens, ambiguity obtrudes into the reader's consciousness, bringing about certain effects.

One such effect is the tension set up by the contrasting nature of ambiguity. 'Tension' appears often as an evaluative term in many works of literary criticism. To Tate (1941), the 'meaning of poetry is its "tension", the full organized body of all the extension and intension that we can find in it' (quoted in O'Connor 1948: 143). 'Extension' and 'intension' are logical terms which Abrams (1981: 199) explains as follows: 'the "intension" of a word is the abstract set of attributes which must be possessed by any object to which the word can be literally applied, and the "extension" of a word is the specific class of objects to which it literally applies.' Tate proposed that deleting the prefixes from the two logical terms would make the equivalent of 'tension'. Tate's definition could be interpreted to mean an incorporation of the abstract and the concrete, but how these are 'organized' may be reconciled to what other critics, in their characterization of tension, describe as a harmonizing of opposing elements or 'a pattern of resolved stresses' (see Abrams 1981: 199 and Crane 1953: 124–5).

The general characterization of tension in the above manner means that any technique which makes use of some form of contrast is likely to generate tension. Thus, there is 'tension between the rhythm of the poem and the rhythm of speech, . . . between the particular and the general, the concrete and the abstract; . . . between the beautiful and the ugly; between ideas' (quoted in O'Connor 1948: 146). Tension arises from other broad comparisons and contrasts, as well as from more specific opposites such as can be found in oxymoron, paradox, irony, ambiguity, and so on. It would seem that any form of foregrounded element causes tension. Despite (or because of) the broadness of its conceptualization, the notion of 'tension' is useful in capturing that aspect of the text or reading experience which relates, *inter alia*, to intensity, resistance, continuing interest and curiosity, and what Dewey describes as 'development and fulfilment' (quoted in O'Connor 1948: 143).

There is no doubt that ambiguity, with its coexistence of different but disparate senses, including mutual exclusives, is an exemplary cause of tension. The effects of lexical ambiguity or tension are not constrained to local occurrences: as O'Connor (1948: 151) observes, 'Tension is also a matter of the relationship or interdependence of line with line.' Similarly, lexical ambiguity, in order to be resolved, understood or appreciated, directs attention to the surrounding text, where not only the meanings of other words are noted, but the interplay between these words will also be considered. In other words, focus on localized linguistic expressions helps to anchor literary discussions in specifics, but poetic value can only be meaningfully interpreted by involving the whole poem. A discussion of the relation between lexical ambiguity and tension should, consequently, take account of the micro- and macro-levels of interpretation, as illustrated in the previous section.

Schneider (1960: 115) warns that 'the richness of symbolic meaning cannot be obtained by reading into the poem a mechanical, dictionary-flavoured ambiguity'. Mechanical enumeration will not help to illuminate literary effects, but interpreting lexical ambiguity within the context of the poem will. In other words, to see how ambiguity serves as a poetic device, we need to take a step further by considering it in terms of the thematic and aesthetic value, which consequently involves interpretation and evaluation.

Since two or more senses are captured in one word, lexical ambiguity has an obvious value as a device of economy. The play on the name *Deutschland* in 'O Deutschland, double a desperate name!' (stanza 20 in 'The Wreck of the Deutschland') is clearly an instance where the reader is invited to associate the name not only with the ill-fated ship but also to the country that expelled the nuns. In this way, the ambiguity is used as an economical and effective means to extend the implications of the particular incident of the shipwreck to comment on the political situation in Germany. In a 'small' way, this economy value is seen as well in *they shook in the hurling and horrible airs* (stanza 15, same poem), where the root form *hurl* for the word *hurling* can mean 'throw with great force' or 'yell' (as in 'hurl insults'). Both senses apply, creating a dramatic situation where sound effect accompanies the physical violence of the shipwreck victims being thrown about in the storm.

An ambiguous word is more likely to call upon a bigger range of collocations and associations than would be possible for an unambiguous word. In 'And frightful a nightfall folded rueful a day' (stanza 15 of 'The Wreck of the Deutschland'), the most immediate interpretation refers to night enclosing and covering the day in its folds, but the word *fold* is a homonym which also means a pen for sheep, so that an effect of foreboding is created in the suggested image of gathering sheep together, perhaps, in the context, for slaughter. Similarly, in the same stanza, there is an association with 'death' in the ambiguous *shrouds*, although its more immediate sense refers to the 'rigging':

Nor rescue, only rocket and lightship, shone,
And lives at last were washing away:
To the shrouds they took, – they shook in the hurling and horrible airs.

In the context of the victims desperately clutching at anything that would save them from drowning, the pun on *shrouds* is particularly poignant and ironical, in that the victims 'took' to, not something that would save them, but death itself.

The play on similar sounding words between *told* and *tolled* in 'A prophetess towered in the tumult, a virginal tongue told' (stanza 17 of 'The Wreck of the Deutschland'), reinforces the 'towering' stature of the prophetess and her strident cry above the 'babble' to Christ. A similar effect is achieved in the homophones of *rein* and *reign* in '. . . and striding / High there, how he rung upon the rein of a wimpling wing / In his ecstasy!' ('The Windhover'). The rather work-a-day horse-training metaphor of 'rung upon the rein' which means 'checked on the end of a very long rein' (Richards 1969: 11) is given an overtone of majesty in its echo of *reign*, an overtone that is apt as the poet glories in the beauty of the windhover's movements.

The above brief description indicates that ambiguity can function to reinforce different levels of interpretation running through a poem, ranging from the physical to the political and religious.

8.3 Some final remarks

This study has been much concerned with defining the concept of ambiguity (in particular, lexical ambiguity) in order that it can be, with some measure of clarity, studied as a poetic device. The redefinition was necessary as it was found that prominent works on ambiguity in literature have not dealt with the concept in a satisfactory manner. Hence, Chapters 2 and 3 took up the issue by offering a theoretical explication. Whereas 'ambiguity' is normally considered to be a semantic phenomenon, the view that has been expounded here was that it is pragmatic. From a logical perspective, whereas semantic-ambiguity exists as an 'either–or', pragmatic-ambiguity is a 'both–and'. The former relates to a potential for more than one meaning, while the latter to the actualization or realization of such polyvalence. The advantage of such a two-level treatment is that it orientates us to view the phenomenon in terms of actual language use, involving linguistic and non-linguistic contexts, and different aspects of experience.

At the semantic level, which forms the springboard for the pragmatic level, it was deemed necessary to delimit the *meanings* of an instance of ambiguity to denotation. Such a delimitation has not been seriously considered by the literature on ambiguity, with the consequence that there has been too much open-endedness in determining what constitutes the phenomenon. Moreover, restricting the examination of ambiguity to denotation offers a basis of objectivity for its identification.

Throughout the book, the focus has been on the lexical type of ambiguity which, together with concrete examples, has helped to anchor the theoretical discussion in specifics. The disadvantage of such a limitation of scope is that it cannot provide as complete a picture as one would like if other types of ambiguity, both at the local and global levels, were included. This problem was partially overcome, however, by giving consideration to the interaction between the ambiguous lexical item(s) and the surrounding text, as well as the text as a whole. Moreover, this allowed us to analyse the relation between micro- and macro-ambiguity, which was especially illustrated in section 8.1. Thus, what was lost in breadth was gained in depth, and it is suggested here that the semantic–pragmatic approach used in this study could be applied to the exploration of other non-lexical types of ambiguity.

The approach to ambiguity as a pragmatic phenomenon places us in a better position to understand it within the cognitive process of interpretation. Chapter 5 in this volume has outlined the role of the reader in the conceptualization of the phenomenon, but it would certainly be useful to undertake empirical tests that could make explicit the ways in which different readers respond to instances of ambiguity. This would address the interesting issue of psychological strategies of interpretation. It may be possible that such an empirical undertaking would help us to gain a better perspective on the kinds of effects ambiguity has on readers, and thence, to uncover in a more systematic way the creative uses of the phenomenon as a poetic device. Such a study would complement the present more theoretical explication, but could not, for reasons of space and time, be included in this book.

Also of interest would be a more detailed examination of the contextual conditions which tend to actualize potential ambiguity; a matter to which this study has been able to give little attention. On a more general level, research could be directed at exploring the relationship of ambiguity to literary history and theory. It is hoped that this book will be a useful foundation for such further studies.

Notes

1. See Woodring (1969: 52) who cited other critics such as Lahey, W. A. M. Peters and Herbert Read who hold this view.
2. This ambiguity is echoed in Nassar's (1970: 30) query as to whether 'things tell only of their own specific nature, or do they give, in addition, analogous spiritual information? The poem, I would assert, is not intended to give a specific answer.'
3. This is a plausible interpretation in the light of Saint Ignatius's exhortation to Christ's servants to 'not only offer themselves entirely to a life of labour [compare line 12: 'sheer plod makes plough down sillion / Shine'], but by acting against their own sensuality, their carnal and worldly love, . . . [to] make offerings of greater value and importance' (quoted in Milward and Schoder 1975: 52). This interpretation is made more likely through the use of *chevalier* which suggests a Jesuit is a knight who serves Christ's cause.
4. Easthope (1985) uses 'The Windhover' to demonstrate that 'the aesthetic text is polysemous and is produced variously by different readers in different contexts of reading' (1985: 326). The readings offered range from author- and text-based interpretations to those imposed on the poem by the reader, giving rise to feminist or gay readings, among others. The validity of the readings is not the issue here; the pertinent observation that may be made about Easthope's article is that lexical ambiguity contributes, to a certain extent, to the diversity of readings. For instance, a sense of *minion* different from the normal one of 'favourite' is adopted in a 'gay reading': 'A *gay reading* . . . might take as its point of departure the word 'minion', which means a man's younger male lover in Elizabethan English.' But, by and large, the less acceptable readings seem to rely more on sheer inference.

References

Abbott, C. C. (ed.) 1935, *The Letters of Gerard Manley Hopkins to Robert Bridges*. London: Oxford University Press.

Abrams, M. H. 1981, *A Glossary to Literary Terms*. New York: Holt, Rhinehart and Winston, 4th edn.

Ackerley, C. J. 1978, 'Linguistic Ambiguity in James Joyce's *Ulysses*'. Unpublished PhD Thesis. University of Toronto.

Adams, V. 1973, *An Introduction to Modern English Word-Formation*. London: Longman.

Ahl, F. 1988, 'Ars Est Caelare Artem (Art in Puns and Anagrams Engraved)'. In J. Culler (ed.), pp. 17–43.

Allan, K. 1986, *Linguistic Meaning*. 2 vols. London: Routledge & Kegan Paul.

Alston, W. P. 1964, *Philosophy of Language*. New Jersey: Prentice-Hall.

Amante, D. J. 1980, 'Ironic Language: A Structuralist Approach'. *Language and Style* **13** (1): 15–25.

Aristotle 1958, *De Sophisticis Elenchis*. Trans. and ed. by W. D. Ross. London: Oxford University Press.

Armstrong, P. 1983, 'The Conflict of Interpretations and the Limits of Pluralism'. *Publications of the Modern Language Association of America (PMLA)* **98**: 341–52.

Attridge, D. 1988, 'Unpacking the Portmanteau, or Who's Afraid of *Finnegan's Wake?*' In J. Culler (ed.), pp. 140–55.

Austin, J. L. 1976, *How to Do Things with Words*. Oxford: Oxford University Press, 2nd edn.

Bahti, T. 1986, 'Ambiguity and Indeterminacy: The Juncture'. *Comparative Literature* **38** (3): 209–23.

Barney, S. A. 1979, *Allegories of History, Allegories of Love*. Connecticut: Archon Books.

Bartsch, R. 1987, *Norms of Language*. London: Longman.

Bauer, L. B. 1979, 'On the Need for Pragmatics in the Study of Nominal Compounding'. *Journal of Pragmatics* **3**: 45–50.

REFERENCES

Bauer, L. B. 1983, *English Word-Formation*. Cambridge: Cambridge University Press.

Beardsley, M. C. 1958, *Aesthetics: Problems in the Philosophy of Criticism*. New York: Harcourt, Brace and World.

Beardsley, M. C. 1962, 'The Metaphorical Twist'. *Philosophy and Phenomenological Research* 22: 293–307.

Beaugrande, R. de 1980, *Text, Discourse, and Process: Toward a Multidisciplinary Science of Texts*. London: Longman.

Bergum, J. E. and Bergum, B. O. 1979, 'Self-Perceived Creativity and Ambiguous Figure Reversal Rates'. *Bulletin of the Psychonomic Society* 14 (5): 313–14.

Black, M. 1949, *Language and Philosophy: Studies in Method*. Ithaca: Cornell University Press.

Black, M. 1962, *Models and Metaphors: Studies in Language and Philosophy*. Ithaca: Cornell University Press.

Blakemore, D. 1987, *Semantic Constraints on Relevance*. Oxford: Basil Blackwell.

Bleich, D. 1978, *Subjective Criticism*. Baltimore: The John Hopkins University Press.

Bloomfield, L. 1935, *Language*. London: Allen and Unwin.

Bolinger, D. L. 1965, 'The Atomization of Meaning'. *Language* 41 (4): 555–73.

Bolton, W. F. and Crystal, D. (eds) 1969, *The English Language*, Vol. 2. Cambridge: Cambridge University Press.

Booth, W. C. 1974, *A Rhetoric of Irony*. Chicago: University of Chicago Press.

Braendlin, H. P. 1988, 'Introduction: Ambiguities in Literature and Film'. In Braendlin, H. P. (ed.), *Ambiguities in Literature and Film: Selected Papers from the 7th Annual Florida State University Conference on Literature and Film*. Tallahassee: The Florida State University Press, pp. 1–9.

Brooks, C. 1947, *The Well Wrought Urn: Studies in the Structure of Poetry*. New York: Harcourt Brace.

Brown, G. and Yule, G. 1983, *Discourse Analysis*. Cambridge: Cambridge University Press.

Brown, J. 1956, 'Eight Types of Pun'. *PMLA* 71: 14–26.

Burgess, A. 1969, 'Words'. In Bolton, W. F. and Crystal, D., *The English Language*. Vol. 2, pp. 294–304. Reprinted from *Language Made Plain*.

Caramazza, A. and Grober, E. 1976, 'Polysemy and the Structure of the Subjective Lexicon'. In C. Rameh (ed.), *Semantics: Theory and Application*. Washington, DC: Georgetown University Press, pp. 181–206.

Carroll, M. C. (SJ) 1949, 'Gerard Manley Hopkins and the Society of Jesus'. In N. Weyand (ed.), pp. 3–50.

Carter, R. 1987, *Vocabulary: Applied Linguistic Perspectives*. London: Allen and Unwin.

Charnley, M. B. 1975, 'The Mechanism of Wordplay'. *RLA: Revista de Linguistica Teorica y Aplicada* 13: 27–30.

Ching, M. K. L. 1975, 'A Linguistic Analysis of Compact Verbal Paradox in Literature: A Semantic Interpretation of the Oxymoron'. Unpublished PhD Thesis. Florida State University.

Chomsky, N. 1962, Syntactic Structures. Prague: Mouton, 2nd edn.

Clark, R. and Welsh, P. 1962, *Introduction to Logic*. New Jersey: D. van Nostrand.

Coates, J. 1983, *The Semantics of the Modal Auxiliaries*. London: Croom Helm.

Cohen, E. H. 1969, *Works and Criticism of Gerard Manley Hopkins: A Comprehensive Bibliography*. Washington: The Catholic University of America Press.

Collins English Dictionary. 1986. Ed. P. Hanks. London: Collins, 2nd edn.

Copi, I. 1961, *Introduction to Logic*. London: Macmillan, 2nd edn.

Cotter, J. F. 1972, *Inscape: The Christology and Poetry of Gerard Manley Hopkins*. Pittsburgh: University of Pittsburgh Press.

Cowie, A. P. 1982, 'Polysemy and the Structure of Lexical Fields'. *Nottingham Linguistic Circular* **11** (2): 51–64.

Crane, R. S. 1953, *The Languages of Criticism and the Structure of Poetry*. Toronto: The University of Toronto Press.

Cruse, D. A. 1982, 'On Lexical Ambiguity'. *The Nottingham Linguistic Circular* **11** (2): 65–80.

Cruse, D. A. 1986, *Lexical Semantics*. Cambridge: Cambridge University Press.

Culler, J. 1975, *Structuralist Poetics: Structuralism, Linguistics and the Study of Literature*. Ithaca: Cornell University Press.

Culler, J. 1980, 'Prolegomena to a Theory of Reading'. In Suleiman and Crosman (eds), pp. 46–66.

Culler, J. 1982, *On Deconstruction*. Ithaca: Cornell University Press.

Culler, J. 1988, 'The Call of the Phoneme: Introduction'. In J. Culler (ed.), pp. 1–16.

Culler, J. (ed.) 1988, *On Puns: The Foundation of Letters*. Oxford: Basil Blackwell.

Davidson, D. 1979, 'What Metaphors Mean'. In S. Sacks (ed.), *On Metaphor*. Chicago: The University of Chicago Press, pp. 29–45.

Deutsch, B. 1969, 'Poetry in Our Time'. In J. Pick (ed.), pp. 61–5.

Donnellan, K. S. 1966, 'Reference and Definite Descriptions'. *Philosophical Review* **75**: 281–304.

Donoghue, D. 1969, 'The Bird as Symbol: Hopkins's Windhover'. In J. Pick (ed.), pp. 91–9.

Dunne, T. 1976, *Gerard Manley Hopkins: A Comprehensive Bibliography*. Oxford: Clarendon Press.

Eagleton, T. 1983, *Literary Theory: An Introduction*. Oxford: Basil Blackwell.

Easthope, A. 1985, 'The Problem of Polysemy and Identity in the Literary Text'. *British Journal of Aesthetics* **25** (4): 326–39.

Eaton, M. M. 1970, 'Good and Correct Interpretations of Literature'. *Journal of Aesthetics and Art Criticism* **29**: 227–33.

Eco, U. 1976, *A Theory of Semiotics*. Bloomington: Indiana University Press.

Edlow, R. B. 1975, 'The Stoics on Ambiguity'. *Journal of the History of Philosophy* **13**: 423–35.

El Batanouny, G. M. M. 1990, 'Readers' Responses to Paradoxical Expressions in Literature: A Linguistic Analysis and Pragmatic Interpretation'. Unpublished PhD Thesis. University of Lancaster.

Eliot, T. S. 1974, *Collected Poems: 1909–1962*. London: Faber and Faber.

Ellis, J. O. 1966, 'On Contextual Meaning'. In C. E. Bazell (ed.), *In Memory of J. R. Firth*. London: Longman.

Empson, W. 1961, *Seven Types of Ambiguity*. Middlesex: Penguin. 3rd edn.

Enright, D. J. 1988, 'Babies'. In L. Sail (ed.), *First and Always: Poems for the Great Ormond Street Children's Hospital*. London: Faber and Faber.

Firth, J. R. 1957, *Papers in Linguistics*. London: Oxford University Press.

Fish, S. E. 1980a, 'Literature in the Reader: Affective Stylistics'. In J. P. Tompkins (ed.), pp. 70–100. Reprinted from *New Literary History* **2** (1): 123–62.

Fish, S. E. 1980b, 'Interpreting the *Variorum*'. In J. P. Tompkins (ed.), pp. 164–84. Reprinted from *Critical Inquiry* 1976, **2**: 465–85.

Fletcher, A. 1964, *Allegory: The Theory of a Symbolic Mode*. Ithaca: Cornell University Press.

Fowler, R. (ed.) 1987, *A Dictionary of Modern Critical Terms*. London and New York: Routledge & Kegan Paul (revised edn).

Fraser, B. 1979, 'The Interpretation of Novel Metaphors'. In A. Ortony (ed.), *Metaphor and Thought*. Cambridge: Cambridge University Press.

Frenkel-Brunswick, E. 1954, 'Intolerance of Ambiguity as an Emotional and Perceptual Personality Variable'. In H. Brand (ed.), *The Study of Personality*. New York: John Wiley.

Freund, E. 1987, *The Return of the Reader: Reader-Response Criticism*. London: Methuen.

Fried, D. 1988, 'Rhyme Puns'. In J. Culler (ed.), pp. 83–99.

Friedrich, P. 1979, *Language, Context, and the Imagination*. California: Stanford University Press.

Frye, N. 1957, *Anatomy of Criticism: Four Essays*. New Jersey: Princeton University Press.

Fulweiler, H. W. 1972, *Letters from the Darkling Plain: Language and the Grounds of Knowledge in the Poetry of Arnold and Hopkins*. Missouri: University of Missouri Press.

Gardner, W. H. 1969, *Gerard Manley Hopkins: A Study of Poetic Idiosyncracy in Relation to Poetic Tradition*. 2 vols. London: Oxford University Press, 2nd edn.

Gardner, W. H. and MacKenzie, N. (eds) 1970, *The Poems of Gerard Manley Hopkins*. London: Oxford University Press, 4th edn.

Gildea, P. M. 1983, 'On Resolving Ambiguity: Can Context Constrain Lexical Access?'. Unpublished PhD thesis. Princeton University.

Gleitman, L. R. and Gleitman, H. 1970, *Phrase and Paraphrase: Some Innovative Uses of Language*. New York: Norton.

Gombrich, E. H. 1977, *Art and Illusion: A Study in the Psychology of Pictorial Representation*. London: Phaidon Press, 5th edn.

Grady, T. J. 1969, 'Windhover's Meaning'. In J. Pick (ed.), pp. 25–9.

Green, G. M. 1989, *Pragmatics and Natural Language Understanding*. New Jersey: Lawrence Erlbaum.

Grice, H. P. 1957, 'Meaning'. *Philosophical Review*. **66**: 377–88. Reprinted in D. Steinberg and L. Jakobovits (eds), *Semantics: An Interdisciplinary Reader*. 1971. Cambridge: Cambridge University Press.

Grice, H. P. 1975, 'Logic and Conversation'. In P. Cole and J. Morgan (eds), *Syntax and Semantics 3: Speech Acts*. New York: Academic Press.

Gruber, J. S. 1976, *Lexical Structures in Syntax and Semantics*. Amsterdam: North-Holland.

Hagenbuchle, R. 1984, 'The Concept of Ambiguity in Linguistics and Literary Criticism'. In R. Watts et al. (eds), *Modes of Interpretation: Essays Presented to Ernst Leisi*. Tübingen: Gunter Narr Verlag.

Halasz, L. 1987, 'Cognitive and Social Psychological Approaches to Literary Discourse: An Overview'. In L. Halasz (ed.), *Literary Discourse: Aspects of Cognitive and Social Psychological Approaches*. Berlin: Walter de Gruyter.

Halliday, M. A. K. 1977, 'Text as Semantic Choice in Social Contexts'. In T. A. van Dijk and J. S. Petofi (eds), *Grammars and Descriptions (Studies in Text Theory and Text Analysis)*. Berlin, N.Y.: Walter de Gruyter.

Harris, W. V. 1988, *Interpretive Acts: In Search of Meaning*. Oxford: Clarendon Press.

Hartman, G. H. 1969, 'The Unmediated Vision'. In J. Pick (ed.), pp. 66–72. Reprinted from *The Unmediated Vision: An Interpretation of Wordsworth, Hopkins, Rilke, and Valéry*. New Haven: Yale University Press.

Hawkes, T. 1972, *Metaphor*. London: Methuen and Co.

Heller, L. G. 1974, 'Toward a General Typology of the Pun'. *Language and Style* **7** (4): 271–82.

Heller, L. G. 1983, 'Puns, Ironies (Plural), and Other Type–4 Patterns'. *Poetics Today* **4** (3): 437–49.

Herman, V. 1986, 'Contexts and Acts in Gerard Manley Hopkins' "I Wake and Feel the Fell. . ." '. In T. D'haen (ed.), *Linguistics and the Study of Literature*. Amsterdam: Rodopi, pp. 89–111.

Herman, V. 1989, 'Subject Construction as Stylistic Strategy in Gerard Manley Hopkins'. In R. Carter and P. Simpson (eds), *Language Discourse and Literature: An Introductory Reader In Discourse Stylistics*. London: Unwin Hyman.

Hill, A. A. 1985, 'Puns: Their Reality and Their Uses'. *International Journal of American Linguistics* **51** (4): 449–50.

Hill, T. E. 1974, *The Concept of Meaning*. London: George Allen and Unwin Ltd.

Hirsch, E. D. Jr 1967, *Validity in Interpretation*. New Haven: Yale University Press.

Holland, N. 1975, *Five Readers Reading*. New Haven: Yale University Press.

Holub, R. C. 1984, *Reception Theory: A Critical Introduction*. London: Methuen.

Horn, L. R. 1985, 'Metalinguistic Negation and Pragmatic Ambiguity'. *Language* **61**: 121–74.

REFERENCES

House, H. and Storey, G. (eds) 1959, *The Journals and Papers of Gerard Manley Hopkins*. London: Oxford University Press.

Hungerland, I. C. 1958, *Poetic Discourse*. Los Angeles: University of California Press.

Iser, W. 1974, *The Implied Reader: Patterns in Communication in Prose Fiction from Bunyan to Beckett*. Baltimore: Johns Hopkins University Press.

Iser, W. 1978, *The Act of Reading: A Theory of Aesthetic Response*. Baltimore: Johns Hopkins University Press.

Jakobson, R. 1960, 'Linguistics and Poetics'. In T. A. Sebeok (ed.), *Style in Language*. London: John Wiley and Sons.

Jensen, James. 1966, 'The Construction of *Seven Types of Ambiguity*'. *Modern Language Quarterly* **27**: 243–55.

Jespersen, O. 1942, *A Modern English Grammar on Historical Principles*. London: George Allen and Unwin.

Kaplan, A. and Kris, E. 1948, 'Esthetic Ambiguity'. *Philosophy and Phenomeno-logical Research*, pp. 415–35.

Kasher, N. and A. 1976, 'Speech Acts, Contexts and Valuable Ambiguities'. In van Dijk, T. A. (ed.), *Pragmatics of Language and Literature*. Amsterdam: North-Holland, pp. 77–81.

Katz, J. J. and Fodor, J. A. 1964, 'The Structure of a Semantic Theory'. In Fodor, J. J. and Katz, J. J. (eds), *The Structure of Language: Readings in the Philosophy of Language*. New Jersey: Prentice-Hall, pp. 479–518.

Keating, J. E. 1963, *The Wreck of the Deutschland: An Essay and Commentary*. Kent State University Bulletin, Research Series 6.

Kempson, R. M. 1977, *Semantic Theory*. Cambridge: Cambridge University Press.

Kempson, R. M. 1979, 'Ambiguity and Word Meaning'. In S. Greenbaum, G. Leech and J. Svartvik (eds), *Studies in English Linguistics for Randolph Quirk*. London: Longman, pp. 7–16.

Kess, J. F. and Hoppe, R. A. 1981, *Ambiguity in Psycholinguistics*. Amsterdam: John Benjamins.

Kess, J. F. and Hoppe, R. A. 1985, 'Bias, Individual Differences, and 'Shared Knowledge' in Ambiguity'. *Journal of Pragmatics* **9**: 21–39.

Kintgen, E. R. 1977, 'Reader Response and Stylistics'. *Style* **11**: 1–18.

Kooij, J. G. 1971, *Ambiguity in Natural Language*. Amsterdam: North-Holland.

Labov, W. 1973, 'The Boundaries of Words and Their Meanings'. In C. J. N. Bailey and R. W. Shuy (eds), *New Ways of Analyzing Variation in English*. Washington DC: Georgetown University Press.

Lakoff, G. and Johnson, M. 1980, *Metaphors We Live By*. Chicago: University of Chicago Press.

Leech, G. N. 1969, *A Linguistic Guide to English Poetry*. London: Longman.

Leech, G. N. 1976, 'Being Precise about Lexical Vagueness'. *York Papers in Linguistics* **6**: 149–65.

Leech, G. N. 1980, *Explorations in Semantics and Pragmatics*. Amsterdam: John Benjamins.

Leech, G. N. 1981, *Semantics*. Middlesex: Penguin, 2nd edn.

Leech, G. N. 1983, *Principles of Pragmatics*. London: Longman.

Leech, G. N. 1985, 'Stylistics'. In T. A. van Dijk (ed.), *Discourse and Literature*. Amsterdam: John Benjamins, pp. 39–57.

Leech, G. N. and Short, M. H. 1981, *Style in Fiction*. London: Longman.

Lehrer, A. 1974, 'Homonymy and Polysemy: Measuring Similarity of Meaning'. *Language Sciences* 3: 33–9.

Levi, J. N. 1978, *The Syntax and Semantics of Complex Nominals*. New York: Academic Press.

Lipking, L. 1981, *The Life of the Poet: Beginning and Ending Poetic Careers*. Chicago: Chicago University Press.

Lyons, J. 1963, *Structural Semantics: An Analysis of Part of the Vocabulary of Plato*. Oxford: Basil Blackwell.

Lyons, J. 1968, *Introduction to Theoretical Linguistics*. Cambridge: Cambridge University Press.

Lyons, J. 1977, *Semantics*. 2 vols, Cambridge: Cambridge University Press.

Lyons, J. 1981, *Language, Meaning and Context*. London: Fontana.

MacKay, D. G. 1966, 'To End Ambiguous Sentences'. *Perception and Psychophysics* 1: 426–36.

MacKenzie, N. H. 1981, *A Reader's Guide to Gerard Manley Hopkins*. London: Thames and Hudson Ltd.

MacKenzie, N. H. (ed.) 1990, *The Poetical Works of Gerard Manley Hopkins*. Oxford: Clarendon Press.

Marchand, H. 1969, *The Categories and Types of Present-Day English Word-Formation*. München: C. H. Beck, 2nd edn.

Mariani, P. L. 1970, *A Hopkins Commentary on the Complete Poems of Gerard Manley Hopkins*. Ithaca: Cornell University Press.

McCarthy, P. 1979, *Hopkins' Rhetoric: A Study in Language Design*. Unpublished PhD thesis. University of Cambridge.

McChesney, D. 1968, *A Hopkins Commentary*. London: University of London Press Ltd.

Meys, W. J. 1975, *Compound Adjectives in English and the Ideal Speaker–Listener*. Amsterdam: North-Holland.

Miller, D. M. 1971, *The Net of Hephaestus: A Study of Modern Criticism and Metaphysical Metaphor*. The Hague: Mouton.

Miller, J. H. 1980, 'The Figure in the Carpet'. *Poetics Today* 1 (3): 107–18.

Milne, R. W. 1983, 'Resolving Lexical Ambiguity in a Deterministic Parser'. Unpublished PhD Thesis. University of Edinburgh.

Milroy, J. 1977, *The Language of Gerard Manley Hopkins*. London: André Deutsch.

Milward, P. 1969, *A Commentary on the Sonnets of Gerard Manley Hopkins*. Tokyo: The Hokuseido Press.

Milward, P., S. J. and Schoder, R. V. 1975, *Landscape and Inscape: Vision and Inspiration in Hopkins's Poetry*. London: Elek Books Ltd.

REFERENCES

MLA International Bibliography of Books and Articles on the Modern Languages and Literatures. 1981–88. New York: The Modern Language Association of America.

Morgan, J. L. and Green, G. M. 1987, 'On the Search for Relevance'. *Behavioral and Brain Sciences* **10**: 726–27.

Morris, C. 1938, *Foundations of the Theory of Signs*. Chicago: University of Chicago Press.

Moynihan, W. T. 1966, *The Craft and Art of Dylan Thomas*. Ithaca: Cornell University Press.

Muecke, D. C. 1969, *The Compass of Irony*. London: Methuen.

Muir, K. 1950, 'The Uncomic Pun'. *Cambridge Journal* **3**: 472–85.

Mukařovský, J. 1970, 'Standard Language and Poetic Language'. In D. Freeman, *Linguistics and Literary Style*. New York: Holt, Rinehart and Winston.

Mukařovský, J. 1976, *On Poetic Language*. Trans. and ed. by J. Burbank and P. Steiner. Lisse: The Peter de Ridder Press.

Nassar, E. P. 1970, *The Rape of Cinderella*. Bloomington: Indiana University Press.

Neustupny, J. V. 1966, 'On the Analysis of Linguistic Vagueness'. *Travaux Linguistiques de Prague* **2**: 39–51.

Nida, E. A. 1975, *Componential Analysis of Meaning: An Introduction to Semantic Structures*. The Hague: Mouton.

Nida, E. A., Louw, J. P. and Smith, R. B. 1977, 'Semantic Domains and Componential Analysis of Meaning'. In Cole, R. W. (ed.), *Current Issues in Linguistic Theory*. Bloomington: Indiana University Press.

Noon, W. T. 1949, 'The Three Languages of Poetry'. In N. Weyand (ed.), pp. 252–74.

Norris, C. 1978, *William Empson and the Philosophy of Literary Criticism*. London: The Athlone Press.

Norrman, R. 1977, *Techniques of Ambiguity in the Fiction of Henry James*. Åbo, Finland: Acta Academiae Aboensis.

Nowottny, W. 1962, *The Language Poets Use*. London: The Athlone Press.

O'Connor, W. V. 1948, *Sense and Sensibility in Modern Poetry*. Chicago: University of Chicago Press.

Oden, G. C. 1978, 'Semantic Constraints and Judged Preference for Interpretations of Ambiguous Sentences'. *Memory and Cognition* **6** (1): 26–37.

Ogden, C. K. and Richards, I. A. 1923, *The Meaning of Meaning*. London: Routledge & Kegan Paul.

Oxford English Dictionary. 1989, ed. J. A. H. Murray, H. Bradley, W. A. Craigie and C. T. Onions, 2nd edn.

Page, R. 1985, *Ambiguity and the Presence of God*. London: SCM Press Ltd.

Palmer, F. R. 1981, *Semantics*. Cambridge: Cambridge University Press, 2nd edn.

Peirce, C. S. 1960, *Collected Papers*. Vols 3 and 4, ed. C. Hartshorne and P. Weiss. Cambridge, Mass: The Belknap Press of Harvard University Press.

Peters, W. A. M. (SJ) 1948, *Gerard Manley Hopkins: A Critical Essay Towards the Understanding of His Poetry*. London: Oxford University Press.

Phillips, C. (ed.) 1986, *Gerard Manley Hopkins*. Oxford: Oxford University Press.

Phillips, M. 1985, *Aspects of Text Structure: An Investigation of the Lexical Organisation of Text*. Amsterdam: North-Holland.

Pick, J. (ed.) 1969, *Gerard Manley Hopkins: The Windhover*. Columbus: Charles E. Merrill.

Pilkington, A. 1989, 'Poetic Effects: A Relevance Perspective'. In *UCL Working Papers in Linguistics* **1**: 119–34.

Pratt, M. L. 1977, *Toward a Speech Act Theory of Literary Discourse*. Bloomington: Indiana University Press.

Preminger, A. (ed.) 1965, *Encyclopedia of Poetry and Poetics*. New Jersey: Princeton University Press.

Quilligan, M. 1979, *The Language of Allegory: Defining the Genre*. Ithaca: Cornell University Press.

Quirk, R. 1951, 'Puns to Sell'. *Studia Neophilologica* **23**: 81–6.

Quirk, R., Greenbaum, S., Leech, G. and Svartvik, J. 1972, *A Grammar of Contemporary English*. London: Longman.

Ransom, J. C. 1941, *The New Criticism*. Norfolk, Conn: New Directions.

Redfern, W. 1984, *Puns*. Oxford: Basil Blackwell.

Richards, I. A. 1936, *The Philosophy of Rhetoric*. London: Oxford University Press.

Richards, I. A. 1969. In J. Pick (ed.), pp. 11–12. Reprinted from *The Dial* 1926, **81**: 198–9.

Richman, R. J. 1959, 'Ambiguity and Intuition'. *Mind*. **68**: 87–92.

Ricoeur, P. 1977, *The Rule of Metaphor: Multi-Disciplinary Studies of the Creation of Meaning in Language*. Trans. by R. Czerny. Toronto: University of Toronto Press.

Ricoeur, P. 1979, 'The Metaphorical Process as Cognition, Imagination, and Feeling'. In S. Sacks (ed.), *On Metaphor*. Chicago: Chicago University Press, pp. 141–57.

Riffaterre, M. 1981, 'Interpretation and Undecidability'. *New Literary History* **12**: 227–42.

Rimmon, S. 1974, ' "Mutual Incompatibility": The Concept of Ambiguity, Illustrated from some Novels and Stories of Henry James'. Unpublished PhD Thesis. University of London.

Rimmon, S. 1977, *The Concept of Ambiguity – The Example of James*. Chicago: University of Chicago Press.

Rimmon, S. 1982, 'Ambiguity and Narrative Levels: Christine Brooke-Rose's *Thru*'. *Poetics Today* **3**: 21–32.

Ronen, R. 1988, 'The World of Allegory'. *Journal of Literary Semantics* **17** (1): 91–121.

REFERENCES

Rosenblatt, L. M. 1978, *The Reader, the Text, the Poem: The Transactional Theory of Literary Work*. Ill: Southern Illinois University Press.

Russell, J. F. J. 1971, *A Critical Commentary on Gerard Manley Hopkins's 'Poems'*. London: MacMillan.

Ruthven, K. K. 1979, *Critical Assumptions*. Cambridge: Cambridge University Press.

Saporta, S. 1967, 'Linguistics and Communication'. In Thayer, L. (ed.), *Communication: Theory and Research*. Ill: Charles C. Thomas.

Schaar, C. 1965, 'Old Texts and Ambiguity'. *English Studies* **46**: 157–65.

Schneider, E. 1960, 'Hopkins' "The Windhover" '. *The Explicator* **18**: 113–15.

Schoder, R. V. 1949, 'What Does "The Windhover" Mean?' In N. Weyand (ed.), pp. 284–303.

Schoorl, S. 1980, 'Opacity and Transparency: A Pragmatic View'. In J. V. Auwera (ed.), *The Semantics of Determiners*. London: Croom Helm.

Selden, R. 1985, *A Reader's Guide to Contemporary Literary Theory*. Brighton, Sussex: The Harvester Press.

Sewell, E. 1952, *The Structure of Poetry*. London: Routledge & Kegan Paul.

Short, M. H. and van Peer, W. 1989, 'Accident! Stylisticians Evaluate: Aims and Methods of Stylistic Analysis'. In M. H. Short (ed.), *Reading, Analysing and Teaching Literature*. London: Longman.

Sinclair, J. M. and Coulthard, R. M. 1975, *Towards an Analysis of Discourse: the English Used by Teachers and Pupils*. London: Oxford University Press.

Small, S. L., Cottrell, G. W. and Tanenhaus, M. K. (eds) 1988, *Lexical Ambiguity Resolution: Perspectives from Psycholinguistics, Neuropsychology, and Artificial Intelligence*. San Mateo, California: Morgan Kaufmann Publishers, Inc.

Smith, N. (ed.) 1982, *Mutual Knowledge*. London: Academic Press.

Sornig, K. 1981, *Lexical Innovation: A Study of Slang, Colloquialism and Casual Speech*. Amsterdam: John Benjamins.

Soueif, A. 1977, 'A Linguistic Analysis of Metaphor with Reference to its Historical Development in English Poetry from 1500 to 1950'. Unpublished PhD Thesis. University of Lancaster.

Sperber, D. and Wilson, D. 1986, *Relevance: Communication and Cognition*. Oxford: Basil Blackwell.

Sperber, D. and Wilson, D. 1987, 'Précis of *Relevance: Communication and Cognition*'. *Behavioral and Brain Sciences* **10**: 697–754.

Stanford, W. B. 1939, *Ambiguity in Greek Literature: Studies in Theory and Practice*. Oxford: Basil Blackwell.

Stempel, D. 1969, 'A Reading of "The Windhover" '. In J. Pick (ed.), pp. 131–5.

Suleiman, S. 1980, 'Introduction: Varieties of Audience-Oriented Criticism'. In S. Suleiman and R. Crosman (eds), pp. 3–45.

Suleiman, S. and Crosman, R. (eds) 1980, *The Reader in the Text: Essays on Audience and Interpretation*. New Jersey: Princeton University Press.

Tate, A. 1941, *Reason in Madness*. New York: G. P. Putnam.

Thomas, J. A. 1985, 'Complex Illocutionary Acts and the Analysis of Discourse'. *Lancaster Papers in Linguistics*.

Tompkins, J. P. (ed.) 1980, *Reader-Response Criticism: From Formalism to Post-Structuralism*. Baltimore and London: The Johns Hopkins University Press.

Traugott, E. C. and Pratt, M. L. 1980, *Linguistics for Students of Literature*. New York: Harcourt Brace Jovanovich.

Ullmann, S. 1971, 'Stylistics and Semantics'. In S. Chatman (ed.), *Literary Style: A Symposium*. Oxford: Basil Blackwell.

Ullmann, S. 1962, *Semantics: An Introduction to the Science of Meaning*. Oxford: Basil Blackwell.

van Dijk, T. A. 1976, 'Pragmatics and Poetics'. In T. A. van Dijk (ed.), *Pragmatics of Language and Literature*. Amsterdam: North-Holland.

van Dijk, T. A. 1977, *Text and Context: Explorations in the Semantics and Pragmatics of Discourse*. London: Longman.

van Dijk, T. A. (ed.) 1985, *Discourse and Literature*. Amsterdam: John Benjamins.

van Peer, W. 1989, 'How to Do Things with Texts: Towards a Pragmatic Foundation for the Teaching of Texts'. In M. H. Short (ed.), *Reading, Analysing and Teaching Literature*. London: Longman.

van Rees, C. J. 1984, ' "Theory of Literature" Viewed as a Conception of Literature on the Premises Underlying Wellek and Warren's Handbook'. *Poetics* **13**: 501–33.

Varga, A. K. 1976, 'Linguistics and Poetry'. In A. Makkai (ed.), *Toward a Theory of Context in Linguistics and Literature*. Proceedings of a Conference of the Kelemen Mikes Hungarian Cultural Society, Maastricht, September 1971. The Hague: Mouton, pp. 13–34.

Veeder, W. 1980, 'Review of R. Norrman, *Techniques of Ambiguity in the Fiction of Henry James* and S. Rimmon, *The Concept of Ambiguity – The Example of James*'. *Style* **14** (1): 67–70.

Vickers, B. 1970, *Classical Rhetoric in English Poetry*. London: Macmillan.

Waldron, R. A. 1967, *Sense and Sense Development*. André Deutsch.

Wales, K. 1989, *A Dictionary of Stylistics*. London: Longman.

Weil, J. 1985, 'Student Performance and Interpreting Ambiguity in Poems and Paintings'. Unpublished PhD Thesis. New York University.

Wellek, R. and Warren, A. 1963, *Theory of Literature*. Middlesex: Penguin, 3rd edn.

Werth, P. 1984, *Focus, Coherence and Emphasis*. London: Croom Helm.

Weyand, N. (SJ) (ed.) 1949, *Immortal Diamond: Studies in Gerard Manley Hopkins*. London: Sheed and Ward.

Wheelwright, P. 1967, 'On the Semantics of Poetry'. In S. Chatman and S. R. Levin (eds), *Essays on the Language of Literature*. Boston: Houghton Mifflin.

Whorf, B. L. 1956, *Language, Thought and Reality*. Cambridge, Mass: MIT Press.

REFERENCES

Widdowson, H. G. 1975, *Stylistics and the Teaching of Literature*. London: Longman.

Wildgen, W. 1983, 'Modelling Vagueness in Catastrophe-Theoretic Semantics'. In T. T. Ballmer and M. Pinkal (eds), *Approaching Vagueness*. Amsterdam: North-Holland.

Wilson, D. and Sperber, D. 1981, 'On Grice's Theory of Conversation'. In P. Werth (ed.), *Conversation and Discourse*. London: Croom Helm.

Wilson, D. and Sperber, D. 1986, 'Pragmatics: An Overview'. *CLCS Occasional Paper No. 16*.

Wimsatt Jr, W. K. (ed.) 1954, *The Verbal Icon*. Lexington: The University of Kentucky Press.

Wolff, M. D. de 1985, 'Irony and Lexical Meaning'. In H. Bennis and F. Benkema (eds), *Linguistics in the Netherlands 1985*. Dordrecht: Foris.

Woodring, C. R. 1969, 'Once More "The Windhover"'. In J. Pick (ed.), pp. 52–56.

Wright, J. 1898–1905, *English Dialect Dictionary*. 6 vols. London: Oxford University Press.

Yasuyoshi, I. 1987, 'The Energeia of Hopkins' Poetry'. Unpublished PhD Thesis. University of California, Santa Cruz.

Zadeh, 1972, 'A Fuzzy-Set-Theoretic Interpretation of Linguistic Hedges'. *Journal of Cybernetics* **2** (3): 4–34.

Zgusta, L. 1971, *Manual of Lexicography*. The Hague: Mouton.

Zwicky, A. M. and Sadock, J. M. 1975, 'Ambiguity Tests and How to Fail Them'. In J. P. Kimball (ed.), *Syntax and Semantics*. Vol. 4. New York: Academic Press.

Index

INDEX

Cooperative Principle, 45, 50–2, 69, 84
Copi, I., 46, 114
Cruse, 28, 36, 41 n11
Culler, J., 92, 95, 104, 105 n4, 112, 127, 129, 161 n8

de Beaugrande, 70, 78
deictic, 49, 76, 157–9
denotation, 20–6, 41 n4, 110, 115, 117, 119, 134–6, 156–7, 160 n3, 171
derivation, 28, 57, 136, 155–6, 162 n24
disambiguation, 7, 22, 23, 48, 56, 58, 63, 67–8, 71, 72, 77, 80–2, 123–5, 128, 151, 154, 162 n23
double/multiple meaning, 26, 107, 145, 154: as equivalent to ambiguity, 1, 7, 11–12, 18, 109; as cognate of ambiguity, 16, 108–12, 131–2 n3; puns, 122, 130–1; in tropes, 133–6, 139–40
double vision, 14, 31, 77, 126, 131, 138, 148–9

Eco, U., 2, 22, 23, 37, 41 n4
either-or, 10, 12, 47, 110, 171
Eliot, T.S., 11, 75, 100, 110, 117, 150
Empson, W., 2, 5, 6–9, 16 n5, 25, 65, 91, 93, 107–11, 113, 131 n2
Enright, D.J., 73–4
etymology, 3, 24, 34, 41 n6, 85, 129, 133
expectation, 70, 76–7, 84, 89 n12, 99, 161 n18

Firth, J.R., 77, 85–6, 89 n2 & n13
Fish, S.E., 92, 95–7, 104
Fletcher, A., 145, 161 n14
foregrounding, 7, 84–5, 88, 122, 166, 168
Frye, N., 2, 5

Gardner, W.H., 83, 84, 112, 163, 166
Gildea, P.M., 73–4
Gombrich, E.H., 14, 93, 132 n5
Grice, H.P., 50–3, 60 n10, 84

Halliday, M.A.K., 77–8
Harris, W.V., 65, 80–1, 110
Hartman, G., 130, 165
Herman, V., 76, 87–8
Hirsch, E.D., 66, 69
homonymy, 30, 132 n10, 170; see also polysemy and homonymy

homophony, 41 n1, 124, 130–1, 132 n9 & n11, 145, 162 n20, 170
Hopkins, G.M., 2–5, 54, 83, 89 n5, 117, 121, 150, 152, 163: 'Andromeda', 37, 130, 144–5, 161 n14; 'As kingfishers catch fire. . .', 137; 'Binsey Poplars', 147; 'Felix Randal', 41 n6; 'God's Grandeur', 85; 'Henry Purcell', 26, 111, 118, 120–1, 141–2; 'I wake and feel the fell of dark', 51, 134, 135, 140, 143, 160 n3; 'In the Valley of the Elwy', 81–4; 'Inversnaid', 106 n10, 118, 154; 'Not, I'll not, carrion comfort', 146–7; 'Peace', 147; 'Spring', 78–9; 'Spring and Fall', 157–8; 'St Alphonsus Rodriguez', 140–1, 149; 'That Nature is a Heraclitean Fire. . .', 31, 100, 148–9, 156; 'The Caged Skylark', 143–4; 'The Candle Indoors', 153–4; 'The Habit of Perfection', 87; 'The Lantern Out of Doors', 49, 72, 117–18, 127; 'The Loss of the Eurydice', 132 n10, 139, 156; 'The Soldier', 142; 'The Starlight Night', 101; 'The Windhover', 57, 129–30, 153, 164–7, 170, 172 n4; 'The Wreck of the Deutschland', 22, 30, 32, 56–7, 74, 84, 116–17, 118, 121, 129, 131, 132 n7, 146, 150, 155, 156, 162 n21, 169–70; 'Thou art indeed just, Lord', 29, 77, 87–8, 112; 'To Seem the Stranger Lies My Lot', 155
Housman, A.E., 130
hyponymy, 45, 59 n2, 110

implicature, 45, 50–3
incompatibility, 13, 24, 45–7, 60 n15, 72, 136
indeterminacy, 2, 16, 107, 108, 112–14, 131
inference, 50–1, 70–1, 75, 83, 172 n4
intentional fallacy, 7, 90 n14
interpretive act, 98–100, 106 n11, 132 n5
interpretive strategies, 104, 120, 161 n16, 171
irony, 2, 11, 12, 25, 52, 80, 107, 108, 133, 147–9, 161 n18, 168, 170
Iser, W., 92, 95–100, 165

Jakobson, R., 5, 130, 140

186